The Status of Student Involvement in University Governance in Kenya

This book is a product of the CODESRIA Higher Education Leadership Programme

The Status of Student Involvement in University Governance in Kenya

The Case of Public and Private Universities

Munyae M. Mulinge

Josephine N. Arasa

Violet Wawire

Council for the Development of Social Science Research in Africa
DAKAR

© CODESRIA 2017
Council for the Development of Social Science Research in Africa
Avenue Cheikh Anta Diop, Angle Canal IV
BP 3304 Dakar, 18524, Senegal
Website : www.codesria.org

ISBN : 978-2-86978-714-8

All rights reserved. No part of this publication may be reproduced or transmitted in any form or by any means, electronic or mechanical, including photocopy, recording or any information storage or retrieval system without prior permission from CODESRIA.

Typesetting: Alpha Ousmane Dia
Cover Design: Ibrahima Fofana

Distributed in Africa by CODESRIA
Distributed elsewhere by African Books Collective, Oxford, UK
Website: www.africanbookscollective.com

The Council for the Development of Social Science Research in Africa (CODESRIA) is an independent organisation whose principal objectives are to facilitate research, promote research-based publishing and create multiple forums geared towards the exchange of views and information among African researchers. All these are aimed at reducing the fragmentation of research in the continent through the creation of thematic research networks that cut across linguistic and regional boundaries.

CODESRIA publishes *Africa Development*, the longest standing Africa based social science journal; *Afrika Zamani*, a journal of history; the *African Sociological Review*; the *African Journal of International Affairs*; *Africa Review of Books* and the *Journal of Higher Education in Africa*. The Council also co-publishes the *Africa Media Review*; *Identity, Culture and Politics: An Afro-Asian Dialogue*; *The African Anthropologist, Journal of African Tranformation, Method(e)s: African Review of Social Sciences Methodology*, and the *Afro-Arab Selections for Social Sciences*. The results of its research and other activities are also disseminated through its Working Paper Series, Green Book Series, Monograph Series, Book Series, Policy Briefs and the CODESRIA Bulletin. Select CODESRIA publications are also accessible online at www.codesria.org.

CODESRIA would like to express its gratitude to the Swedish International Development Cooperation Agency (SIDA), the International Development Research Centre (IDRC), the Ford Foundation, the Carnegie Corporation of New York (CCNY), the Norwegian Agency for Development Cooperation (NORAD), the Danish Agency for International Development (DANIDA), the Rockefeller Foundation, the Open Society Foundations (OSFs), TrustAfrica, UNESCO, the African Capacity Building Foundation (ACBF) and the Government of Senegal for supporting its research, training and publication programmes.

Table of Contents

Acknowledgements vii
List of Abbreviations ix
List of Tables xiii
Authors xv
Preface xvii
Foreword xix

1. Introduction 1
　Background to the Study 1
　The Research Problem 6
　Objectives of the Study 7
　Justification of the Study 8
　The Structuring of the Study 9

2. The Growth of University Education in Kenya 11
　Origins and Growth of University Education in Kenya 12
　Factors Responsible for the Growth of University Education in Kenya 20
　The Quality of University Education in Kenya 23

3. The Governance of Higher Education 37
　The Concept of (Good) Governance 37
　Governance in University Education 43
　Students' Involvement in University Governance 53
　Relationship between University and Student Leaderships 64
　The Governance of University Education in Kenya 65
　Research Issues 70
　Theoretical Framework 73

4.	**Research Design and Methodology**	79
	Research Design	79
	The Sites of the Study	80
	Sample Size and Sampling Design	86
	Data Collection Techniques	89
	Data Management and Analysis	91
	Ethical Considerations	92
	Limitations of the Study	92
5.	**Findings**	95
	Respondents' Socio-Demographic Characteristics	95
	Mainstreaming of Involvement in Governance in Policy Documents, Governance Structures and Practices	96
	Importance Students Attach to Involvement in University Governance	100
	Extent, Adequacy of and Satisfaction with Involvement in Governance	106
	Incentives for Enhancing Students' Involvement in Governance	121
	Level of Influence of National Politics on Student Self-governance Processes	123
	Impediments to Effective Students' Participation in Governance	125
	Testing for Cross-University Differences	130
6.	**Summary, Discussion, Conclusions and Recommendations**	139
	Summary of Findings	139
	Discussion of Findings	146
	Conclusions	160
	Recommendations	162

References 165
Appendices 179
Index 215

Acknowledgements

The authors acknowledge the contribution of the many individuals, groups and organizations/ institutions that were involved in one way or another in the completion of this study. First, we are indebted to the Council for the Development of Social Science Research in Africa (CODESRIA) not just for funding the research that led to the authoring of this book, but also for organizing, funding and facilitating the review workshops that helped sharpen the quality of the final product. The study was funded through CODESRIA's National Working Groups Programme themed Leadership in Higher Education in Africa.

Further, we immensely acknowledge the two universities that provided the sites for this study; Kenyatta University (KU) and the United States International University-Africa (USIU). In particular, we wish to thank the management of the two institutions for permitting us to conduct the study and for allowing us to access records and documents required for the study as well as to use selected administrators, student leaders and the general student body as respondents. Still within the context of the two institutions, our special tribute goes to the individuals – administrators (e.g., Deputy-Vice Chancellor and Deans of Students), student leaders and students – who served as the respondents for this study. To all of you we say: thank you very much for finding the time to sit and chat with us despite your obviously busy schedules. No amount of words can express our sincere gratitude to all of you. It is the invaluable information that we gathered from you and from existing records in your institutions that made it possible for us to author this book.

Many thanks are owed to the individuals who served as research assistants during the data collection stages of this study. Your efforts and especially the diligence with which you executed your roles and responsibilities are highly appreciated. To all of you, we will be eternally grateful. Also meriting mention here is the USIU-Africa research office which assisted with the analysis of the quantitative data utilized for the study. In this regard, we wish to single out Mr. Paul Ruto for his invaluable assistance.

We expressly thank our fellow grantees (researchers), the anonymous reviewers of our work, and our academic colleagues in our respective universities. Their criticisms and invaluable suggestions contributed immensely in enhancing the quality of this book. Individually, our special and sincere appreciation goes to our families for their unwavering support and understanding. Their patience, empathy, reassurance and, in some cases, periodic critique of the work in progress contributed immensely to the completion of this work.

List of Abbreviations

AAU	Africa Association of Universities
AIU	African International University
AGM	Annual General Meeting
AKU	Aga Khan University
ANU	Africa Nazarene University
AUA	Adventist University of Africa
BWI	Bretton Woods Institutions
CHE	Council on Higher Education
CODESRIA	Council for the Development of Social Science Research in Africa
CORD	Coalition for Reform and Democracy
CU	Chuka University
CUE	Commission of University Education
CUEA	Catholic University of Eastern Africa
DBA	Doctor of Business Administration
DKUT	Dedan Kimathi University of Technology
EMOD	Executive Master of Science in Organizational Development
EU	Egerton University
FGDs	Focus Group Discussions
GEMBA	Global Executive Master of Business Administration
GLUK	Great Lakes University of Kisumu
GOK	Government of Kenya
HELB	Higher Education Loans Board
IAU	International Association of Universities
ILO	International Labour Organization
ILU	International Leadership University
IMF	International Monetary Fund
IUCEA	Inter-University Council for East Africa
JKUAT	Jomo Kenyatta University of Agriculture and Technology
JOOUST	Jaramogi Oginga Odinga University of Science and Technology
KABU	Kabarak University

KACE	Kenya Advanced Certificate of Education
KARU	Karatina University
KCAU	KCA University
KCSE	Kenya Certificate of Secondary Education
KeMU	Kenya Methodist University
KHEU	Kenya Highlands Evangelical University
KIs	Key Informants
KNEC	Kenya National Examination Council
KSU	Kisii University
KU	Kenyatta University
KUC	Kenyatta University College
KUSA	Kenyatta University Students Association
KWUST	Keriri Women's University of Science and Technology
KYMs	Kanda ya Mikono
LIA	Letter of Interim Authority
LU	Laikipia University
MBA	Master of Business Administration
MKU	Mount Kenya University
MMARAU	Maasai Mara University
MMU	Multi Media University of Kenya
MMUST	Masinde Muliro University of Science and Technology
MU	Moi University
MUA	Management University of Africa
MUST	Meru University of Science and Technology
NACOSTI	National Council for Science Technology and Innovations
NWU	North-West University
ODM	Orange Democratic Movement
OECD	Organization for Economic Cooperation and Development
PAC	Pan Africa Christian University
PIU	Pioneer International University
PU	Pwani University
PUEA	Presbyterian University of East Africa
RU	Riara University
SAC	Student Affairs Council
SAPs	Structural Adjustment Policies
SCU	Scott Christian University
SEKU	South Eastern Kenya University
SONU	Student Union of Nairobi
SPU	St Paul University

SU	Strathmore University
TAWS	Tanganyika African Welfare Society
TEAU	The East Africa University
TNA	The National Alliance
TUK	Technical University of Kenya
TUM	Technical University of Mombasa
URP	United Republican Party
UEAB	University of Eastern Africa, Baraton
UFS	University of the Free State
UNESCO	United Nations Educational, Scientific and Cultural Organization
UoE	University of Eldoret
UoK	University of Kabianga
UoN	University of Nairobi
UP	University of Pretoria
URP	United Republican Party
USA	United States of America
USIU-A	United States International University, Africa
WASC	Western Association of Schools and Colleges
WERK	Women Educational Researchers of Kenya
USIU	United States International University

List of Tables

2.1	Universities and Allied Constituent Colleges Accredited to Operate in Kenya, 2015	14
4.1	Chartered Public and Private Universities in Kenya by Year of Establishment	87
5.1	Distribution of Respondents by Age Group	96
5.2	Mainstreaming of Students' Involvement in Governance in Institutional Strategic/ Policy Documents and Practices	98
5.3	Importance Attached to Students' Involvement in University Governance and Decision-making	101
5.4	Positive Consequences of Students' Participation in Governance	103
5.5	Negative Consequences of Students' Participation in Governance	104
5.6	Remedies for Negative Consequences of Students' Participation in Governance	105
5.7	Percentage Distribution of Respondents by Ranking of Major "Players" in University Decision-making	107
5.8	Overall Involvement by Students in University Governance	108
5.9	Level of Involvement in Governance Structures and Decision-making Activities	109
5.10	Adequacy of Involvement in Governance and Decision-making	114
5.11	Extent of Inclusivity of Student's Involvement in University Governance	116
5.12	Satisfaction with Students' Involvement in University Governance Processes	118
5.13	Satisfaction with Involvement in Governance Structures and Decision-making Activities	119
5.14	Incentives for Enhancing Students' Involvement in University Governance	123
5.15	Influence of National Politics on Students' Self-Governance Processes	125
5.16	Impediments to Effective Student's Participation in Governance	127
5.17	Overcoming Challenges to Effective Students' Involvement in Governance	129
5.18	Significant Cross-University Differences in Policies, Practices and Students' Involvement in Decision-making	131

Authors

Munyae M. Mulinge is a Professor of Sociology, School of Humanities and Social Sciences, United States International University (USIU) in Nairobi, Kenya. He holds a BA (First Class Honours) in Sociology and an MA in Urban and Regional Planning from the University of Nairobi, Kenya, plus a PhD in Sociology from the University of Iowa, USA. Prof. Mulinge has taught Sociology in various colleges and universities in the United States, Botswana, and Kenya. He has conducted research in varied areas, including Higher Education (focusing on governance and the quality of postgraduate training), job satisfaction and organizational attachment, corruption and economic mismanagement, ethnicity and HIV/AIDS, leading to the authorship and publication of many research works with internationally acclaimed journals and publishing houses.

Josephine Nyaboke Arasa (PhD), is currently an Assistant Professor of Psychology, School of Humanities and Social Sciences, United States International University, Nairobi, Kenya. She holds a Bachelor of Education (Science), a Master of Education in Educational Psychology and a PhD in Educational Psychology from Kenyatta University, Kenya, as well as a Postgraduate Diploma in Clinical Neuro-Psychology from the Niilomaki Institute in Finland. Dr Arasa is closely involved with issues of quality in higher education in Kenya and the East African region. She has carried out training in quality assurance in a number of African countries and has written on the quality of postgraduate research in Africa. She has also researched the motivation and achievement of children in Kenyan slums. Her research activities have culminated in the authorship and publication of a wide spectrum of research works with internationally acclaimed journals.

Violet Wawire holds a PhD from Kenyatta University and has over 18 years' experience of teaching Sociology of Education, Higher Education and Health Education at the university. She is also a member and lead researcher of the Women Educational Researchers of Kenya (WERK). Her areas of research interest include educational study relating to social inequality issues including gender, disability and poverty. Dr Wawire has initiated, developed and managed various competitively won grant research projects in the above interest areas sponsored by international organizations including Ford Foundation, FAWE, SSRC, CODESRIA and OSSREA. As a consultant, she has conducted educational research evaluations for organizations including Hewlett Foundation, Uwezo, Cornell University, WERK and Loreto Sisters. Dr Wawire has presented papers at both local and international conferences and is an accomplished author of several journal papers.

Preface

The book is based on the study on the status of student involvement in University Governance in Kenya using experiences of one public and one private university. It addresses the critical area of governance of higher education in Kenya, given the role universities play in socio-economic and political development for most African countries. Governance of universities has been a challenging issue on the African continent with most universities experiencing poor governance characterized by poor quality of university education and staff and student strikes. The book is conceptualized around the theoretical framework of shared governance to interrogate how students, who are key members of the university community, have been mainstreamed in the democratization of higher education processes that have taken place in Kenya in the last decade. It is premised on the reality that collaborative governance is essential if universities are to attain their visions, missions and goals. The level and nature of student involvement in university governance is interrogated through the examination of key student self-governance processes including the inclusiveness of policies and organizational structures as well as the role of and support provided to, student governance bodies to ensure participation in university decision making. In addition, the objectives of the study center on whether students value and are satisfied with, their involvement in the decision making processes.

The book is organized in six chapters. The first three chapters set the stage for the study by providing a background on the history and state of university governance in Kenya. They highlight the issues that relate to student involvement in decision making processes at the university. Chapter one introduces the book by spelling out the problem statement, objectives, and justification and research issues of the study. In chapter two, the growth of university education in Kenya is discussed providing a platform for analysis of governance in higher education for proceeding chapters. Here, factors responsible for university growth and challenges faced that have implications on the quality of university education in Kenya are highlighted. Chapter three which is on the governance of higher education is mainly a literature and theoretical conceptualization of the study. The concepts of leadership and good governance are not only debated but their intersection is also established and contextualized to the governance of university education. Specifically, the chapter uses Kenya to provide an understanding of the structures and practices of university governance from a student involvement perspective. Chapters four, five and six delve into how the study was done, its findings and the conclusions that can be drawn from it. In chapter four, details of the study methodology and protocols are underscored. In chapter five, after providing a background on the socio-demographic characteristics of the study respondents, the study findings are discussed along the study objectives. Chapter six concludes the book by discussing the study findings and drawing some implications of the findings in terms of conclusions and recommendations on how to ensure a democratic culture in the governance of Kenyan universities in general and student involvement in particular.

Foreword

For many years in Kenya, universities have been conceived as battlefields where spasmodic violent protests by students, over a variety of grievances, break out frequently. Quite often, lecturers and professors have also taken their own turn to go on the streets to demonstrate against poor remuneration. This perception has overshadowed the mission of university education presented in this book as the production of graduates who respond to the needs of the society, with regards to upgrade of skills of the existing workforce, development of community and business leaders of tomorrow, as well as the empowerment of beneficiaries ability to start new businesses to employ Kenyans and contribute to the country's economic well-being. As institutions of higher learning where the country's top human resource is trained, universities have attracted attention for the wrong reasons. It is against this background that this book, well researched and written by Prof. Mulinge, Dr Arasa, and Dr Wawire, reputable academics, prolific researchers with big publication portfolios and long careers in the service of universities in Kenya, the East African region and abroad, sets to interrogate the governance in universities often blamed for these conflagrations of protest. For the large numbers of academics, politicians, policy makers, and members of the public, this is the book that answers the big question that is often asked: "what is ailing our universities?"

To answer the questions that frequently come to mind about the difficulties that bedevil universities, this book sets a background by exploring the role of university education as the single most important driver of socio-economic development in societies and the sole agent of social mobility and national cohesion, particularly in Kenya and Sub-Saharan Africa. This is the justification for the huge budgetary allocations governments, non-governmental organizations, and aid agencies keep giving to ministries and agencies manning education. The 21st century has however seen the emergence of other influences that have impacted the delivery of quality education. Chief among them have been what the authors call the "massification" of education to accommodate growing populations and human resource needs, the need to ensure efficiency in the delivery of education, and the democratization of nations. These factors have triggered close scrutiny of leadership and governance in higher learning institutions including universities.

Kenya, for example, has experienced turbulence in higher education institutions with frequent strikes which have been accompanied by violence and destruction of property. An intellectual *exposé* of the nature that this book provides is a welcome effort in directing the spotlight on leadership and governance issues in universities that would other wise be lost in the maze of occurrences blamed on a host of societal shortcomings.

Situating their study of governance in university education in Kenya, Prof. Mulinge, Dr Arasa, and Dr Wawire demonstrate the exclusive value of university education in the design and productive use of new technologies for a nation's innovative capacity that outstrips any other social institution in the development of the civil society. They confirm the role of university education in social, cultural, political and economic development of nations through knowledge creation and dissemination. They achieve this by exploring, as part of the background, the evolution of university education from beginnings when the institutions had no focus on the development role through the 'Accra Declaration' to the 1990s and 2000s, when the focus fell squarely on the revitalization of university education to forge a tighter link with development. But for university education to accomplish this link and the noble objectives the country has set for it, it has to be effective. The authors are persuaded that governance issues, in as far as they relate to he shared governance principle of good governance in the running of the universities, is critical in enabling the institutions to achieve the mission of university education. Their investigation reveals that the country's university education is afflicted by violation of the core principles of good governance, particularly shared governance; students, easily recognizable as major stakeholders in university education, are largely excluded from significant structures of governance thereby limiting their influence and participation. Even though their representation is provided via student government organs, such organs do not retain the trust and confidence of the student body. The authors urge a paradigm shift in the involvement of students in the governance of universities in ways that encourage and entrench democratic principles.

This book provides a deeply and exhaustively researched *exposé* of governance issues in university education and shows why the relationship between students and university leadership has been characterized by turmoil. It is incisive as it is exhaustive. It also offers pragmatic solutions for the enhancement of participation by all stake holders of this vital sector of Kenya's development engine.

Tom Onditi Luoch, PhD
Dean, School of Humanities and Social Sciences
United States International University – Africa
Nairobi, Kenya

1

Introduction

Background to the Study

The production, accumulation, transfer and application of knowledge is the major factor in socio-economic development. This has pushed virtually all world countries to put these processes at the core of national development strategies for gaining competitive advantage in the global knowledge (Santiago, Tremblay, Basri and Arnal 2008; World Bank 2002; World Bank 2009). Among the major players in delivering the knowledge requirements for development are higher education institutions, including universities (Cloete, Bailey, Pillay, Bunting and Maassen 2011). Current research available, for example, suggests the existence of a strong association between higher education participation rates and levels of development (Cloete *et al.* 2011). Furthermore, high levels of education in general, and of higher education in particular, have been proven to be essential for the design and productive use of new technologies and to provide the foundation for a nation's innovative capacity and to contribute more than any other social institution to the development of civil society (Carnoy, Castells, Cohen, and Cardoso 1993; Serageldin 2000). Most recently, studies such as Bloom, Canning and Chan (2006), Kamara and Nyende (2007) and the World Bank (2009) have empirically demonstrated a relationship between investment in higher education and gross domestic product in Africa. Given such evidence, many countries are putting knowledge and innovation policies, as well as higher education, at the core of their development strategies

In the light of the above, the importance of higher education in societal socio-economic development is not a moot issue. The sector is expected to serve the primary function of nation-building and development (Kauffeldt 2009; Mosha 1986; World Bank 2009). Universities are expected to make a sustained contribution to development by equipping human resource with relevant knowledge, skills and value systems through their diversified academic programmes and through the generation and dissemination of relevant knowledge (Bailey, Cloete and Pillay 2013). Higher education should enable individuals to develop their capabilities to the highest potential; serve the needs of an adaptive, sustainable and knowledge-based economy and play a major role in the shaping of a democratic, civilized and inclusive society (Okioga, Onsongo and Nyaboga 2012). The sector should produce graduates that are able to compete in a global economy with those that are products of the well-established Western higher education systems (Kauffeldt 2009; Santiago *et al.* 2008; World Bank 2002, 2009).

On the African continent, following independence, universities were expected to play a central role in social, cultural, political and economic development in the continent by contributing significantly to the human resource needs and through knowledge creation and dissemination (Okioga, Onsongo and Nyaboga 2012). With a particular focus on the development of human resources for the civil service and the public professions, universities were supposed to address the acute shortages of human capital resulting from the gross underdevelopment of universities under colonialism, and the departure of colonial administrators and professionals following independence (Cloete *et al.* 2011). The importance of the university in newly-independent African countries was underscored by the 'Accra declaration' that all universities must be 'development universities' (Yesufu 1973). Those who participated in the workshop leading to the declaration concurred that the role of universities in development was such an important task that, rather than leave the university to academics alone, governments should be responsible for steering universities in the development direction. Subsequently, the central role of the university in the continent's development was to be captured by Sherman (1989: 4) in the following quote:

> The emergent African university must, henceforth, be much more than an institution for teaching, research and dissemination of higher learning. It must be accountable to, and serve, the vast majority of people who live in rural areas. The African university must be committed to active participation in social transformation, economic modernization, and the training and upgrading of the total human resources, not just of a small elite.

Despite the above recognition of higher education as a key driver of socio-economic development in Africa, initially, governments did little to promote the development role of universities, partly because many of them had not developed a coherent development model and also because many had become increasingly embroiled in internal power struggles, and the external politics of the Cold War and funding agencies such as the World Bank (Cloete *et al.* 2011). It was not until the 1990s and early 2000s that some influential voices started calling for the revitalization of the African university and for linking higher education to development (Sawyerr 2004). The World Bank (2000), for example, inspired by Castells' (1991) path-breaking paper, 'The University System: Engine of development in the new world economy', started recognizing the role of higher education in the knowledge economy and in development in the developing world. This was subsequently strengthened by the findings of other empirical studies (e.g., Bloom *et al.* 2006; Kamara and Nyende 2007; World Bank 2009) that associated higher education with gross domestic product in Africa. The resurgence of support for the university as an avenue for development in Africa was best captured by Kofi Annan, the then Secretary general of the United Nations, when he stated that:

> The university must become a primary tool for Africa's development in the new century. Universities can help develop African expertise; they can enhance the analysis of African problems; strengthen domestic institutions; serve as a model environment for the practice of good governance, conflict resolution and respect for human rights, and enable African academics to play an active part in the global community of scholars (quoted in Bloom *et al.* 2006: 2).

Annan's sentiments were endorsed by a group of African ministers of education at a preparatory meeting for the United Nations Educational, Scientific and Cultural Organization (UNESCO) World Conference on Higher Education in 2009 who demonstrated support for the role of higher education in development by calling for improved financing of universities and a support fund to strengthen training and research in key areas (MacGregor, 2009). Born of the resurgence of higher education as a key factor in socio-economic development in Africa is the recognition of the twenty-first century 'as a knowledge era' (Damtew and Altbach 2004: 21). This has given the sector added impetus on the continent.

In Kenya, university education is an indispensable element for socio-economic and political and technological development (Republic of Kenya 2005). Access to university education is an important tool for sustainable socio-economic development and for rapid development and improvements in human capital (Ndegwa 2008; Republic of Kenya 2005) and also plays a major role in the alleviation of poverty (Republic of Kenya 2003, 2005). Education in general, and university education in particular, is viewed as the primary means of social mobility but also as a basis for national cohesion and socio-economic development (Kinuthia 2009; Ministry of Education 2012; Nyangau 2014). The government recognizes that the education and training of all Kenyans is a fundamental development. In particular, it sees the country's future as a prosperous and internationally competitive nation to be dependent on the university education system. The sector has the responsibility of creating a knowledge-based society that upholds justice, democracy, accountability and encourages issue-based and results-oriented political engagements. According to the Ministry of Education (2012), the country will rely on the university education system to create a sustainable pool of highly trained human resource capital equipped with the knowledge (understanding) and skills required for the country to experience socio-economic development, actualize its ambition of becoming a knowledge-based economy and to remain globally competitive in a rapidly changing and more diverse economy. The university sub-sector is also expected to equip citizens with understanding and knowledge that enables them to make informed choices about their lives and to confront the challenges facing the Kenyan society. Among the middle class, university education is seen as guaranteeing lifelong secure careers. That is, it enables individuals to cope with the changing nature of the job market characterized by frequent changes of jobs; university education enhances one's chances for advancement in current employment and creates prospects for future careers (Gudo, Olel and Oanda 2011).

Across the African continent, the growing awareness of the critical role of university education in socio-economic development, coupled with the recognition of the twenty-first century as 'a knowledge era' has pushed governments in virtually all countries to endeavour to improve access to relevant and quality university education by building new universities while, at the same time, increasing enrolment at existing ones (Okioga, Onsongo and Nyaboga 2012; Reisberg 2010). This has resulted in massive expansion both in the number of public and private university institutions as well as in enrolment, with most of the growth occurring since 1990. Building on tiny and initially elitist universities, many African countries have witnessed rapid expansion in higher education since independence. In Kenya, for example, the government has invested heavily in all sectors of education with the view to widening access to education at all levels. Such investments resulted in the country experiencing exponential growth in primary, secondary and tertiary and university education. The growth has been accompanied by the revision of curricula and the upgrading of educational standards or quality. The term 'massification of higher education' has often been used to refer to the dramatic growth in public and private sector universities coupled with astronomical increments in the number of students enrolled (Jowi 2003; Kaburu and Embeywa 2014). By massification of university education we mean growth of enrolment beyond the capacities of universities (Jowi 2003). The meaning of the term though transcends the growth in numbers of institutions and students to include the absence of corresponding increases in budgetary allocation and investments in facilities and staff (Kaburu and Embeywa 2014).

For the higher education system to make a meaningful contribution to national development, it must be effective (Kauffeldt 2009). This calls for a university education system that is focused, efficient and able to deliver accessible, equitable, relevant and quality training and to create and disseminate quality knowledge through research. However, in many African countries the sector faces many daunting challenges that erode its capacity to perform (Reisberg 2010; Ngome 2003; Damtew and Altbach 2004; Sawyerr 2004). These have occasioned a decline in quality; an attribute that is essential if the sector is to play its expected role in development and if the goal of the twenty-first century being a knowledge era is to be realized. To illustrate: in most universities the rising number of students has outpaced the expansion and improvement of facilities and other important resources, such as finance and qualified human resources (Reisberg 2010). In countries such as Kenya and Uganda, for example, the massification of university education has occasioned the establishment of public and private universities and colleges that lack the infrastructural facilities (such as lecture theatres, laboratories, libraries, and faculty offices) essential for quality learning and training (Ngome 2003; Musisi and Muwanga 2003). In addition, institutions of higher learning in Africa must contend with inadequate and poorly trained (unskilled) faculty coupled with the lack of qualified professors with graduate degrees or research experience (Reisberg 2010). This has mainly been occasioned by the continuing brain drain or the departure of the skilled and experienced scholars and scientists (Seth 2000; Kelly 2001; Effah 2003; Ngome 2003; Wondimu 2003) to Europe, North America and Southern Africa in search of better remuneration. In some countries, the situation is compounded by long-standing economic and social crises and rampant corruption which siphons resources allocated for socio-economic development (Seth 2000; Kelly 2001; Effah 2003; Ngome 2003; Wondimu 2003; Damtew and Altbach 2004; Saint 2004).

An often forgotten challenge facing many African universities is the crisis of governance. Governance has been demonstrated to play a pivotal role in the success of institutions of higher learning and is a crucial factor in sustaining and improving quality and performance (Gibbs, Knapper and Picinnin 2009; Osseo-Asare, Longbottom and Murphy 2005; Martin, Trigwell, Prosser and Ramsden 2003). To deal with the governance crisis affecting them and to fulfil their roles, universities must embrace good governance. The existence of good governance in universities is a function of a combination of factors. First, it requires visionary, creative (innovative) and inclusive leadership equipped with good communication skills capable of driving change (Brookes 2006; Craig 2005; Lownsborough and O'Leary 2005; NCSL 2008a). Second, it demands adherence to the key principles of good governance; that is, academic freedom, shared governance, clear rights and responsibilities meritocratic selection, financial stability and accountability (Kauffeldt 2009; Obondo 2000; OECD 2003; Task on University Education and Society 2000). Third, universities can achieve good governance harnessing the following tools and practices effectively: faculty councils (or senates), governing councils (or board of trustees), institutional charters and handbooks, visiting committees and accreditation, budget practices and financial management, data-driven decision making, style of identifying leaders (appointing or electing), faculty appointment and promotion decisions and security of employment (Task on University Education and Society 2000).

This study focuses on the status of governance in universities. In particular, it keys on the shared governance principle of good governance to interrogate the status of students' participation (or involvement) in university governance processes, with the view to understanding the extent to which students, as major stakeholders, have been mainstreamed in the democratization of governance in universities in Kenya. The study is premised on the reality that collaborative governance is essential if universities are to attain their visions, missions and goals. Also, students are the majority of the institutions' community and finance the larger part of the institutions' budgets. As such, they have a right to representation in decision making and policy formulation. For students to effectively participate in the governance of their institution, their leadership should not just be involved in some matters. Instead it should be adequately involved in all major decision and policy issues affecting the university. The university should also provide the student leadership with the resources they require to be adequately involved.

The Research Problem

In Kenya, the vision for the university sub-sector is to provide globally competitive quality education, training and research for sustainable development (Ministry of Education 2012). Its mission is to produce graduates who respond to the needs of the society, to upgrade the skills of the existing workforce, to develop the community and business leaders of tomorrow, as well as the ability to start new businesses to employ Kenyans and contribute to the country's economic well-being. To realize its vision and mission, the sub-sector has the objectives to promote socio-economic development in line with the country's development agenda; achieve manpower development and skills acquisition; promote the discovery, storage and dissemination of knowledge; encourage research, innovation and application of innovation to development and; contribute to Community Service (Ministry of Education 2012). From the perspective of these objectives, it is very clear that the government's goal is to have a sustainable, quality and relevant university education for national development.

Like elsewhere in the world, for the Kenyan university sector to meet its goals, it must meet high quality standards and its contents must remain relevant to the needs of the economy and society. One of the factors that infringes on the sector's capacity to deliver a quality and relevant education is the way the sector is governed. The existing evidence suggests that consistent with the practice in other African countries, Kenya's university education sector suffers from the violation of the core principles of good governance, including that of shared governance. As a result, poor governance prevails across most universities in the country (Klemenčič 2014; Leuscher-Mamashela 2013; Mutula 2002). This calls for renewed efforts to democratize governance in Kenyan universities by making decision making and policy formulation truly participatory. However, doing so can be an uphill task without the support and active involvement of students. Student leadership and student voice must be integrated into the governance of institutions of higher learning not just in principle (or as an act of tokenism) but also in practice. This demands the input of the total student body through the officials of student government and other organized students' groups (e.g. associations and clubs). Given that students are the majority members of the university community, administrators at all levels of management of universities must be seen to forge a strong collaborative partnership with student leadership. Such partnership must exist from the department as the lowest administrative unit, to the office of the vice-chancellor, who is the chief executive of the institution. For the partnership to be functional it should be truly consultative and characterized by shared decision making by both parties, with students having co-decision rights.

Unfortunately, existing evidence tends to suggest that the relationship between university management and the student body has been characterized by frustration and mistrust that in extreme cases has resulted in student riots (Luescher-Mamashela, Kiiru, Mattes, Mwollo-ntallima, Ng'ethe, and Romo 2011; Otieno 2004). As such, there is a need for studies that not only assess the extent to which student leadership has been mainstreamed into the governance of universities but also spotlight the quality of student leadership in our universities, its capacity to serve effectively as well as identify the factors that stand in the way of strong and effective student leadership. It is in this spirit that this study has been designed. In addition, although the existing literature shows that the subject of student leadership in general in Kenyan universities has been the locus of previous studies (see e.g., Klemenčič 2014; Luescher-Mamashela et al. 2011; Obondo 2000; Mwiria 1992), not much investigation has been conducted focusing on the mainstreaming of student leadership into the governance of universities and how the quality of student leadership infringes on that process in a comprehensive fashion. Furthermore, no studies that we are aware of have been conducted in Kenya systematically focusing on the public and private contexts of student involvement in university governance. This study is designed with the broad purpose to address the above gaps.

Objectives of the Study

The broad purpose of this project is to investigate issues surrounding student leadership as it relates to the democratic governance of universities in Kenya. This endeavour is premised on the reality that collaborative governance is essential if universities are to attain their visions, missions and goals. The specific objectives of the study are to:

1. Determine the extent to which official university policy documents as well as governance structures and practices in Kenya accommodate (or mainstream) student participation in governance and decision making processes.

2. Assess the level of importance students in Kenyan universities attach to their involvement in governance and decision making processes.
3. Establish the extent, adequacy of and level of satisfaction with student participation in governance and decision making processes in Kenyan universities.
4. Document existing structural and material (rewards) incentives used by universities in Kenya to nurture and entrench student involvement in university governance and decision making processes.
5. Gauge the extent of national political influence on student governance processes in Kenyan universities today.
6. Identify the impediments to effective student involvement in University governance, from the perspective of different stakeholders.

Justification of the Study

This study is important for its theoretical value and applied utility. At the theoretical realm, the study is expected to contribute invaluable knowledge On student leadership as it relates to the democratic governance of universities in Kenya. It is hoped that, through the study, the level of understanding of the subject matter of governance in Kenyan universities in general and of student involvement in the governance process in particular has been expanded considerably. The study generates data that help unlock our understanding of this subject matter by focusing on the important elements such as the following: the democratization of governance in universities; the extent to which official university policy documents as well as governance structures and practices mainstream student participation in governance and decision making; the importance students in Kenyan universities attach to their involvement in governance; the extent of political meddling with the governance processes in universities; and, the impediments to effective student involvement in university governance, among others.

Whereas empirical studies exist focusing on universities in Kenya, many of them have tended to concentrate on effects of the massification of the sector with particular emphasis on the challenges facing university education and how these have undermined the quality of the education provided by these institutions (e.g., Gudo, Olel and Oanda 2011; Kaburu and Embeywa 2014; Kinuthia 2009; Munene 2016; Mutula 2002; Nganga 2014; Nyangau 2014; Odhiambo 2011; Okioga, Onsongo and Nyaboga 2014). The governance element, for the most part, remains under-researched. In particular, to our knowledge, no comprehensive analysis of student involvement in university governance has been undertaken by any single study; where as a systematic public-private universities comparison is lacking in the existing empirical literature. This despite the fact that governance is one of the umbrella challenges facing institutions of higher education in Kenya today; universities in the country continue to be dogged by poor governance. Poor governance is not only detrimental to the quality of education offered – and, hence, the quality of graduates produced by universities – poor governance also intensifies the effects of other challenges such as inadequate funding, inadequate teaching and learning facilities, lack of transparency and accountability, and, rising academic fraud.

At the applied realm, the study has generated data that should inform the efficient development of democratic (participatory/inclusive) governance in universities, as well as inform capacity building programmes and activities for university student leaders in the country. Concerning the latter, the findings of this study point out specific training needs for student leaders based on the knowledge, attitudes and skill gaps that exist and form the basis for the development of relevant training manuals. Capacity building in leadership skills and knowledge for students should create a leadership that enjoys legitimacy and trust of, and has a positive relationship with, fellow students; enable them to gain key skills and to develop competences that enhance their participation in the governance process of universities; whlst providing a more effective link with the management on issues that directly affect the student body as a whole. This should strengthen governance systems of higher education institutions that are in most instances, faced with cases of failed dialogue between the two sides (Luescher-Mamashela *et al.* 2011; Otieno 2004) and reduce the frustration and mistrust that has tended to punctuate the relationship between university management and the student body.

The Structuring of the Study

This study is organized into six chapters. Chapter One, as introduction, gives an overview of the study subject and presents the research problem, its objectives and its justification. Chapter Two presents the historical development of higher education in Kenya. This includes the profiling of the historical growth of both public and private universities and their attendant student enrolments in the country as well as some of the major challenges facing the sector. The third chapter presents a comprehensive review on the governance of the university education sector. The chapter commences with the definition of the concept of governance. Here the relationship between governance and leadership is also explored before delving into the concept of good governance. The chapter analyzes subject of university governance including the principles of good university governance and some of the tools and practices that universities can employ to achieve good governance. This is followed by a descriptive profiling of students' involvement in university governance, including its historical origins; the forms it takes; and its benefits for society, the student and the university. The final four sections of the chapter focus on the relationship between students and university leadership, the governance of universities in Kenya, the research issues emanating from the review, and the theoretical framework anchoring the study, respectively.

Chapter Four deals with the research methodology, including the research design, sample selection techniques, data collection methods and the techniques of data analysis as well as a presentation of the study sites. Also presented in the chapter are ethical considerations and the limitations of the study. The study's results are presented in Chapter Five, commencing with a socio-demographic profiling of the study respondents. This is followed by the systematic presentation of the core results anchored on the objectives of the study. The final chapter (six) concludes the study. It presents a systematic summary and discussion (interpretation) of the major findings of the study guided by its specific objectives. In addition, the chapter presents data-driven conclusions and policy recommendations for action, again anchored on the specific objectives of the study.

2

The Growth of University Education in Kenya

As pointed out earlier, having recognized the importance of education in general and of higher education in the socio-economic development of the continent (see e.g., Bailey, Cloete and Pillay 2013; Damtew and Altbach 2004; Kauffeldt 2009; Mosha 1986; Nyangau 2014, 2009; Okioga, Onsongo and Nyaboga 2012; Sawyerr 2004; World Bank), African governments have declared the twenty-first century 'as a knowledge era' (Damtew and Altbach 2004). Education, more so university education, is expected to play an increasingly greater role in socio-economic development by training skilled manpower and producing and disseminating the knowledge required for a knowledge-driven economy. It should enable individuals to develop their capabilities to the highest potential; serve the needs of an adaptive, sustainable and knowledge-based economy and play a major role in the shaping of a democratic, civilized and inclusive society (Okioga et al. 2012). It is on the basis of such convictions about and anticipations on university education that many governments have laboured over the years to improve access, quality and relevance of university education. This has culminated in the 'massification' of higher education (Jowi 2003; Kaburu and Embeywa 2014) across many countries, including those of Africa in general and Kenya in particular. Bornout of that 'massification' of university education are multiple challenges facing the sector (Damtew and Altbach 2004; Kaburu and Embeywa 2014; Munene 2016; Musisi and Muwanga 2003; Mwebi and Simatwa 2013; Nganga 2014; Ngome 2003; Nyangau 2014; Okioga et al. 2012; Sawyerr 2004; Wondimu 2003) that impair the functioning of the sector, thereby severely undermining its capacity to deliver a quality and relevant education accessible to all.

This chapter keys on the growth of university education, with an emphasis on the Kenyan situation. Doing so is important because it provides the necessary background and context against which the analysis of governance in higher education in Kenya, the subject matter for this study, will take place. The chapter focuses not just on the historical development of university education in the country but also on the factors responsible for that growth and the quality of university education in the country, including the multiple challenges that the sector is faced with. The many challenges that the sector must contend with have implications for its ability to deliver the envisioned quality and relevant education required for socio-economic and other forms of development in the country.

Origins and Growth of University Education in Kenya

The initial origins of university education in Kenya can be traced back to 1947, when the then colonial government came up with a plan seeking to establish a technical and commercial institute in Nairobi (Bailey, Cloete and Pillay 2013). In 1949, the plan mutated to encompass the East African region with the aim to provide higher technical education for the three territories of East Africa, namely Kenya, Uganda and Tanzania. However, it was not until 1951 that this concept received a Royal Charter, under the name of the Royal Technical College of East Africa. The College was initially designed to provide instruction in courses leading to the Higher National Certificate offered in Britain and to prepare matriculated students for university degrees in engineering, and commercial courses not available in Makerere in Uganda (Mwiria and Nyukuri 1994). It opened its doors to the first intake of students (A-level graduates for technical courses) in April 1956 (Bailey, Cloete and Pillay 2013; Olel 2006), to become the first Kenyan higher educational institution (Ngome 2003). A working party established in July 1958 recommended, among other things, that through a process of reconstruction and addition of appropriate facilities, the College be transformed into the second Inter-Territorial University College in East Africa, a recommendation that the East African governments accepted. On 25 June 1961, the Royal Technical College was transformed into the second university college of East Africa, renamed the Royal College of Nairobi (Bailey *et al.* 2013).

Following Kenya's attainment of independence in 1963, the Royal College was elevated to the University College of Nairobi on 20 May 1964, following the establishment of the University of East Africa with Makerere, Dar-es-Salaam and Nairobi as constituent colleges. This constituted the first step towards the introduction and development of university education in Kenya (Mutula 2002). The University College prepared students in the faculties of Arts, Science and Engineering for the BA and BSc general degrees of the University of London (Bailey *et al.* 2013). Later, in 1970, the University of East Africa was dissolved and the University College of Nairobi was transformed into the University of Nairobi by an Act of Parliament, the 1970 University of Nairobi Act (Mutula 2002; Ngome 2003; Nyaingoti-Chacha 2004; Nyangau 2014; Odhiambo 2011; Sifuna 2010). Since then, the University has grown to become one of the leading universities in the region, having the highest concentration of scholars and academic programmes in the country. In 1972, Kenyatta College, a teacher-training institution located on the outskirts of Nairobi City, became a constituent college of the University of Nairobi.

After attaining political independence in 1963, the Kenya government produced a blueprint to guide development in the country titled, 'African Socialism and Its Application to Planning in Kenya'. The document recognized education and training of skilled manpower as one of the pillars of the development process. It emphasized that economic growth required ample supplies of skilled, trained and experienced manpower. As such, it was concluded that the provision of education and training to all Kenyans was fundamental to the success of the government's overall development strategy (Republic of Kenya 1965). Concerning higher education, the 1963 policy document saw its (higher education's) long-term objective to be the enhancement of ability of Kenyans to preserve and utilize the environment for productive gain and sustainable livelihoods. In this regard, quality human resources were considered essential for the attainment of national development goals and for industrial development (Republic of Kenya 1965). Buoyed by such convictions, the Kenya government enthusiastically came up with programmes to assist Kenyans to access education in general and higher education in particular. The consequence has been the rapid growth in education in Kenya that has occurred at all levels, including the university level.

Since 1972, Kenya has experienced massive growth in university education to have the largest university education system in East Africa (Bailey *et al.* 2013; Mutula 2002; Nyangau 2014; Olel 2006; Onsongo 2007). From one national university, the University of Nairobi, and one constituent college, Kenyatta University College, catering for only a few fortunate high school graduates, the country's public university system has grown exponentially, both in terms of the number of institutions and the number of students enrolled in those institutions. The genesis of that growth appears to have been the 1981 Government-appointed Presidential Working Party on Establishment of the Second University in the country, chaired by Dr. Colin B. Mackay, a Canadian legal scholar (Government of Kenya 1981). Its mandate was to investigate and report on the feasibility of establishing a second university in Kenya with emphasis on technical courses. Following the recommendations of the Presidential Working Party, Moi University was established in 1984. Soon after, Kenyatta University College and Egerton University College were elevated to full University status in 1985 and 1987, respectively, to become the third and fourth public universities in the country.

The most dramatic growth in public universities has occurred after 1990 as more Kenyans demanded access to university education and the system opened up rapidly. From four fully-fledged universities in 1987, the number had risen to seven public universities by 2007 (Onsongo 2007), with the establishment of Jomo Kenyatta University of Science and Technology (1994), Maseno University (2000) and Masinde Muliro University of Science and Technology (2007). In 2013 the number of public universities had more than trebled, rising to 22 fully-fledged universities after the government, in its push to meet rising demand for university education, upgraded 15 university colleges into fully-fledged universities. Today, Kenya has a total of 23 fully-fledged chartered public universities (see Table 2.1 for details) and 10 public university constituent colleges. Kibabii University is the newest of the fully-fledged universities having been chartered in 2015.

Private higher education is the fastest growing sector worldwide; it is estimated that about 30 per cent of higher education enrolments are in private institutions (Duderstadt 2002). The growth in private universities has been particularly strong in former Soviet bloc countries, East Asia and Latin America, while many English-speaking African countries have experienced growth in the sector (Kihara 2005; Sharma 2009). According to Kihara (2005), by 2005 there were 85 private (and 316 public) universities in Africa. In Kenya, like elsewhere in the world, growth in public sector universities has been complemented by that in private universities. Kenya's private higher education though has a longer history, compared to most of Africa, and antedates the public privatization movement. Conditions for the development of private education in Kenya evolved in the late 1970s and in the 1980s. In particular, limited government funding for university education meant restricted supply of university education against a rising demand for the same, a gap that required the entry of other non-governmental players to fill (UNESCO 2005a). In lieu of this, private universities emerged as a viable option of acquiring higher education in Kenya (Mutula 2002) and have continued to flourish and coexist with public universities in the country. These offer market-driven courses and provide a conducive environment for academic excellence (Okioga *et al.* 2012).

Although the first private institutions of higher learning in Kenya were the St. Paul's United Theological College and the Scott Theological College established in 1955 and 1962, respectively (Onsongo 2007), the actual initial entry of private university education into the country can be traced to 1970 when the San Diego-based United States International University (USIU) established a campus in Nairobi (Waweru 2013), offering degrees in the names of the parent university in the United States of America (USA). Subsequently, in 1978.

Table 2.1: Universities and Allied Constituent Colleges Accredited to Operate in Kenya, 2015

	Name of Institution	Year Established	Year Chartered
	Public Chartered Universities		
1	University of Nairobi (UoN)	1970	2013
2	Moi University (MU)	1984	2013
3	Kenyatta University (KU)	1985	2013
4	Egerton University (EU)	1987	2013

5	Jomo Kenyatta University of Agriculture and Technology (JKUAT)	1994	2013
6	Maseno University	2001	2013
7	Masinde Muliro University of Science and Technology (MMUST)	2007	2013
8	Dedan Kimathi University of Technology (DKUT)	2007	2013
9	Chuka University (CU)	2007	2013
10	Technical University of Kenya (TUK	2007	2013
11	Technical University of Mombasa (TUM)	2007	2013
12	Pwani University (PU)	2007	2013
13	Kisii University (KSU)	2007	2013
14	Maasai Mara University (MMARAU)	2008	2013
15	South Eastern Kenya University (SEKU)	2008	2013
16	Meru University of Science and Technology (MUST)	2008	2013
17	MultiMedia University of Kenya (MMU)	2008	2013
18	Jaramogi Oginga Odinga University of Science and Technology (JOOUST)	2009	2013
19	Laikipia University (LU)	2009	2013
20	University of Kabianga (UoK)	2009	2013
21	University of Eldoret (UoE)	2010	2013
22	Karatina University (KARU)	2010	2013
23	Kibabii University	2011	2015
Public University Constituent Colleges			
24	Murang'a University College (JKUAT)	2011	
25	Machakos University Collecge (KU)	2011	
26	The Co-operative University College of Kenya (JKUAT)	2011	
27	Embu University College (UoN)	2011	
28	Kirinyaga University College (JKUAT)	2011	
29	Rongo University College (MU)	2011	
30	Garissa University College (MU)	2011	
31	Taita Taveta University College (JKUAT)	2011	
32	Kimosi Friends University College (MMUST)	2015	
33	Alupe University College (MU)	2015	
Private Chartered Universities			
34	University of Eastern Africa, Baraton (UEAB)	1989	1991
35	Catholic University of Eastern Africa (CUEA)	1984	1992
36	Daystar University (DU)	1989	1994
37	Scott Christian University (SCU)	1989	1997

38	United States International University (USIU)	1989	1999
39	St Paul University (SPU)	1989	2007
40	Pan Africa Christian University (PAC)	1989	2008
41	African International University (AIU)	1989	2011
42	Kenya Highlands Evangelical University (KHEU)	1989	2011
43	Africa Nazarene University (ANU)	1993	2002
44	Kenya Methodist University (KeMU)	1997	2006
45	Strathmore University (SU)	2002	2008
46	Kabarak University (KABU)	2002	2008
47	Great Lakes University of Kisumu (GLUK)	2006	2012
48	KCA University (KCAU)	2007	2013
49	Mount Kenya University (MKU)	2008	2011
50	Adventist University of Africa (AUA)	2008	2013
Private University Constituent Colleges			
51	Hekima University College (CUEA)	1993	
52	Tangaza University College (CUEA)	1997	
53	Marist International University College (CUEA)	2002	
54	Regina Pacis University College (CUEA)	2010	
55	Uzima University College (CUEA)	2012	
Private Institutions with Letter of Interim Authority (LIA)			
56	Keriri Women's University of Science and Technology (KWUST)	2002	
57	Aga Khan University (AKU)	2002	
58	GRESTA University	2006	
59	Presbyterian University of East Africa (PUEA)	2008	
60	Inoorero University	2009	
61	The East Africa University(TEAU)	2010	
62	GENCO University	2010	
63	Management University of Africa (MUA)	2011	
64	Riara University (RU)	2012	
65	Pioneer International University (PIU)	2012	
66	UMMA University	2013	
67	International Leadership University (ILU)	2014	
68	Zetech University	2014	
69	Lukenya University	2015	
Registered Private Institutions			
70.	KAG -EAST University	1989	

Source: Commission for University Education 2016, the Seventh

Day Adventists sponsored the creation of the University of Eastern Africa Baraton, Eldoret, followed in 1984 by the starting of the Catholic University of East Africa (CUEA). These three were to become the pioneer accredited private universities following the relaxation of the Kenya government's grip on the provision of higher education in 1990 (Waweru 2013). Despite such growth in private university education, it was not until the 1990s that private university education approached the takeoff threshold in Kenya. While for a long time the Kenya government did not give accreditation to private colleges and universities, in the 1990s, with increased demand for university education, the government began to encourage the establishment and accreditation of private universities (Onsongo 2007). Private providers took advantage of the slow pace of expansion of the public higher education sector to venture into the university education market, thereby accelerating the growth of the private sector. Today, the sector boasts about 20 per cent of all students currently enrolled in Kenya's universities.

By 1994/1995 the number of privately funded university institutions operating in Kenya had increased to 12. These were offering mainly theological-based university-level education. Today there are 37 private institutions of higher education in the country, comprising 17 fully-fledged chartered universities, 5 university constituent colleges, 14 institutions with Letter of Interim Authority (LIA) and one registered institution. Lukenya University is the most recent private institution to be awarded an LIA in 2015. The fully-fledged chartered institutions include University of Eastern Africa, Baraton, Catholic University of Eastern Africa, Daystar University, Scott Christian University, United States International University, St Paul University, Pan Africa Christian University, African International University and the Kenya Highlands Evangelical University. Others are Africa Nazarene University, Kenya Methodist University, Strathmore University, Kabarak University, Great Lakes University of Kisumu, KCA University, Mount Kenya University and the Adventist University of Africa. It should be noted that the CUE has recommended the de-gazetting of two of the private institutions with LIA, namely Inoorero University and GENCO University, as well as the awarding of a charter to KAG-East University, the only registered private institution. When effected, this step will increase to 18 the total number of fully-fledged chartered private universities while reducing to 12 the number of private institutions with an LIA.

Private university education is not homogeneous. The institutions can be differentiated in terms of their missions, mandates and sources of finance. Specifically, there are the 'not for profit' religious institutions, mainly established by religious bodies. These account for the largest number of private universities in the country and base their curricula on some evangelical Christian beliefs and teachings. Among others, they include University of Eastern Africa at Baraton in Eldoret, the Catholic University of East Africa, Daystrar University, Africa

Nazarene University, Kenya Methodist University, Scott Christian University, St. Paul's University, Pan Africa Christian University, Kenya Highlands Evangelical University, African International University and Adventist University of Africa. The second category comprises for-profit institutions. These include the United States International University, Kabarak University, Aga Khan University, Mount Kenya University, Strathmore University and Keriri Women's University of Science and Technology, to name but some.

Unlike public universities, private universities offer comparatively fewer programmes, with a bias toward business studies, information communication and technology and the social sciences. Most recently, though, a few private universities such as the United States International University and Mount Kenya University have ventured into science-related disciplines such as nursing, pharmacy and actuarial sciences. In addition, unlike their public counterparts which are mainly dependent on direct funding from the state (and are highly subsidized by the state), private universities depend on endowments, tuition fees and direct funding from founders and sponsors. They have to recover most of their costs from instruction and other services such as hostel accommodation. As a result, private universities are notably expensive compared to the public institutions. The only form of public funding for these universities comes in the form of student loans; but this is notably small compared to the amounts received by public universities.

To sum up, since independence Kenya has experienced phenomenal growth in university education with the public and private sectors growing side by side and complementing each other in the drive to make higher education more accessible in the country. From a single public university (the University of Nairobi) and a single private university (the USIU) in 1970, the total number of fully-fledged universities had increased to 33 (seven public and 26 private) universities and 24 university constituent colleges by 2012 (Ministry of Education 2012). By 2013 the number had risen to a combined total of 53 fully-fledged chartered public and private universities and 14 public and private constituent colleges. As evident from Table 2.1, today Kenya's higher (university) education sector comprises a total of 70 institutions, making it one of the largest higher education systems in Africa. These include 33 public and 37 private institutions. Of the 33 public institutions, 23 are fully-fledged chartered public universities. The remainder include 10 public university constituent colleges. However, the CUE has recommended the awarding of charters to four of the 10 public university constituent colleges – that is, Rongo University College, Taita Taveta University College, Murang'a University College and Machakos University College – a process that will increase to 27 the total number of fully-fledged public universities in the country. The remainder (37) are private institutions and include 17 fully-fledged chartered universities, five university constituent colleges, 14 institutions with LIA and one registered institution. This number could drop to 37 if the degazetting of Inoorero University and GENCO University, as suggested by CUE, occurs.

The growth in the number of public and private universities in Kenya has been accompanied by an impressive growth in student enrolments (Ministry of Education 2002, 2012; Munene 2016; Nganga 2010; Owuor 2012). The rise in new courses offered by universities, the upgrading of public university constituent colleges to fully-fledged universities, the establishment of more constituent colleges and the expansion of private universities has boosted access to university education (Nganga 2014; Munene 2016; SoftKenya n.d). Thus, while at independence in 1963 only about 1,000 students were attending university in Kenya, over the years the overall number has grown very steadily. For instance, the total number of university students rose steadily from 67,558 in 2003/04 to about 240,551 in 2012 (ICEF Monitor 2015; SoftKenya n.d). By 2013, the number had grown to 361,379 students, reaching 443.783 and 470,152 students in 2014 and 2015 respectively (ICEF Monitor 2016). This 2014 number represents a 22.8 per cent growth over the 2013 enrolment figure. The dramatic growth in student numbers has been propped by a government policy of absorbing as many students as possible that meet the minimum admissions qualification (Boit and Kipkoech 2012; Gudo, Olel and Oanda 2011; Nyaigotti-Chacha 2004; Odhiambo 2011; Owuor 2012; Wangenge-Ouma 2012).

The rise in student numbers has been most dramatic in public universities compared to their private sector counterparts, with the bulk of enrolments occurring in the public sector (Mutula 2002; Ngome 2013). Enrolments in public universities increased steadily from 3.443 students in 1970 to about 20,000 students by 1989/1990 (Ministry of Education 2012). The numbers skyrocketed with the 1990 intake of 21,450 students, increasing to a total of 41,000 students. By 1998/1999, total enrolment in public universities had climbed to 42,020 students (Mutula 2002), reaching 67,558 students in 2003/2004. The number increased to 159,752 students by 2009/2010, reaching 198,260 students in 2010/11 and about 240,551 students in 2011/12 (ICEF Monitor 2015; Ministry of Education 2012; Nganga 2014; SoftKenya n.d). By the end of 2013, enrolments in public universities had reached 276,349 students (ICEF Monitor 2015; Nganga 2014). The dramatic growth in enrolments in 2013 resulted from the admission of record numbers of students by public universities, beating their fast-growing private sector rivals and defying infrastructure constraints that have been dogging them.

In contrast, the contribution of the private sector remains minimal, mainly because the majority of private institutions have limited capacity with annual admissions ranging from 500 to 2,000 students (Ngome 2013). In 1998/1999, for example, despite the large number of private universities in Kenya, their enrolments remained relatively low compared to the public sector, standing at 4,181 students (Mutula 2002). This number had reached 9,541 students in 2003/2004 and rose to 37,179 students in 2009/2010 (Ministry of Education 2012). By 2012, enrolments in private universities had reached 45,023 in 2012 (Ministry of Education 2012), climbing to 48,211 students in 2013 (Nganga 2014). Today, the sector is estimated to accommodate only about 20 per cent of all students enrolled in universities in the country

Despite the massive expansion in numbers of students attending university in Kenya, the proportion of females' enrolment remains relatively low. According to Ngome (2003), for example, of the 1999-2000 enrolments in public universities, female students made up only about 30 per cent, with their under representation being especially noticeable in engineering and technical-based professional programmes. The situation, though, was better in private universities where females comprised 54.5 per cent of the 1999-2000 total student enrolment (Ngome 2003). This is understandable because relative to public universities, private universities admit students with relatively lower average mean grades; overall males tend to outperform females in national examinations and dominate admission to public universities. In addition, most private universities offer social sciences, education, arts, business administration, accounting, and computer studies and therefore easily admit most females who fail to secure admission into the public universities (Ngome 2003). Of the 324,560 students enrolled in universities by the end of 2013, at least 60 per cent were males. During 2013, for example, female student enrolment increased by 25 per cent to 131,375 compared to male enrolment which surged by 42 per cent to 193,185 (Nganga 2014).

Factors Responsible for the Growth of University Education in Kenya

The rapid growth in higher education has been occasioned by a number of factors (Gudo *et al.* 2011; Ngome 2003; Okioga *et al.* 2012). From the broader perspective, the expansion of university education can be understood mainly within the context of the undue emphasis that governments, the world over, have placed on education in general and on university education in particular as an engine of socio-economic growth and development (see e.g. Bailey, Cloete and Pillay 2013; Damtew and Altbach 2004; Kauffeldt 2009; Mosha 1986; Nyangau 2014; World Bank 2009). In virtually all nations, universities are expected to make a sustained contribution to development by equipping human resources with relevant knowledge, skills and value systems through their diversified academic programmes and through the generation and dissemination of relevant knowledge (Bailey *et al.* 2013). Kenya, for example, recognizes that the education and training of all Kenyans is fundamental for socio-economic development (Ministry of Education 2012). The government sees the country's future as a prosperous and internationally competitive nation to be dependent on the university education system. By recognizing the importance of university education in fostering national development, many governments, including those on the African continent, have endeavoured to improve access to, relevance and quality of education (Okioga *et al.* 2012). This has been responsible for the 'massification' of higher education that has occurred on the African continent as a whole and in Kenya in particular, since the 1990s.

A second broad factor accounting for the expansion in university education is the increasing complexity of modern societies and economies, thereby demanding a more highly educated and trained workforce (Okioga *et al.* 2012). In addition, globally universities have increased in response to the expanded roles and occupations in contemporary societies that require university testing and certification (Chacha 2004; Okioga *et al.* 2012). As Chacha (2004) underlined, academic certification is necessary for most positions of power, authority and prestige in most societies. There is also the perception that university education guarantees a lifelong secure career (Gudo *et al.* 2011). This bestows great power on universities. In this regard, education is considered the answer to the changing nature of the job market characterized by frequent changes of jobs that create the need for further education and training, the desire to advance current employment and create prospects for future careers (Gudo *et al.* 2011).

A leading factor specific to the Kenyan context that is responsible for the expansion in university education is the growing segments of the population that demand university education (Onsongo 2007; Republic of Kenya 2006). In particular, the widespread belief that a degree is required to get a good job, or to advance in a job demand has elevated the importance attached to university education, making it a necessity for success. This in turn has increased the need among many Kenyans, especially those in the middle class, to access university education. The expanding demand for university education has been associated with the increase in the number of secondary school leavers meeting the minimum qualifications (average grade of C+) for university admission that was triggered in part by the massive expansion of primary education (Onsongo 2007), accompanied by increased transition rates from primary to secondary school.

A second factor explaining the growth of university education within the specific context of Kenya is the flexibility afforded by university institutions. According to Gudo *et al.* (2011), individuals who attain lower qualifications are finding universities more flexible than before. Previously, the only way of entering a university was a convincing pass in the Kenya Advanced Certificate of Education (KACE) or, since 1987, the Kenya Certificate of Secondary Education (KCSE). Today though, individuals who scored lower passes are joining universities, sometimes through the longer route of studying for a certificate, followed by a diploma before one can enroll for a degree programme. Such flexibility has been responsible for Module II group of students which thrives in virtually all public universities in the country.

Concerning private universities in particular, several factors have favoured their emergence and expansion in the country. First, as elsewhere in Africa, private university expansion sprang forth largely due to the public system's failure to meet the demand for higher education. With an ever-growing need to increase higher education provision in the country, it became increasingly impossible for the public sector in Kenya to cater for all those who qualify for university admission (Mwebi and Simatwa 2013; Ngome 2003). Despite the phenomenal growth in the number of public universities, these could only absorb a small proportion of secondary school graduates who met the minimum requirements for university entry. The situation was compounded by the financial inability of the government to continue subsidizing an ever-expanding public university system (Graham and Stella, 1999). This was especially so after the implementation of the Structural Adjustment Programmes (SAPs) in 1985 as part of the reform initiatives driven by the World Bank and bilateral donors. The programme called for reforms in the education sector, including the reduction of subsidies to university education. The inability of the public sector to meet the demand for a university education created the need to complement government-managed higher institutions of learning (Mwebi and Simatwa 2013) as well as a gap that called for the entry of other non-governmental players to fill such gap (UNESCO 2005a). According to the Ministry of Education (2012), the government recognized that, without a working partnership between the public and the private sectors in the financing of education, it was going to be hard to address the problems of access, equity and quality. As such, it strongly encouraged private sector partnership as articulated in Sessional paper No. 1 of 2005 and in the Kenya Education Sector Support Programme (Government of Kenya 2005). This resulted in the privatization and liberalization of higher education (or the opening up of the sector to private players) and to the provision of incentives to encourage the growth of private sector education (Ministry of Education 2012). This explains the mushrooming of private universities as a viable alternative for acquiring university education in the country (Mutula 2002; Okioga *et al.* 2012).

A second catalyst to the growth in private university education in Kenya is the instabilities that characterize many public universities. Because of poor governance (Mutula 2002), public universities have been pervaded by indiscipline among students. The situation has been aggravated by political meddling, manipulation and intervention (Mwiria, Ngethe, Ngome, Ouma-Odero, Wawire and Wesonga 2007) that has persisted in these institutions. Jointly, indiscipline and political meddling have not only disrupted academic life; they also did occasion major strikes, demonstrations and frequent closures. This has resulted in the prolonging of the minimum time required to complete degree programmes (Mutula 2002; Mwiria *et al.* 2007). According to Mutula (2002), some students take up to six years to complete what should be a four-year basic degree. Matters are compounded by the double intakes that force cohorts to take long vacations to allow others to be on campus. The growth of private universities has provided alternative avenues for acquiring university education to those who do not desire to deal with such rot in public universities.

The Quality of University Education in Kenya

Like most of her counterparts on the African continent, Kenya recognizes that the education and training of all Kenyans is fundamental to development. As such, the country has always placed education as a priority at all levels, promoting it not just as a basis for social mobility but also as a factor of national cohesion and socio-economic development (Kinuthia 2009; Ministry of Education 2012; Nyangau 2014). In particular, the government sees the country's future as a prosperous and internationally competitive nation to be dependent on the university education system. According to the Ministry of Education (2012), the country's university education system is expected to create sustainable pools of highly trained human resources equipped with the skills required for the country to experience socio-economic development and to remain globally competitive in a rapidly changing and more diverse economy. This will enable the country to actualize the national ambition of being a knowledge-based economy. Given the centrality of (university) education in Kenya's development, the government has, since independence, invested heavily in all sectors of education with the goal to widen access at all levels. Such investments resulted in the country experiencing exponential growth in primary, secondary, tertiary and university education. The term 'massification', which refers to the transformation of a previously elite system to a mass-oriented one as participation expands dramatically (Trow 2000), is frequently utilized to denote the phenomenal growth experienced at the level of university education.

For the university education sector to deliver its mandate, quality of education is of essence. This means that the education delivered by universities must not only be accessible, equitable and relevant to the needs of the economy and society, but must also meet high quality standards. For private universities in particular, quality education is also a major factor for survival. To compete effectively with their private counterparts and to justify the high fees charged to clients, private universities can only rely on the quality factor; they must offer quality education (Kalai 2010). It is the quality aspect of university education that is the subject of the debate ensuing hereafter. Although the construct of quality in higher education is subjective and its meaning contested, with different stakeholders contextualizing it differently relative to their contexts (Nyangau 2014), in our, view a quality university education should be one that produces graduates who are fit for (having the requisite skills to discharge) their roles and responsibilities in the labour market. We share the sentiments expressed by Harvey and Green (1993) that the quality of an education system can be evaluated in terms of the fitness for purpose or the extent to which it is able to facilitate the attainment of the stated goals and objectives; in this case by producing graduates who have the knowledge and skills to drive the country's socio-economic growth and development. As Cheng and Tam (1997) indicated, that quality is, by and large, a function of input, process and output of the system.

The centrality of quality for the university sub-sector in Kenya is underlined by the sub-sector's vision of providing a globally competitive quality education, training and research for sustainable development (Ministry of Education 2012). This is accompanied by the mission to produce graduates who respond to the needs of the society, whilst upgrading the skills of the existing workforce, developing the community and business leaders of tomorrow, as well as the ability to start new businesses to employ Kenyans thereby contributing to the country's economic well-being. So to speak, to realize its mission, university education in Kenya has to promote socio-economic development in line with the country's development agenda; achieve manpower development and skills acquisition; promote the discovery, storage and dissemination of knowledge; encourage research, innovation and application of innovation to development; and, contribute to community service (Ministry of Education 2012). Jointly, the vision, mission and objectives of the university sub-sector echo the Kenya government's goal of having a sustainable, quality and relevant university education for national development.

Existing research suggests that in Kenya, like in most other African countries, the 'massification' of university education raises questions about the quality of higher education. The fast growth of the sector has occurred without effective strategies for ensuring the maintenance of a healthy balance between quality and quantity. Specifically, the rapid expansion in university education in the country has not been accompanied with the provision of resources necessary for the maintenance of high standards, quality and relevance (Okioga *et al.* 2012). This has undermined considerably the quality of the education offered by the sector as well as that of the final product, i.e. the graduates themselves (Kaburu and Embeywa 2014; Munene 2016; Nganga 2014; Nyangau 2014; Odhiambo 2011; Okioga *et al.* 2012). To illustrate, Kaburu and Embeywa (2014) concluded that in many Kenyan universities, quality has become a misnomer (it does not exist). According to them, universities have become production lines where they are biting more than they can chew. Similar sentiments were expressed by Odhiambo (2011), who concluded that universities in Kenya produced graduates who are ill-equipped to compete effectively in a globalized economy. These sentiments are inconsistent with the anticipation that universities in the country will prepare a well-educated, highly-trained workforce for industrialization, modernization, and global citizenship (Nyangau 2014).

Factors Affecting the Quality of University Education in Kenya

The source of the declining quality of university education is the myriad of serious challenges consequent from the phenomenal growth in university education that the sector is faced with (Nganga 2014; Nyangau 2014; Munene 2016). The leading challenges include insufficient or declining funding, inadequate teaching and learning facilities, inadequate and poorly trained academic staff, increasing academic fraud and poor governance. Jointly, these challenges constitute major catalysts to the declining quality of education that is facing universities in Africa in general, and in Kenya in particular. They not only impair the functioning of the sector they also undermine its capacity to effectively deliver on its mandate of a quality and relevant education (Munene 2016; Nganga 2014; Nyangau 2014; Okioga *et al.* 2012; World Bank 2000a). In sum, the challenges as identified have resulted in declining academic achievement and quality of university education. A more detailed profiling of these is presented below starting with insufficient or declining funding.

Insufficient or Declining Public Funding

For the university system to guarantee quality it must be adequately funded. This means that the providers of higher education must be prepared to infuse the finances necessary for the system to deliver quality education that meets the human capital requirements and research demands of the country (Kauffeldt 2009). Unfortunately for Kenya, the dramatic expansion of enrolments in the public universities has occurred simultaneously with declining funding received from government through the Ministry of Education. Government subsidies to public universities are no longer enough, making the funding of the sector one of the biggest concerns in Kenya. According to Munene (2016), for example, the 1990s, as the period marking the rapid increase in the number of universities in the country the bulk of which are public, coincided with the adoption of a market-based policy of financing public universities by the government, thereby ushering in an era of reduced state support for higher education. Since then, government funding for public universities, including the average per capita expenditure per student, has continued to diminish. To illustrate this fact, the *Economic Survey 2014* showed that subsidies to public universities grew by six per cent during the period to reach US$624 million, from US$588 million in 2012 (Kenya National Bureau of Statistics, 2014); meaning that enrolments to public universities rose seven times faster than funding.

Funding cuts by government have made it difficult for universities to cater to the growing numbers of students taking courses. This has forced public universities to explore alternative strategies (or avenues) for expanding their revenue bases (Ministry of Education 2012; Nganga 2014; Munene 2016;

Mutula 2002; Nyangau 2014). The implementation of the so-called 'Parallel' or 'Module II' programme, which allows public universities to admit privately-sponsored students who fully pay for the cost of their education, is a step in this direction. Such programmes have become increasingly common in Africa. Recent research shows that self-sponsored students are dominating public universities in Kenya (Odhiambo 2011; Sifuna 2010; Wangenge-Ouma 2012). Other measures put in place by public universities to generate extra revenue to augment meagre government allocation include cost-recovery measures and introduction of commercial ventures such as shopping malls, funeral homes, industrial parks, rented-out property and provision of catering services (ICEF Monitor 2015; Nganga 2014; Nyangau 2014; Munene 2016).

The admission of fully-paying students in public universities through Module II and other paid programmes has created the partial privatization of the public sector of university education. This has become a major challenge to the growth of the private sector of university education. It should be noted that, unlike public universities which are heavily dependent on government funding, private universities mainly depend on tuition fees for their revenue and, therefore, are self-sustaining and less likely to suffer the financial crunch evident in the public service. The strategy of the public sector relying on paid programmes to supplement government funding though could be undermined considerably if the directive by the CUE to universities to terminate the offering of diploma and certificate courses by July 2015 (ICEF Monitor, 2015) is eventually effected. By increasing student numbers as well as being good sources of revenue, these courses have become a major cash cow for many public sector higher education institutions. As such, ending them would be a major financial blow to many public universities. Of course, such a move would also hurt private universities. A large number of them experience their highest enrolments at the Certificate and Diploma levels. The only exception is the United States International University which does not offer Certificate and Diploma programmes.

That dwindling financial resources undermine the quality of education provided by public universities is not a moot issue. As stated earlier, to guarantee quality education the university system must be adequately funded. Among other things, sufficient funding is required to develop, maintain and equip teaching and learning facilities such as libraries, laboratories, classroom and office space; to develop and constantly improve the quality of programmes offered; to create a conducive living environment for students; to train and remunerate staff well so as to keep them motivated and committed to their work and to fund research activities. This is consistent with the sentiments expressed by the Ministry of Education (2012) that, among other key ingredients, the quality of education must be founded on not just the students admitted but also on the learning environment created, the curriculum or programmes adopted and the academic staff in the institution. Although commercial ventures and other entrepreneurial activities offer what appear to be viable alternatives to government funding, if not handled carefully they can be detrimental to the quality of the education provided by (public) universities. Where universities become too focused on revenue generation (commercial ventures), for example, their attention is likely to be diverted from their core business of providing a quality education. This is consistent with the sentiments expressed by Santiago, Tremblay, Basri and Arnal (2008) that universities are no longer viewed as centres of academic progress but of entrepreneurship, with professors, heads of departments viewed as line management and the vice-chancellor being the chief executive. In addition, where students must pay for their education, sometimes the need to attract, retain and satisfy customers may be met at the expense of quality of the education provided to them. In this regard, 'Module II' can thrive at the expense of regular programmes as well as lead to the lowering of academic standards as universities lower minimum entrance requirements to attract those who did not find admission into regular programmes.

Inadequate Teaching and Learning Facilities

Most universities on the African continent in general, and in Kenya in particular, lack the physical facilities required for effective teaching and learning (Akinwumi 2008; Kaburu and Embeywa 2014; Mwebi and Simwata 2013). The rising enrolments in the midst of declining government funding and support and the consequent crisis occasioned by it, have left (public) universities without decent teaching and/ or learning facilities (Munene 2016; Mutula 2002; Nyangau 2014; Okioga, *et al.* 2012). The institutions are experiencing acute shortages of facilities that are essential for the existence of a suitable learning and teaching environment (Okwakol 2008). In some instances, universities have experienced a general decay and a near collapse of the good physical facilities that existed during the 1970s and 1980s (Okioga *et al.* 2012) when universities enjoyed significant budgets from government.

The acute shortage of teaching and learning facilities in many public universities manifests itself in many forms. First, public universities experience shortages of classroom (lecture halls) space (Nyangau 2014; Munene 2016; Okwakol 2008) due to the lack of funds to facilitate the necessary ongoing development and maintain such facilities. Some institutions are littered with deteriorating and crumbling buildings (Kauffeldt 2009). Second, public universities are also characterized by the lack of spacious libraries that are adequately equipped (stocked) with current reading materials (Kauffeldt 2009; Munene 2016; Mwebi and Simatwa 2013). Despite serving large numbers of students, such libraries tend to have outdated collections and restricted internet connectivity as a result of funding cuts. This means that students and faculty often work without access to essential components of university work, such as current textbooks and academic journals.

A third manifestation of inadequate learning and teaching facilities in public universities is the lack of basic computer laboratories that are well maintained and have adequate supplies, tools and equipment (Munyasi 2010; Mwebi and Simatwa 2013; Nyangau 2014; Odebero 2010). This restricts students' access to communication technology, denies them access to current information sources and restricts teaching to traditional methods (Munyasi 2010; Mwebi and Simatwa 2013; Nyangau 2014; Odebero 2010; Okwakol 2008).

The fourth pointer to the inadequate teaching and learning facilities characteristic of public universities in Kenya is the lack of adequate and sufficiently equipped science laboratories and workshop equipment for effective teaching and learning (Gudo *et al.* 2011) in institutions offering scientific and technical subjects. This undermines considerably the practical elements of the curricula offered. In addition, many universities lack sufficient funds to sustain a meaningful research capacity (Kauffeldt 2009; Munene 2016; Mwebi and Simatwa 2013). Finally, students in public universities must also contend with distracting living conditions, due to poor quality hostels and official accommodation without adequate healthcare facilities (Mwebi and Simatwa 2013; Okioga *et al.* 2012).

As compared to public universities, private universities tend to have good facilities and infrastructure (Mutula 2002; Okioga *et al.* 2012), on account of having always remained under the microscopic watch of the CUE, formerly CHE, which insists on adherence to strict standards and regulations by these institutions. Library facilities are well endowed with book budgets compared to those in the public sector (Mutula, 2002). They tend to have sufficient as well as current books, journals. Most private universities also have modern infrastructure such as classrooms and offices as well as information and communication technology and internet connectivity allow access to electronic sources of information (Okioga *et al.* 2012).

Inadequacies in teaching and learning facilities in public universities in Kenya undermine their capacity to offer quality education (Gudo *et al.* 2011; World Bank 2000a). Existing research evidence suggests that rising enrolments without corresponding increases in facilities pose a great threat to quality of education provided by universities (Akinwumi 2008; Mwebi and Simatwa 2013; Ngolovoi 2006; Odebero 2010; Ogot 2002). The poor quality and shortage of physical facilities subject students to difficult learning conditions, thereby causing the quality of education provided and hence the quality of the graduates produced by these institutions to deterioration. According to Gudo *et al.* (2011), the ultimate consequence is the mass production of graduates who have certificates without matching academic and technical competence, which in turn makes attempts by universities to meet their objectives a mirage and an exercise in futility. Speaking specifically about the Kenyan situation, Ogot (2002) posited that the quality of higher education in Kenya could be questionable because of inadequate facilities.

A major outcome of insufficient teaching and learning facilities facing many Kenyan public universities is overcrowding. The significant growth in enrolments coupled with declining funding has resulted in more and more students joining universities whose facilities were originally designed to accommodate far fewer students (Boit and Kipkoech 2012; Mutula 2002; Nyangau 2014; Odhiambo 2011; Sifuna 2010; Teferra and Altbach 2004). The obvious outcome of this is overcrowding especially in classrooms. In some universities, for example, sometimes as many as 1,000 students occupy a single classroom. According to Nyangau (2014: 12), 'so severe is the crisis of overcrowding that it is not uncommon to find students standing inside or outside of lecture halls or even perched on windows during lectures'. Similar sentiments are expressed by Gudo *et al.* (2011) who posited that the shortage in classroom space causes students to miss sitting space or to attend lectures sitting outside of the classroom. Overcrowding makes classes increasingly hard to teach and manage effectively (Gudo *et al.* 2011). It also leads to students' lack of concentration and attention to lectures. This has obvious detrimental effects on the quality of student learning, the overall quality of the education received by learners and on the quality of graduates.

Inadequate and Poorly Trained Academic Staff

Central to the success of higher education institutions are the educational resources (or inputs) available to them (Kauffeldt 2009; UNESCO 2005b). These, in addition to buildings and equipment, include the people (staff), necessary to be able to offer well-designed academic programmes (Kauffeldt 2009). A sufficient, highly qualified and effective faculty and sufficient supporting staff are crucial for a quality university education. These should also have sufficient resources to support their efforts, including adequate classroom space, adequate and well-equipped laboratories, adequate library space equipped with current reading materials, access to the most up-to-date computer and other communication technology and access to adequate research funds. Unfortunately, many universities experience tremendous growth in enrolments without an equivalent growth in staffing, thereby suffering severe deficiencies in the academic staff vital to deliver a quality education. In Kenya, for example, the demand for teaching staff outstrips the supply in both public and private universities (Gudo *et al.* 2011). Furthermore, because of the funding crisis affecting Kenyan (public) universities, lecturers are poorly trained and, thus, not properly qualified (Nyangau 2014; Munene 2016).

The staffing situation in most African countries is compounded by brain drain (see e.g., Damtew and Altbach 2004; Kauffeldt 2009; Kelly 2001; Effah 2003; Ngome 2003; Saint 2004; Seth 2000; Wondimu 2003) that has involved the flight of well-qualified academics mostly to North America and Europe, and in some cases to Southern Africa, where pay is much better. This is mainly caused by the poor remuneration of academics, the undervaluing of faculty and non-conducive working environment (Gudo et al. 2011; Kauffeldt 2009). These make it difficult for universities to recruit and retain good scholars in their fields as there are often more lucrative opportunities in the business world or in some foreign lands. As a result of brain drain, a significant proportion of faculty teaching in many universities in Africa in general, and in Kenya in particular today, do not have the minimum academic qualification of a PhD.

To cope with the severe shortages in academic staff, universities have adopted varied strategies. In some universities, survival tactics have included assigning graduate students and tutorial fellows full teaching responsibilities (Odebero 2010); some of them teaching both junior and senior students. A second coping mechanism is increased workloads for faculty (Gudo *et al.* 2011; Owuor 2012). According to Owuor (2012) in many Kenyan universities lecturers who teach 36 hours a week, lecturers who have no offices, overcrowded lecture halls/rooms; and, limited library facilities, commonplaces. In addition, the shortage of qualified academics has forced many to fill existing academic positions with under-qualified (or incompetent) persons, including graduates from unaccredited universities in India and North America (Gudo *et al.* 2011; Kauffeldt 2009), with public universities being the most affected. Normally, such persons would not have qualified to join the university system. Other survival tactics include encouraging Master's students to elect to take the project instead of the thesis option because it is less rigorous compared to the thesis and the appointing of supervisors from other disciplines where they have no basis on content (Odebero 2010). With specific reference to supervision, for one to be effective, one must not only be in the same discipline as the student but, most important, also share the research interests of the student.

No doubt, the quality of university education suffers a great setback due to inadequate, poorly trained and incompetent academic staff (Gogo 2010; Ngolovoi 2006; Ogot 2002; Oketch 2009). For effective teaching to occur at the university, it requires a minimum ratio of lecturing staff against the number of enrolled students. Based on the Commission for University Education (CUE), the recommended lecturer-student ratio should be 1:50 for theoretical-based courses and 1:20 for practical-based courses [Commission for University Education, n.d (b)]. The shortage of academic staff has rendered it impossible to meet these thresholds.

Poor pay, lack of incentive or reward for good performance and the undervaluation of academic staff by universities (Kauffeldt 2009) cause those who occupy teaching positions in Kenyan universities to have low commitment to their work and to play a limited role in the life of their employing institution (Okioga *et al.* 2012; Standa 2007). Many of them spend most of their time moonlighting: doing consultancy work, working part-time at several institutions or engaging in other forms of income-generating activities so as to be able to supplement the meagre pay earned from their full-time job. This distracts them from performing their roles effectively. They devote little attention to research or improving their teaching. The situation is best summed up by Bloom and Ahmad (2000:24) who stated that:

> Many faculty work part time at several institutions, devote little attention to research or to improving their teaching and play little or no role in the life of the institution employing them. Faculty members are often more interested in teaching another course – often at an unaccredited school – rather than increasing their presence and commitment to the main institutions with which they are affiliated. With wages so low, it is difficult to condemn such behavior.

Bloom and Ahmad's (2000:24) sentiments are echoed in a commentary appearing in a copy of the *Chronicle for Higher Education*, titled 'When family Ties Bind African University', in which Holm (2010) writes:

> Many, if not most African academics dedicate surprisingly little time teaching, advising students, conducting research, writing scholarly articles and serving as administrators. Often they are away from their universities for a combined period equals as much as half or more of the academic year.

A closer look at some of the coping mechanisms embraced by universities to deal with the shortage of academic staff reveals that they are detrimental to the delivery of quality education and negatively influence academic rigour (Gudo *et al.* 2011). For instance, assigning tutorial fellows and graduate students full teaching responsibilities undermines the quality of education provided by universities. The gravity of the adverse effects of this practice is best understood within the context of the reality of the poor quality of (lack of rigour in) postgraduate training in many universities today. The heavy workloads many lecturers have to carry render them ineffective in their teaching, supervision and assessment of learners. This is supported by Ngolovoi (2006), who expressed that increased workload and lack of competence among lecturers could be affecting the delivery of quality education to university students in Kenya. Moonlighting and the consequent excessive absenteeism also negatively impact on quality. The net effects of these are poorly trained graduates who employers must invest in considerably for them to acquire the knowledge and skills required to perform competently the duties and responsibilities assigned in the work environment. The effect of poorly trained lecturers is especially evident in the training of postgraduate students, where students are expected to acquire research skills which most of their mentors (lectures) may have a poor mastery of.

Increasing Academic Fraud

The declining quality of universities must also be viewed within the context of the entire education system in Kenya (Mutula 2002). Specifically, the rising rate of examination cheating and grade inflation that pervades the primary and secondary levels of education in the country is responsible for students who join the universities with high grades that do not mirror their intellectual capacity (Mutula 2002). Although this has gone on for many years, the peak of cheating in examination appears to have occurred in 2015, with students even in the most rural of areas being able to download and openly discuss examination questions for most courses using social media engines such as *WhatsApp*. This prompted the government, through the Ministry of Education, to suspend the top officials of the Kenya National Examination Council (KNEC). In their place new officials were appointed with the mandates to investigate the causes of the rampant fraud and to streamline the management of the examination process in the country. The fraud and grade inflation that have characterized the lower levels of education have serious implications for the quality of students joining public and private universities in the country.

The culture of fraud and cheating affecting the lower levels of education in Kenya has infiltrated universities, further undermining the quality of the graduates produced. The situation is complicated further by the mediocre academic climate prevailing in many universities. Because of such a climate, the quality of teaching and learning has been eroded significantly and there has occurred a surge in academic fraud, evident through acts such as plagiarism, fabricated references, students impersonating each other in exams and lecturers demanding money or sexual favours in exchange for passing grades (Nyangau 2014; Munene 2016). To illustrate, most recently, the CUE cancelled five doctoral degrees awarded by Kisii University after it emerged that the five students had only studied for six months each before receiving their doctorates. The situation has been aggravated further by the sprouting of essay writing 'mills' and other assignment completion businesses, which is occurring is in tandem with the increasing numbers of university students. This has prompted the Commission for University Education to issue the warning that undetected cheating is damaging the quality of graduates; sentiments that are shared by many other stakeholders. The ultimate outcome is degree holders with limited intellectual capacity. Some universities have initiated steps to cut on the level of academic dishonesty among students by introducing technological software, such as *Turnitin* and *Blackboard*, to detect plagiarism. However, there are indications that technological loopholes are allowing savvy students to beat academic plagiarism software (see e.g., Heather 2010; Fearn 2011). In his paper titled, 'Turnitoff: Identifying and Fixing a Hole in Current Plagiarism Detection Software', Heather (2010) revealed that beating the plagiarism detection system is simple. These sentiments were echoed by Fearn (2011) who indicated plagiarism detection systems are open to simple cheats allowing students to evade detection when submitting copied material. This definitely erodes the utility of such software is the fight against poor quality of education in universities.

Poor Governance

Another major challenge facing higher education in Kenya today is poor governance (Kauffeldt 2009; Nyangau 2014; The World Bank/UNESCO Task force on Higher Education and Society 2000). Good governance is essential for the performance of higher education systems, particularly in countries suffering from scarce or limited resources like Kenya. To be effective, universities require visionary, creative and inclusive leadership. According to the Task Force on Higher Education and Society (2000), good governance promotes education quality. Whereas good governance alone may not be a sufficient condition for attaining quality education, it is certainly a necessary one. A poorly governed institution will neither flourish nor deliver quality education (The Task on Higher Education and Society 2000). This study focuses on the broad subject of governance in higher university education with a specific emphasis on students' participation (or involvement) in governance and decision making processes. A detailed review of the status of governance in universities and of student participation in the governance process is presented in Chapter Three.

For good governance to exist in universities, the institutions must uphold the following six key principles of governance: academic freedom; shared governance; clear rights and responsibilities; meritocratic selection; financial stability; and accountability (Kauffeldt 2009). Academic freedom denotes the right of scholars to teach and publish without controls or restraints from the institutions that hire them or the primary stakeholder, that is, government (Kauffeldt 2009). The principle of shared governance involves notions of cooperative governance and participation in critical decision-making by all those involved in higher education. It expresses the need for faculty and student representation and participation in decision-making (Kauffeldt 2009). It is this principle that is the locus of this study. The study interrogates the extent of students' involvement in the governance processes in both public and private universities in Kenya. The existence of clear rights and responsibilities in universities is manifested in mutually agreed conditions for university operations that provide a stable environment for decision-making. Adherence to the meritocratic selection principle of good governance requires that the selection and promotion of faculty, administrators and students be based on broadly defined merit (Kauffeldt 2009). This is essential to the functioning of higher education. The principle of financial stability refers to the adequacy of funding for universities to be able to meet their demands and to execute their mandates effectively. The final principle of good governance is accountability. It represents the obligation universities and their managers have to justify their activities, accept responsibility for them, and to disclose the results of their activities in a transparent manner.

Existing evidence suggests that universities in many African countries in general, and in Kenya in particular, routinely violate the principles of good governance with great frequency. This means that universities in Africa suffer poor governance. In particular, political interference especially in public universities makes adherence to the principles of good governance a near impossibility (Kauffeldt 2009). In many instances, the intervention is based on the perception that universities constitute a potential threat to fragile and often not well-established political systems and therefore must be closely monitored (Saha 1993). Political meddling can impact negatively on the learning environment and stability in universities. While political activity on campuses has helped address injustices and promote democracy the world over (Okioga *et al.* 2012), it has also inappropriately disrupted campus life including research, teaching and learning. This affects adversely the quality of education provided by universities.

Existing evidence suggests that political meddling has continued to undermine the implementation of this principle. In addition, the lack of cooperation in institutional governance abounds in many universities. Turning to rights and responsibilities, the evidence suggests that whereas many universities have drafted and passed legislation to guide academic freedom, the tendency is for events to occur outside of or around the policy framework, thus creating a culture of uncertainty (Kauffeldt 2009). Another pointer to the existence of poor governance practices in many universities is the politicization of appointments and promotions (Kauffeldt 2009), thereby defeating the very principle of meritocracy that is core to good governance. Concerning the financial stability principle, evidence abounds showing that university education in many African countries, including Kenya, often functions under turbulent financial conditions. The situation is further compounded by the limited financial resources available especially to public universities (Kauffeldt 2009; Ministry of Education 2012; Nganga 2014; Munene 2016; Mutula 2002; Nyangau 2014). In Kenya some progress has been made to instil a sense of accountability especially through the establishment of semi-autonomous agencies, like the CUE, to regulate university education. However, there is still a fair degree of state and higher education system enmeshment that leaves little space for these agencies to operate with the independence necessary to actualize true accountability (Bloom and Ahmad 2000; Kauffeldt 2009).

Other

Other challenges facing university education in Kenya worth mentioning here include the mushrooming of new satellite campuses all over the country and the existence of a weak regulatory framework. To cope with the rising numbers some universities, in the name of meeting the high demand for tertiary education and to raise money for the parent university, have established campuses in cities and towns located in environments that are not conducive to learning such as next to pubs, restaurants and supermarkets, among others. Such satellite campuses are normally cheap and of low quality. They lack even the most basic facilities, such as libraries and internet access and are normally staffed by a handful of academic staff who in most cases do not have more than a Master's degree; in some instances even that Master's degree is of questionable credibility. The mushrooming of satellite campuses creates a mediocre academic environment that is not conducive to quality education. As a result, the sprouting of such campuses has become a major concern for Kenya's Commission of University Education (CUE), which has ordered the closing of sub-standard campuses by both public and private universities.

Although the Kenya government established a body, the Council on Higher Education (CHE) later renamed Commission for University Education (CUE), to regulate university education as early as 1995, the body initially focused on the accreditation of private universities, leaving public universities' growth virtually unregulated (or unchecked) for years. It was not until 2013 that the CUE's mandate was expanded to cover public universities. The CUE recognizes the need to regulate, coordinate and assure quality in university education. The body, though, has continued to perform poorly on account of the lack of organizational, technical and human capacities to monitor and enforce quality compliance (Munene 2016).

Strategies for Alleviation of Poor Quality of Education

According to Munene (2016), a combination of strategies is necessary to restore quality, especially at Kenya's public universities. For such strategies to succeed, though, it calls for the involvement of the state, regulatory authorities and the institutions themselves. As a first step, Munene (2016) recommends a differentiated public university system for Kenya, with a small number of research universities specializing in high-level research and graduate training. In this regard, he identified the University of Nairobi, Kenyatta University, Moi University, Egerton University and the Jomo Kenyatta University of Agriculture and Technology, which are older and more established, as having the academic and other resources to assume such a role, leaving other newer institutions established to focus on good-quality undergraduate and Master's level training. A second recommendation for addressing the poor quality of education in Kenya offered by Munene (2016) is change in the funding model utilized by the government. According to him, the current 'one-size-fits-all' approach has failed, and instead programmes should be financed according to how expensive they are to prepare and teach. Thirdly, Munene (2016) emphasizes the strengthening of the university education regulatory oversight. More specifically, he recommends the upping of the budget allocated to CUE if the commission is to harness its technical and human resources for effective monitoring and quality enforcement. However, to be effective, the commission must work very closely with professional associations and internal university quality assurance units. In addition, Munene (2016) suggested that universities must set up faculty development programmes to train academic staff about the complexities and changing nature of an academic career. Such training is imperative if Kenyan academics are to be introduced to modern teaching strategies that appeal to an evolving student demographic.

Staying with academic staff, it is imperative that universities rethink the remuneration and incentive packages offered to them, as well as initiate improvements in the overall working conditions faced by staff. In our view, it is only through the payment of livable wages to academics that Kenya will move closer to having professional academics who are committed to their work of teaching and research as well as to the life and activities of their organizations. Today's full-time academic employees have perfected the art of functioning like part-time employees whose loyalty lies elsewhere. As indicated earlier, many university academic staff spent the bulk of their time moonlighting; doing consultancy work, working part-time at several institutions or engaging in other forms of income-generating activities so as to be able to supplement the meagre pay earned from full-time employment (Bloom and Ahmad 2000; Holm 2010; Okioga *et al.* 2012; Standa 2007). For the majority of them, the institution employing them provides a contact address rather than a source of livelihood. Finally, to grow quality research among faculty, universities must invest more money in the sector. There is need to supplement the money set aside by universities for research; though the institutions must create capacity among faculty for grant application and competition.

3

The Governance of Higher Education

This chapter presents a review of literature in relation to the subject of student involvement in university governance. The chapter is organized into six sections. Section one examines the meaning of the concept of governance, bringing in the related concepts of leadership and good governance. This is followed by the profiling of the practice of governance in higher education. The discussion here incorporates the identification and profiling of the principles that universities must observe for good governance to exist and the tools and practices they can rely on to enhance good governance. The third section of the chapter delves into the subject matter of student involvement in university governance. Here the presentation centres on the historical development of student involvement in governance, the forms that involvement assumes and the benefits of participation for the society, the student and the institution. Whereas section 4 of the chapter focuses on the relationship between students and leadership, section five examines the governance of university education in Kenya, including structures and practices used. The final section of the chapter (section six) identifies some of the research issues emanating from the historical analysis of student involvement in the governance of higher education.

The Concept of (Good) Governance

Governance is a complex and highly contested concept that is difficult to capture in a simple definition. Because the concept means different things to different people, diverse definitions of it abound in the literature. As advanced by Plato when referring to the term 'Kubernao' in Greek, governance is the act of governing or steering a government, or for that matter any other appropriate entity (www.gdrc.org/u-gov/governance-understand.html). This definition is consistent with the one offered by the Webster's Third New International Dictionary (1986:982) that governance is a synonym for government, or 'the act or process of governing, specifically authoritative direction and control'. A similar definition is offered by the Cambridge Advanced Learner's Dictionary and Thesaurus when it views governance as the way that organizations or countries are managed at the highest level and the systems for doing this. The concept of governance has also been defined as 'a process whereby elements in society wield power, authority and influence and enact policies and decisions concerning public life and social upliftment' (www.gdrc.org/u-gov/governance-understand.html). This is close to Santiso's (2011) view that governance is a multifaceted concept that captures the manner in which power is exercised in the management of a country's economic and social resources for development. The definition is also closely allied to the one advanced by the World Bank (1992, 1994, 2000a) that governance is the manner in which power is exercised in the management of a country's economic and social resources for development and includes the capacity of governments to design, formulate and implement policies and discharge functions.

What emerges from the sample definitions presented above is that governance is not just a broad concept whose meaning transcends the notion of government but also a highly contextual concept whose meaning cannot be captured using one monolithic definition. As such, the process and practices that will apply will vary significantly given the environment in which they are applied. For instance, governance in the public sector needs to take into account legal and constitutional accountability and responsibilities; whereas in the non-governmental sector, representing stakeholder interests may take precedence over all else in the governance to be applied (Task Force on Higher Education and Society 2000).

Within the context of higher education, the term governance has been used to refer to the means by which universities and other higher education institutions are organized and managed (ESMU 2009). The Task Force on Higher Education and Society (2000) defined it as the formal and informal arrangements that allow higher education institutions to make decisions and to establish, implement and continuously monitor the proper implementation of policies. Whereas the arrangements are official and explicit, their informal equivalents refer to unwritten rules governing how people within higher education institutions relate to each other. For the purpose of this study, the term governance is employed to refer to all those structures, processes and activities that are involved in planning and directing of higher education institutions and the people working in them. Since governance is about interest articulation and goal realization, it raises the questions about who decides when on what; and in the case of higher education this introduces the two levels of governance, i.e.: the internal and external levels or dimensions of governance. Internal or institutional governance refers to the organizational arrangements within institutions that contribute to the smooth running of these organizations and constitute the lines of authority, decision-making processes and policies, staffing and financing mechanisms. External governance, in most cases, refers to the macro system or state control of higher education institutions and entails the laws, decrees, funding arrangements and evaluations they subject these institutions to (Eurydice 2008; OECD 2008). Higher education governance is therefore understood as the external (system) and internal (institutional) coordination of higher education and research. Consequently, in relation to this study, while the involvement of students in governance is mainly an internal governance issue, its implementation has a lot of influence from State policies and practices especially relating to democratic politics that have close ties to whether higher education institutions practice participatory decision-making or not.

The Relationship between Governance and Leadership

Closely related to the concept of governance is the concept of leadership. Although the literature presents the two as distinctive items, in practice they often overlap (Task Force on Higher Education and Society 2000). Leadership can be defined as an influential relationship among leaders and followers who are bound together by a mutual goal that constitutes the basis for their quest for change (Gordon 1955; Rost 1993). It manifests an interaction between a person and the members of a group in which one person, the group leader, influences, while the other persons respond (Gordon 1955:10). Kouzes and Posner (1995:30) define leadership as 'the art of mobilizing others to want to struggle for shared aspirations'. For Davis (2003:4), leadership implies movement, taking the organization or some part of it in a new direction, solving problems, being creative, initiating new programmes, building organizational structures and improving quality.

According to Bolman and Deal (1995: 102), 'The essence of leadership is not giving things or even providing visions. It is offering oneself and one's spirit.' As can be gleaned from the above definitions, leadership is a 'collaborative endeavor'; that is, leadership is not the leader, but the relationship that exists between the leader and those following him/her. It is crucial for a leader to be able to share power, empower and co-operate with others. According to Bennis and Bennis (2003), a leader has a focus on the people and the interest of everyone. He/she motivates, earns trust of others through integrity and notably has a vision of what they want to achieve in the present and in the future. Leadership may be seen as an inborn ability that is only in a few people and not in others. However, Kouzes and Posner (1988) differ with this and explain that leadership is a set of learnt and observable skills. As such, people who have the aspiration and persistence can acquire the much needed skills and abilities for the role. Basham (2000) echoes similar sentiments, arguing that few leadership skills are naturally endowed but are learned through enthusiasm and training.

The literature identifies a variety of leadership types. These include transformative, participative, transactional and distributed leaderships (Gous 2003; Parrish n.d; Rost 1993). Transformational leadership entails a leader who motivates others through a shared vision of where they want to go and what they want to achieve. These leaders tend to delegate duties, and monitor and inform the people what they are supposed to do (Parrish n.d). They share power, learn from others and identify with the needs of others to also achieve and grow (Gous 2003). This kind of leadership is change oriented (Basham 2010; Gardiner 2005); leaders guide their followers in confronting the status quo. Participative leadership, on the other hand, is about inclusivity. The leadership engages everyone in decision-making, with the view to making people own what is being created (Diamond 2006). However, vested interests and the lack of a culture of openness may undermine participation at different levels (Obondo 2000). The transactional type of leadership is more concerned with productivity rather than changing the environment (Basham 2010; Connor 2004). The leader is the authority figure and he/she simply wants his/ her objectives to be followed and will attempt to make changes only when the paradigm in play seems not to be working. Others are not given space to be creative or even to appreciate their resourcefulness (Connor 2004). Finally, distributed leadership involves several individuals, who have diverse skills that enable achievement of goals, contributing to the leadership (Pearce 2004; van Ameijde, Nelson, Billsberry and Meurs 2009). This form of leadership has been associated with higher performance compared to old 'leader dominated' leadership forms.

The running thread across most definitions of governance is the way issues affecting the entire institution, or one or two components thereof, are decided. Consequently, governance is intertwined with leadership. Specifically, there exists a reciprocal (two-way) link between leadership and governance. Leadership represents the organization of people into manageable groups and influencing them into a specific direction for the purpose of harnessing available resources for the good of all. Hence, it is a significant component of any governance arrangement, including that of higher education institutions, because it provides an opportunity for members of the institutions to participate in running their organizations. In an academic community, student leadership arises from the way governance is structured within a college or university. The governance structure in place in terms of policies, goals and procedures as well as the organizational structure articulates the rights and responsibilities of various actors in the institution in addition to legitimizing the kind of groups and power relations that an institution will have. The governance structure and particularly a policy on stakeholder participation in governance, therefore, must be accommodative of all members of the institution, including students through their leaders.

Leaders play an important role in (effective) governance (Department for Education and Skills 2006). For good governance to thrive it requires quality leadership that is capable of giving it direction by fostering interagency collaboration and shared understanding (Brookes 2006; Craig 2005; Lownsborough and O'Leary

2005; NCSL 2008a); promoting clarity of roles and responsibilities between actors (Brookes 2006; Craig 2005); and growing collaboration and team work (Harker, Dobel-Ober, Berridge, and Sinclair 2004; National College for School Leadership 2008b; University of East Anglia with the National Children's Bureau 2007). Strong leadership also contributes to effective governance by ensuring that people's and institutional needs remain at the forefront of the agenda, focusing on the clear issues and outcomes and, by encouraging commitment at all levels (Department for Education and Skills 2006; Robinson 2008).

In turn, governance supports leadership through arrangements and frameworks. In addition to setting the right goals and procedures for ensuring institutional aims are met, the governing body must appoint personnel and give them power to make decisions on behalf of the organization. Furthermore, the existence of good governance arrangements (frameworks), such as partnership agreements and 'outcome-based' accountability frameworks, support effective leadership by providing strategic direction for leaders (Brookes 2006; Thompson and Uyeda 2004); fostering agreed and shared objectives and vision, including clarifying roles and responsibilities (National College for School Leadership 2008a; Brookes 2006; Thompson and Uyeda 2004) and; by helping leaders to foster commitment and shared aims (Department for Education and Skills 2006; Utting, Painter, Renshaw and Hutchinson 2008). These are features of effective leadership for narrowing the gap (Martin, Lord, White, Mitchell, and Atkinson 2009). Governance frameworks also help leaders to establish accountability. Accountability is central to the purpose and function of governance and important for effective leadership. The National College for School Leadership (2008b) found that effective leaders think creatively about governance arrangements so as to guarantee shared participation, shared responsibility and accountability, and sustainable partnerships.

The Concept of Good Governance

Emanating from the broad concept of governance is the concept of 'good governance'. The concept denotes the quality of the governance process, in particular the effectiveness of government (Santiso 2001). The quality of governance is ultimately attributable to its democratic content. Neither democracy (in our case participation) nor good governance is sustainable without the other; the two should converge. Good governance represents the best possible process for making decisions. It is not about making 'correct' decisions but about the processes for making and implementing decisions. For the Wold Bank (1994), good governance is epitomized by predictable, open and enlightened policy-making and a bureaucracy imbued with a professional ethos acting in furtherance of the public good. This is consistent with the sentiments expressed by Healey and Robinson (1994) who opined that 'good governance' implies a high level of organizational effectiveness in relation to policy-formulation and the policies actually pursued, especially in the conduct of economic policy and its contribution to growth, stability and popular welfare. A good governance system puts further requirements on the process of decision-making and public policy formulation. It extends beyond the capacity of public sector to the rules that create a legitimate, effective and efficient framework for the conduct of public policy (Santiso 2001).

There exist a number of characteristics or practices of 'good governance' that set it apart from bad (or poor) governance. Poor governance tends to be associated with arbitrary policy making, unaccountable bureaucracies, unenforced or unjust legal systems, the abuse of executive power, a civil society unengaged in public life, and widespread corruption (Kaufmann, *et al.* 1999; World Bank 1994, 2000a; http://www.goodgovernance.org.au/about-good-governance/what-is-good-governance/). The first characteristic of good governance is participation (Santiso 2001; World Bank 1994, 2000a). Good governance requires that all stakeholders have a voice in decision-making, either directly or through legitimate intermediate institutions that represent their interests. Anyone affected by or interested in a decision should have the opportunity to participate in the process for making that decision. Members' participation could be direct or delegated through an entity created to represent them in the decision-making process. The delegated model is especially applicable where the group is too large to efficiently make all necessary decisions by involving everyone, as is the case with universities where the student body delegates the responsibility for involvement in university decision-making to elected (or appointed) representatives.

The second characteristic of good governance, one that is closely related to participation, is consensus orientation. Good governance mediates differing interests to reach a broad consensus on what is in the best interest of the group and, where possible, on policies and procedures (http://www.goodgovernance.org.au/about-good-governance/what-is-good-governance/). The third fundamental requirement of good governance is accountability (Kaufmann *et al.* 1999; Santiso 2001; World Bank 1994, 2000a). Where good governance is the norm, decision-makers are accountable to the public and/ or to institutional stakeholders. Accountability means that administrators (or managers) have an obligation to report, explain and be answerable for the consequences of the decisions they make on behalf of the stakeholders they represent (World Bank 1994, 2000 a; http://www.goodgovernance.org.au/about-good-governance/what-is-good-governance/). Closely linked to accountability is transparency. Normally built on the free flow of information, transparency represents the extent to which people (stakeholders) follow and understand the decision-making process. Transparency exists where stakeholders are able to clearly see how and why a decision was made; what information, advice and consultation decision makers considered, and which legislative requirements were followed (http://www.goodgovernance.org.au/about-good-governance/what-is-good-governance/;World Bank 1994, 2000a). Where transparency exists, processes, institutions and information are directly accessible to those concerned with them, and enough information is provided to understand and monitor them.

In addition, good governance is responsive. It ensures that the needs of the entire community/ stakeholders are served while balancing competing interests in a timely, appropriate and responsive manner (http://www.goodgovernance.org.au/about-good-governance/what-is-good-governance/). In this scheme of things, institutions and processes are designed to serve all stakeholders. Furthermore, Good governance is effective and efficient. This means that processes and institutions produce results that meet needs while making the best use of resources (http://www.goodgovernance.org.au/about-good-governance/what-is-good-governance/). Equity and inclusivity are other distinguishing features of good governance. All community members and/ or stakeholders should be satisfied that their interests have been considered by decision-makers during the decision-making process. This means that all groups should have opportunities to participate in the process. The final characteristic of good governance is adherence to the rule of law. Where good governance obtains legal frameworks should be fair and enforced impartially, particularly the laws on human rights (http://www.goodgovernance.org.au/about-good-governance/what-is-good-governance/).

Governance in University Education

Governance is essential whenever a group of people come together to accomplish an end (Institute on Governance 2016). The higher education setting is a case in mind. For universities to service their role effectively, they need governance. University governance can be construed in terms of the framework of rules and practices by which management ensures accountability, fairness and transparency in the institution's relationship with all its stakeholders, such as regulation agencies, students and faculty (Task Force on University Education and Society 2000). This framework consists of contracts between the university and its stakeholders for the distribution of responsibilities, rights and rewards; the procedures for settling the sometimes conflicting interests of stakeholders in accordance with their duties, privileges, and roles and; procedures for proper supervision, control, and information flows to serve as a system of checks and balances.

Around the world, higher education is under pressure to be revolutionized, in response to the changing needs of the society and its growing contribution to economic and social development. Universities, which expected to create knowledge, improve equity, respond to students' needs and do so efficiently, have undergone some transformations including rapid expansions of student enrolments and diversity in the composition of students, a relative decrease in public funding, increasing importance of research and innovation in the knowledge-based economy and wider competition between higher education institutions. The factors precipitate the call for scrutiny of governance systems to ensure effectiveness in their operations (Fieden 2008). Institutional structures have also evolved away from the traditional mode of academic self-governance towards new modes of managerial self-governance, thereby increasing the importance of providing effective governance systems in higher education and heightening the interest of scholars on how decisions are made in higher education institutions (Jones 2011). The ultimate aim of the scrutiny of governance structures in universities is the attainment of good governance in the higher education sector.

Good governance and leadership are attributes that have been shown to have a major bearing on the capacity for the higher education sector to succeed and to play its expected role in development and to fulfil the goal of the twenty-first century being a knowledge era. Whereas good governance alone may not be a sufficient condition for attaining quality education, it is certainly a necessary one. Based on existing research (see e.g., Gibbs, Knapper and Picinnin 2009; Osseo-Asare, Longbottom and Murphy 2005; Martin, Task Force on Higher Education and Society 2000; Trigwell, Prosser and Ramsden 2003), governance plays a pivotal role in the success of institutions of higher learning and is a crucial factor in sustaining and improving quality and performance. Universities require visionary, creative (innovative) and inclusive leadership equipped with good communication skills capable of driving the change anticipated in them. A poorly governed institution will neither flourish nor deliver quality education. To be effective universities require leadership that is characterized by outstanding qualities which can earn them legitimacy from other stakeholders (Bryman 2007; Goleman 2000a, 2000b; Diamond 2006; Kozner and Posner; Obondo 2000).

Despite the centrality of good governance to the success of universities, most African universities are facing a governance crisis that often manifests itself in terms of conflict between management and students and staff that flares up from time to time over issues such as living allowances, pay, terms and conditions of service, limited representation in university governing bodies and perception of university authority as defender of state interests as opposed to the interests of the university (Mwiria 1992). Existing evidence shows that the principles of good governance are routinely flouted with great frequency in many African countries (Kauffeldt 2009; Mutula 2002; Obondo 2000; Task Force on Higher Education and Society 2000), resulting in poor governance. In particular, regular political interference, especially in public universities, makes adherence to the principles of good governance a near impossibility (Kauffeldt 2009). In many instances, the intervention is based on the perception that universities constitute a potential threat to fragile and often not well-established political systems and therefore must be closely monitored (Saha 1993).

While there is growing recognition across the African continent that higher education is critical to development, policy and institutional reforms in many countries in Africa tend to focus on the economic impact of higher education neglecting the governance dimension (Petlane 2009). Yet, attention to governance issues is particularly crucial given that African universities have not been good examples of good governance. They have been characterized by the same management ills that have plagued national administrations and other sectors of society. They are distinguished by the inability to directly contribute to policy making, and the development of a national vision, produce usable outputs, as well as corruption, patronage and power struggles. Specifically, apprehension over the internal governance of universities is manifested in the administrative deficiencies observed in the appointment of institutional leaders, particularly vice chancellors, who are perceived to be politicized and dominated by government, persistent Government over-expenditures and, more importantly for this study, weak or non-existent decision-making processes (Sifuna 2012; Petlane 2009).

Throughout the continent, the quality of governance in institutions of higher learning is a reflection of the leadership responsible for the running of these institutions. Based on EDULINK (n.d.) many African universities lack the strong management and leadership systems that are necessary to promote responsive academic and research activities. While many of the individuals who occupy leadership positions in institutions of higher learning in Africa are accomplished scholars, few are adequately equipped for the task of managing these institutions (Reisberg 2010); top managers lack the modern management skills that are crucial for such positions. In addition, many African universities continue to rely on paternalistic leadership that is focused on a single individual (i.e. the vice chancellor) who is the super leader (Bolden, Petrov and Gosling 2008). EDULINK (n.d.) singled out ineffective communication between the various levels of management and lecturers, students and other stakeholders and the poor management, and sometimes misuse, of resources, as suggested/shown by some of the pointers to the weak management systems in universities.

For good governance to obtain in universities, the institutions must uphold a number of principles of good governance (Kauffeldt 2009; Task Force on University Education and Society 2000) and rely on a number of tools and practices (Task Force on University Education and Society 2000). A brief profiling of these principles and tools is presented below, starting with the principles of good governance.

Principles of Good Governance in University Education

The key principles of good governance in higher education include academic freedom, shared governance, clear rights and responsibilities, meritocratic selection, financial stability and accountability. According to the Task Force on

University Education and Society (2000), not all the principles apply with equal force to all institutions of higher education. Whereas all these principles may be applicable to research universities, academic freedom or shared governance may be less important in vocational schools.

Academic Freedom

Academic freedom refers to the rights of scholars to pursue their research, teach, and publish without controls or restraints from the institutions they work for or from the primary stakeholder (Kauffeldt 2009; Task Force on Higher Education and Society 2000); being in our case government for the public sector, and trustees/owners for the private sector such primary stake holders. Academic freedom plays a significant role in promoting not just the quality of universities as institutions of higher learning but also the quality of the education they deliver. On the contrary, the absence of academic freedom impairs universities from fulfilling one of their primary functions, which is to be a catalyst and sanctuary for new ideas, including even unpopular ones.

Academic freedom is anchored on the UNESCO report concerning the Status of Higher Education Teaching Personnel, adopted by the Paris-based United Nations agency's general conference in 1997, after a thorough process of consultation with academic and legal experts and international NGOs, in particular the International Labour Organization (ILO). It is recognized by the African Charter on Human and Peoples' Rights. The charter does not specifically guarantee academic freedom. However, a landmark ruling in the case of 'Kenneth Good versus Botswana' recognized academic freedom under the African Charter (Appiagyei-Atua1 2015). Despite this and the fact that many African countries have returned to an ethos of a democratic culture and a refinement of the role of the university in the globalization era, an assessment of the level of compliance with the UNESCO document indicates that the level of breach exceeds its observance (Appiagyei-Atua1 2015). This means that many countries continue to suppress or restrict academic freedom. Even where in principle academic freedom has been embraced, there appear to be limits beyond which it cannot be tolerated. This curtails academics from propagating what are considered to be unpopular ideas without negative consequences, including sanctioning by the State. The repeated attempt by the Kenya government to control the freedom of expression through untenable media bills could be viewed in this light.

Shared Governance

Stakeholder involvement in decision-making has become one of the key principles of the practice of good governance which is increasingly being embraced by higher education institutions worldwide. Also known as cooperative governance, shared governance entails giving various groups of people a share in the decision-making process often through elected representation and allowing certain groups to exercise primary responsibility for specific areas of decision-making. This perception is in line with the stakeholder theory that emerged in the 1980s from the organizational field and whose main tenet was that individuals who have a stake in any institution should be involved in the matters pertaining to that institution (OECD 2003). Shared governance entails the devolving of decision-making to those who are best qualified to make them and ensures that individual's and/ or institutional priorities are based on broad consensus and that the voices of all, including the most vulnerable, are heard in decision-making over.g. the allocation of resources. This bolsters the inclusivity of the governance process and enhances co-decision rights and consensus in decision-making. Shared governance arose out of the recognition that broad participation in decision-making increases the level of employee investment in an institution's success and improves the productivity of an organization; advantages that are relevant to quality assurance of higher education (OECD 2003). The principle of shared governance stands in sharp contrast to the traditional model of university governance, which emphasized one supreme leader, with the State having a strong hold on the universities. Other levels of university management did not have the power to make decisions (Parrish n.d). They were regulated and controlled in every way including policies, human resource issues and all forms of expression.

In a university setting, shared governance means that all those involved in higher education, including administrators, faculty and students, participate in the making of critical decisions affecting the institution (Kauffeldt 2009; Task Force on Higher Education and Society 2000). Specifically, it ensures that faculty, students and other stakeholders have a meaningful voice in policy formulation and decision-making in general. In this regard, students who constitute the majority of the institution's community, and finance the larger part of the institution's budgets, have a right to representation in decision-making through a group of student leaders.

Challenges to the participation principle of good governance have been noted in the literature (Kauffeldt 2009; Obondo 2000). According to Kauffeldt (2009), for example, the lack of cooperation in institutional governance abounds in many universities. Obondo (2000) pointed out that people with vested interests may hinder participation at different levels of the university. In addition, higher education institutions tend to lack the culture of openness and frequent dialogue on issues, which is counter to the participation principle. In such cases when decisions are made, the partakers of the decisions feel disenfranchised and do not embrace the change they embody even where it is beneficial and necessary. As a result, externally (public) university governance remains a state-controlled system, while internally the process remains the preoccupation of top management (Task Force on Higher Education and Society 2000). Internally, decisions are made from the top and imposed on subordinate bodies, with faculty, lower cadre administrators and students hardly having any voice and/ or influence in decision-making. As the Task Force on Higher Education and Society (2000) stated, students are rarely considered as part of the higher education administrative process. As such, they are hardly consulted on many matters related to their education. Overall, the status of shared governance in universities reflects the society in which they operate. To illustrate, this fact the existence of undemocratic practices in many African countries hinders the growth of shared governance in universities. In addition, the corruption that pervades many African countries has encroached on universities, leaving them tainted (Task Force on Higher Education and Society 2000).

To deal with the governance crisis affecting them and to fulfil their roles, African universities must move away from a leadership focused on a single individual, the super leader, to a more inclusive leadership that will function broadly within the institution. Although governance structures in many universities have, in principle, shifted away from the traditional mode of academic self-governance towards new models of managerial self-governance that is concerned with the participation of all internal stakeholders in universities and colleges (Euryduce 2008) – mainly because of the benefits accrued from shared governance – the practices are still rooted in the traditional model of governance. African universities must also embrace transformational leadership; 'a style of leadership that engenders a shared-power environment with followers/ stakeholders (Bryman 2007; Rost 1993; Parrish n.d.). Transformational leadership is characterized by power sharing, collaboration, inclusiveness, collectivity, constructive dialogue collegiality and shared and dispersed decision-making, among others (Gibbs, Knapper and Picinnin 2006, 2009; Bolden *et al.* 2008; Bryman 2007; Rantz 2002; Pounder 2001; Rost 1993; Parrish n.d.). It focuses more on empowering others as opposed to an individual assuming sole responsibility for leading (Rowley 1997). The leader inspires followers through a shared vision for the future, empowers them by delegating responsibilities to them and equipping them to play their roles to the best of their abilities and, by regularly monitoring and communicating with them with regard to the tasks for which they have responsibility (Parrish n.d.: 2). This form of leadership has been acknowledged as being highly appropriate as well as needed in the higher education sector (Middlehurst, Goreham and Woodfield 2009; Anderson and Johnson 2006; Bolden *et al.* 2008; Rowley 1997).

Clear Rights and Responsibilities

The third principle of good governance in universities is the existence of clear rights and responsibilities. For good governance to be obtained/realized in higher education, mutually agreed rights and responsibilities for all stakeholders are essential (Kauffeldt 2009; Task Force on Higher Education and Society 2000; http://www.businessdictionary.com/definition/corporate-governance.html). There should exist explicit and implicit contracts between the institution and the stakeholders for distribution of rights and responsibilities. This will ensure that both external stakeholders (e.g., government, sponsors, external supervisors etc.) and internal stakeholders (students, faculty, administrators, etc.) should have a clear grasp on their rights and responsibilities. These can be explicated through laws, institutional charters and faculty and student handbooks. The existence of clear rights and responsibilities in universities is manifested in mutually agreed conditions for university operations that provide a stable condition for decision-making.

While many universities have drafted and passed legislation to delineate stakeholder rights and responsibilities, events still occur outside of or around the policy framework, creating a culture of uncertainty (Kauffeldt 2009). In Kenya, for example, whereas the roles and responsibilities of the Ministry of Education and of other external higher education regulatory agencies, such as the Commission for University Education, may be explicit, those of internal stakeholders have not been adequately formalized. Charters establishing universities only gloss over these and detailed specification is lacking in many areas of decision-making (Task Force on Higher Education and Society 2000).

Meritocratic Selection

For higher education to function efficiently, it requires a broadly defined merit system to anchor the selection and promotion of faculty, administrators and students (Kauffeldt 2009; Task Force on Higher Education and Society 2000). Where merit lacks, practices such as ideology, nepotism, cronyism and intimidation are allowed to determine selection and/or advancement. In addition, in some cases decision-making is influenced by distant bureaucrats and politicians and legal barriers stand in the way of recognition of merit. The evidence suggests that the implementation of the meritocratic selection principle in many universities has continued to be undermined by political meddling. In many African countries, the tendency for politicians to intervene in universities has left many institutions hostage to factional policies and the inability to rely on merit for important decisions such as the admission of students and the appointment and promotion of faculty (Kauffeldt 2009; Task Force on Higher Education and Society 2000).

Financial Stability

The fifth principle of good governance in higher education is financial stability. For higher education to function efficiently, financial stability is imperative (Kauffeldt 2009; Task Force on Higher Education and Society 2000). As such, the providers of higher education must infuse the finances necessary for universities to deliver quality and relevant education. Unfortunately, evidence abounds showing that higher education in many African countries often function in turbulent financial conditions, a situation compounded by the limited financial resources available especially to public universities (see e.g. Nganga 2014; Munene 2016; Mutula 2002; Nyangau 2014; Task Force on Higher Education and Society 2000). In most African countries, the dramatic expansion of enrolments especially in public universities has occurred without a corresponding growth in the funding of the sector. The shortage of funding has made it difficult for universities to cater to the growing numbers of students, in many cases forcing (public) universities to turn to entrepreneurial activities to expand their revenue bases (Nganga 2014; Munene 2016; Mutula 2002; Nyangau 2014). This creates conditions for poor governance and makes rational planning impossible (Task Force on Higher Education and Society 2000).

Accountability

Universities, whether public or private, must be accountable to all stakeholders (Bloom and Ahmad 2000; Kauffeldt 2009; Task Force on Higher Education and Society 2000; World Bank 1994). While this does not necessarily imply uncontrolled interference by stakeholders, it imposes a requirement on the institutions to periodically explain actions and to have their successes and failures examined in a transparent fashion. Accountability is important in monitoring performance in change management (Brookes 2006; Department for Education and Skills 2006; Thompson and Uyeda 2004). It ensures that decision-making is transparent across the collaborating agencies (Her Majesty's Government 2005). For the accountability principle to operate smoothly, interactions between universities and their stakeholders must be guided by clearly agreed on rights and responsibilities. In addition, there must exist mechanisms for determining the appropriate balance between autonomy and accountability (Task Force on Higher Education and Society 2000).

Some progress has been made to instil the sense of accountability especially through the establishment of semi-autonomous agencies to regulate university education, such as the Commission for University Education in Kenya. However, there is still a fair degree of State and higher education system enmeshment that leaves little space for these agencies to operate with the independence necessary to actualize true accountability (Bloom and Ahmad 2000; Kauffeldt 2009).

Tools and Practices for Achieving Good Governance

Beyond adherence to the principles of good governance in higher education, the Task Force on University Education and Society (2000) enumerated the following as important tools that universities can rely on to achieve good governance:

Faculty Councils (or Senates), Governing Councils (or Board of Trustees), institutional charters and handbooks, visiting committees and accreditation, budget practices and financial management, data-driven decision-making, style of identifying leaders (appoint or elect), faculty appointment and promotion decisions and security of employment (Task Force on University Education and Society 2000). Faculty councils and/or Senates are representative bodies of faculty members responsible for making decisions about selected academic policy such as programmes offered, curricula, degree requirements and admissions policy. Where they exist and function optimally, they facilitate delegation of power and hence promote shared governance by limiting the extent of reliance on top-down governance (Task Force on Higher Education and Society 2000). On the other hand, governing councils are independent bodies that act as a buffer between the institutions and external bodies to which the institutions are accountable, e.g., the State, and sponsors (Task Force on Higher Education and Society 2000). These represent the institutions to the outside world, thereby insulating them from excessive external interference. The Governing Council should be involved in developing the long-term plans for the institution as well as in monitoring their implementation. Where they operat optimally, they are likely to boost accountability and transparency, foster clear roles and responsibilities for all stakeholders and reduce external meddling.

The third tool for fostering good governance is institutional charters and handbooks. Charters establish the legal basis and define the mission of the institution and lay down the rules governing the institution's relation with the State or private sponsor. They may specify some internal rules of operation too (Task Force on University Education and Society 2000). Handbooks (faculty and students), on the other hand, apply to the internal governance of universities. To be effective though, they must be comprehensive, clearly written and frequently updated. Faculty handbooks articulate faculty rights and responsibilities. The objective is to guide faculty conduct within the context of teaching and research activities and their broader life in the institution and in the profession (Task Force on University Education and Society 2000). Students' handbooks regulate students' academic lives by defining the objectives, rules and requirements of different academic programmes as well as the students' non-academic rights and responsibilities (Task Force on University Education in Society 2000). Where clearly formulated charters and handbooks exist, they facilitate the institution to spell out the roles and responsibilities of faculty and students as major stakeholders.

The fourth tool that universities can rely on to nurture good governance is Visiting Committees and Accreditation. For the university sector to uphold its goal of quality education amidst expanding enrolments, it needs to come up with procedures for performance measurements and for having regular audits and evaluation of services (Task Force on University Education in Society 2000). Comprising of international, regional and national experts, visiting committees, are an important tool for monitoring performance and promoting the responsible exercise of authority. By offering objective assessments of achievements of faculty and programmes in relation to international, regional and national standards, they serve to promote quality (Task Force on Education and Society 2000). Generally speaking, accreditation improves attraction of students, faculty and other resources to the institution. Whereas internal accreditation provides a focus for improving standards and enhancing institutional pride, external accreditation provides the market information vital for competition (Task Force on Education and Society 2000). Concerning budget practices and financial management, the Task Force on University Education and Society (2000) advances that transparent, logical and well understood budgeting and accounting rules improve the operation and performance of higher education institutions. Such rules encourage flexibility, financial stability and transparency as opposed to bureaucratic rigidity which tends to cause inefficiency. This in turn strengthens the institution's culture of good governance.

Another tool for enhancing good governance in universities is data for decision-making. According to the Task on University Education and Society (2000), to be effective in decision-making, universities need adequate data on teaching and research performance, student-based achievement, institutional financial status etc. Data are also necessary for effective monitoring and accounting. It can be argued that decisions anchored on adequate data are more objective, balanced and likely to be acceptable to the stakeholders concerned. This will reduce the level of conflict that may undermine the governance process in universities. In addition, data-driven decisions are likely to increase honesty, transparency and accountability as well as promote meritocracy, all of which are important ingredients for nurturing good governance. The style of appointment of leaders used by a university can also enhance good governance. The Task Force on University Education and Society (2000) is categorical that universities in developing countries require strong leadership regardless of the selection methods. According to them, universities across the world tend to rely more on election to fill leadership positions. Although this promotes shared governance which is an essence of good governance, more often than not it results in weak leadership that is prejudiced in favour of the status quo (Task Force on University Education and Society 2000). The Task Force considered appointed leaders to be better placed to make unpopular decisions where required but noted that these often lack widespread support, diluting the sense of shared governance. However, this can be eased through in-depth consultation with all stakeholders, which should increase the appointed leader's legitimacy.

Faculty appointments and promotion decisions and job security are two other tools that universities can rely on to enhance good governance. Based on the Task Force on University Education and Society (2000), faculty quality is the most important determinant of quality in university education. Such quality though is significantly undermined by nepotism, cronyism, and inbreeding. On the contrary, reliance on external peer review when making appointments and promotions will greatly improve the quality of faculty by allowing quality to be judged on proper technical grounds and free of conflict of interests. Peer review also promotes the quality of publication decisions and efficient allocation of funds. Concerning security of employment, the Task Force on University Education and Society (2000) argued that its importance lies with its ability to enhance academic freedom among faculty. According to the Task Force, academic freedom – which is a basic principle of good governance in university education – tends to be greater among employment-secure faculty (those on permanent or long contract appointment) relative to their counterparts who are temporary because they can be dismissed at will. Employment security also acts as a form of non-wage benefit that reduces turnover among talented faculty.

Students' Involvement in University Governance

Students' involvement in university governance has been shown to have a major bearing on the capacity for the sector to succeed and to play its expected role in development and to fulfil the goal of the twenty-first century being a knowledge era. This study focuses on the subject student participation (or involvement) in university governance processes, in an attempt to understand the extent to which students have become part of the democratization of governance in universities in Kenya. This endeavour is premised on the reality that collaborative governance is essential if universities are to attain their visions, missions and goals. For students to effectively participate in the governance of their institutions, it requires that the student leadership is not just involved in some matters. Rather, it should be adequately involved in all major decisions and policy issues affecting the university and the university must provide the students' leadership with the resources they need to be adequately involved. In Africa, the massification and marketization of higher education that has occurred since the 1990s have given students' involvement in governance greater impetus (Klemenčič 2014). Although they may not hold co-decision rights, they are supposed to be consulted in decision-making and their views solicited during the framing of policy.

Origins of Students' Participation in University Governance

Historically, students' involvement in the governance of their universities has never been guaranteed the world over except in the thirteenth century Bologna University, known as the "student university" where students were in charge of their studies. However, this practice was quickly phased out to give way to the Parisian model of university governance that was in operation at the time, where the guild of professing teachers managed the university with the assistance of an elected student rector (Luescher-Mamashela 2005). Students have had to struggle to have their voice heard in matters that concern the running of their institutions. Student movements and fights characterized the struggle for students to have their issues addressed by universities in most of the 1960s and early 1970s in Europe and North America. A similar picture was witnessed in Africa during this period just before and after most countries attained independence. For example, students used movements like the Tanganyika African Welfare Society (TAWS) and the Student Union of Nairobi (SONU), both from East Africa, to agitate for better conditions for students and modernization of the system of education and curriculum from the previous one that was racially inclined to favour the white populations (Boahen 1994; Munene 2003). Later, when student movements were banned by the governments, students turned to the use of other innovative avenues like publications, books, newspapers, periodicals, journals, pamphlets, organizing meetings, congresses, holding symposia, debates, lectures, seminars, rallies and demonstrations to continue their course (Boahen 1994; Munene 2003; Chege 2009).

Appreciation for the need to involve students in university governance was prompted by the wave of university democratization that swept across most industrialized countries in the 1970s. This involved making universities more democratic in their practices especially as it pertains to ensuring that the decision-making process in universities was more representative. The membership of university governing structures was extended to staff members and elected student representatives (Boer and Stensaker 2008; Luescher-Mamasheal 2005). Given that higher education institutional practices reflect the social realities in which they operate, where the democratization in the political sphere in Africa has taken time to mature, university governance practices have mirrored the national contexts. Anyang' Nyon'go describes the political state of African countries in the 1970s and 1980s in terms of disintegration of the national coalitions and a rise in authoritarianism in the existing governments exemplified by multiple military coups, prevalence of military regimes and one-party State (Anyang' Nyon'go 1989). In this context, universities that were incubators of critical thought began to take on the veneer of the opposition, giving rise to confrontations by students and academic staff that often led to strikes and showdowns (Mamdani 2008).

In Kenya, the post-colonial Kenyatta and Moi governments that were distinguished by dictatorship, suppression of discourse in the wider society and curtailed political pluralism by dissolution of other political parties contributed to limited application of participatory governance in universities. Universities through academic members of staff and student movements became voices of dissent for their individual institutions and society at large. The government suppressed these efforts by arresting, detaining without trial and sometimes killing of anti-establishment academics and students. In 1972, the Student Union of Nairobi (SONU) was banned because they staged riots demanding for curriculum and examination reforms, improved conditions on campus and participation in all decisions affecting students' welfare. Specifically, during the Moi era, when sycophancy was a prerequisite for political, professional and personal survival, university administrations collaborated with the government to suspend and expel students on flimsy accusations (Chege 2009).

The opening up of the democratic space in Africa in general, and by extension Kenya, in terms of political liberalization and multiparty politics entailing the return to competitive electoral processes, rebuilding adherence to human rights and democratic institutions, came with some progress; self-governance in higher education (Aina 2009). In Kenya, President Mwai Kibaki relinquished his position as chancellor of all public universities and instead appointed eminent persons. Further, vice chancellors and top university officials were now to be appointed by the university councils in a competitive process (Chege 2009; Sifuna 2012). This change is now legally supported in the University Bill 2012 (Government of Kenya 2012). This democratic wave was echoed in the electoral practices of universities where deans and student leaders were elected through the ballot. It is, however, imperative to establish where this practice has been sanctioned by the new university statutes that are in the process of being revised by individual universities allegedly without the substantial input of members of the academic and student bodies. Besides, there is a downside to these gains given that the growing ethnic rivalry witnessed nationally during this period has crept into universities where student leadership election campaigns have taken on an ethnic face because they are heavily supported financially by national political parties (Mwindi 2009). This issue is compounded by university administrations interfering with student politics to ensure that, as much as possible, pro-administration and ethnically correct students assume office in the student government (Sifuna 2013). It is therefore evident that students' concerns are unlikely to be adequately addressed by student leaders who have been compromised by the administration that is responsible for providing solutions needed.

Implications on the involvement of students in university decision making can also be historically drawn from the other transformations that have occurred in the higher education sector in Africa, and in Kenya specifically. Growth in enrolments at the university level is one such transformation that began immediately after independences stemming from the significant role of higher education in the social and economic development of post-independent African countries (Assie-Lumumba 2006). Unfortunately, this growth in numbers coincided with the economic downturn that hit most African countries in the 1970s due to the crash in commodity markets and the rapid rise in oil prices that forced most governments to turn to multinational and private international financiers for credit and the universities to be under-resourced. The solution to this crisis proposed by the Bretton Woods Institutions (BWI) mainly the World Bank and the International Monetary Fund (IMF) had negative effects on the place of students in the governing processes of universities (Aina 2009). The Structural Adjustment Policies (SAPs) imposed on governments account for changes that occurred in the university including introduction of privatization and cost sharing, financial decentralization, retrenchments of staff and dilution of academic programmes.

In Kenya, the implementation of SAPs in the higher education sector and consequent legalization of privatization of higher education was spearheaded by the recommendations by the committee mandated to analyze university educational expansions popularly known as the Mackay report of 1981 (GOK 1981). The application of this policy explains the growth in the number of private universities that followed and the introduction of privately-sponsored students in public universities attending what are popularly known as parallel degree programmes that currently account for half of the revenue generated by public universities (Oanda, Chege and Wesonga 2008). On the other hand, these new developments have introduced a new set of students into the universities through the innovative and flexible modes of learning delivery including distance learning, evening classes, credit transfers, and short courses that require adequate representation by the student governance structures to ensure that their unique needs are addressed by the university administration. It is not apparent whether this is actually happening both in the private and public universities in Kenya.

In line with these developments has been the growing application of the market approach to the governance of universities, also known as the rise in managerialism – a trend that began in the western universities and is quickly catching on in Africa (ESMU 2009; Luescher-Mamashela 2005). The application of leadership styles and management approach developed in the business world to the academic context is encouraged to enhance efficiency and relevance to the labour market environment. Consequently, emphasis on strategic goal-setting and attainment through the development of institutional mission and vision statements, strategic planning and legitimization of the authority of university executives as professional managers has become common practice in universities (ESMU 2009; Luescher-Mamashela 2005). At face value, this setup presents a huge opportunity for students' involvement in university governance given that they are the prime consumers of university courses offered; yet their prospect of benefitting in this way depends on whether self-governance, in terms of support for student government affairs is an important feature of strategic and implementation plans that are becoming more and more business-inclined (Mwiria *et al.* 2007).

Forms of Students' Involvement in Governance

Students' participation in governance can occur through a range of informal (passive) and formal mechanisms (Kulati 2000; Lodge 2005; Luescher-Mamashela 2005). The level of informality and formality applied by the university affects the quality of students' participation (Lizzio and Wilson 2009). At the realm of passivity, student feedback might be informally sought on specific issues (Lodge 2005) from student councils or committees. Beyond this, informal participation takes the form of students employing a range of protest forms, stretching from cooperative-informative forms to highly confrontational and militant forms (Luescher-Mamashela 2005).

On the contrary, formal involvement entails a more systematic incorporation of students' voices into governance forums through formal membership of students on various university-level governance bodies and committees such as the University Council, Academic Senate, Faculty Board and disciplinary committees aimed at ensuring adequate representation of constituencies (Kulati 2000; Luescher-Mamashela 2005). Students could also be allowed formal representation in School-wide/ Faculty-wide as well as in departmental/ programme committees and working groups. Representation on departmental committees appears to be the most strategic and potentially useful participative mechanism because it aids problem-solving at a local level, on issues that have an immediate impact on students, while offering the greatest potential for building a sense of community and social capital between staff and students (Zuo and Ratsoy 1999). Where practiced effectively, formal representation should give students co-decision rights. In Africa, formal inclusion of students in university governance has taken three principal forms (Luescher-Mamashela 2005) 1) Establishment of student government on university campuses; 2) Representation of the institutional student body in certain structures of university governance and; 3) Involvement of national (or institutional) student organizations in higher education policy formulation.

An inherent part of democratic university governance is student governments (Badat 1999; Klemenčič 2014; Luescher-Mamashela 2005). Student governments or self-governance structures are the most recognizable and widespread platforms from which students' involvement in university governance occurs. The practice of democratic governance by higher education institutions and the resultant moulding of effective leaders entails participation of all students in student representation through elective selection of their leaders, active participation of regular students in student organizations and societies which promote dialogue among their members, and democratic internal procedures and diversity within their structures. Further, student governing bodies should have mechanisms in place to ensure continuity in student representation in terms of efficient ways to transfer knowledge to the new generation of leaders (May 2009; Astin 2000).

Although membership to student governments is voluntary (Badat 1999), it is normally assumed that all members of the student body are members of the organization. This means that student organizations operate like the one-party states of the pre-1990s in Africa where every citizen was assumed to be a bona fide member of the ruling party.

Student governments exist in different forms and designations such as student unions, councils, parliaments, boards, guilds, associations, etc. Regardless of their forms or designations, these operate as governments in the sense that they present a system of rules, norms and institutions by which the student body within an institution is organized and governed (Klemenčič 2012a, 2014). Their primary function is to represent the students' interests in institutional governance. This involves mediating the interests of the student body to the institution's management by relating to management, engaging with the structures and agenda of management and engaging in management's policy networks (Klemenčič 2014). Student governments also provide the framework for student social and political activities and student organizations on campus, as well as serve the professional function of providing academic and welfare support services to students and managing student facilities (Klemenčič 2014; Luescher-Mamashela 2005).

Student governments can be institution-specific, national or regional (Badat 1999; Klemenčič 2014; Luescher-Mamashela 2005). Whereas university-level governments are almost universally accepted, student organizations at the national and regional levels are less widespread (Klemenčič 2014). This might be explained by the fear governments, especially authoritarian regimes, have of the potency of student interest groups. To illustrate, national student associations can be very powerful political institutions that cannot be easily ignored by national governments. As Klemenčič (2014) pointed out, they can rely on varied networks to establish close connections with different actors within government and political parties. Frequently, national or institutional student governments initiate and organize student protests. Student unions also have a tradition of being training grounds for future political leaders (Day 2012; Leusher-Mamashela and Mugume 2014). Furthermore, if organized into a representative student government or movement, students have been shown to be a highly influential agency shaping higher education policy (Luescher-Mamashela 2005).

Student governments stand in implicit or explicit exchange relationship with authorities whom they seek to influence. In this relationship student governments possess and can supply important resources, such as professional expertise, legitimation of policy, social control of their members, and other services that may be of value to the authority (Klemenčič 2012a). Authorities reciprocate by providing funding and other material and/ or symbolic resources and by defining the relational structures through which student governments can formally or informally intermediate their interests. The relations between university and representative student structures can assume one of three forms: an authoritarian paternalistic form, a democratic form or a managerial or corporate form (Klemenčič 2014; Leuscher-Mamashela 2013). In the authoritarian paternalistic approach, a student government is integrated into the institutional structure and given limited discretion for involvement on issues strictly concerning students (e.g., student services and teaching quality) and only in an advisory role rather than on a co-decision capacity. Here students constitute a junior member of the academic community who are not capable of contributing to decisions on an equal level as academics (Leuscher-Mamashela 2013).

The democratic institutional governance form, which is characterized by the existence of fairly autonomous student governments is the locus of this study. It involves student representatives being granted participation in the institution's decision-making process, often with co-decision rights (Klemenčič 2014). Finally, in the managerial or corporate governance model, institutional leadership involves student unions together with other stakeholders, with external stakeholders holding a considerable leverage. Student representatives (as well as academics) are engaged as consultants rather than as co-decision makers (Klemenčič 2012b).

While in principle most African universities may encourage the democratic governance model, in practice they tend to rely on the authoritative, paternalistic model. This is consistent with Johnson and Deem (2003), who argued that, more often than not, incongruence between espoused and practical participation characterizes university institutions, a fact that Argyris and Schon (1978) consider to be an enduring aspect of social and organizational life. Whereas university policy may emphasize student-centerdness, its practical implementation often focuses on 'managing the student body' more than responding to the experiences of the students.

The role of students in a system of shared governance, though, can be controversial given the transient nature of studentship and the rapid turnaround of student elected officials (Klemenčič 2014; Task Force on Higher Education and Society 2000). Unlike faculty and administrators, students stay in universities for a short period of time, often four years, and their elected officials normally serve a one-year term. Because of this, faculty and administrators tend to have natural authority over students in many matters of internal governance, particularly academic matters such as admission standards, grading policy, and degree requirements. Students are only allowed to play key roles in those areas that affect their lives and in which they have the competence to provide constructive input (Task Force on Higher Education and Society 2000). In addition, student governments tend to be more susceptible to change under the influence of individual 'agents' or external circumstances (Klemenčič 2014). This undermines their capacity to effectively participate in decision-making. Matters can be complicated further by the cultural assumptions of a particular academic community. For instance, the institution may routinely make conscious efforts to protect students' rights in university policy and procedures but the often hierarchical structures of educational institutions can, perhaps inadvertently, privilege 'staff discourse' and marginalize students' views (Johnson and Deem 2003; Lizzio and Wilson 2009). Similar sentiments were expressed by Klemenčič (2014) who indicated that the relations between institutional leaders and student representatives often contain some forms of domination by authorities over students as manifested through subtle and implicit actions.

There is also the element of apathy that tends to affect the level of students' participation in governance processes. As Klemenčič (2014: 399) pointed out, despite the significant legitimate power conferred on student governments as key university stakeholders through legislation and institutional rules and the significant coercive power of student movements, the 'majority of students rarely get politically engaged in student government, even if this involves only casting a vote in student elections" (Klemenčič, 2014: 399).

Some scholars have argued for the total exclusion of students from university governance (see e.g., Lee 1987; Wood 1993; Zuo and Ratsoy 1999). These have advanced a number of factors to justify their stance, including the following: students may not be in a position to effectively represent the interests of their groups; students have no place in university boards because only trustees have been assigned the responsibility of serving the public through board membership; students promote the interests of specific groups, which can lead to conflict of interest; and, students are not suitable for participation in boards due to limited knowledge and experience (Wood 1993). In addition, it has been argued that students have no interest in academic matters and that their involvement could distract them from their studies, thereby undermining their educational progress. Others indicate that students should be excluded from the discussion of 'sensitive' issues such as student grading and faculty tenure (Lee 1987; Zuo and Ratsoy 1999).

The Benefits of Students' Involvement in Governance

Various grounds, all hinged on the principle of participatory governance, have been put forth to elucidate why university students should be involved in university governance. These can be viewed from three perspectives: social, developmental and functional (Cress, Astin, Zimmerman, Oster, Burkhardt 2001; Kuh 1994; Kuh and Lund 1994; Lee 1987; Lizzio and Wilson; Menon 2005, 2009; Obondo 2000; Sabin and Daniels 2001). The social perspective deals with the benefits accrued to society while the developmental perspective relates to the benefits accruing to the student participants. On the other hand, the functional perspective deals with the benefits of involvement to the university.

The benefits of students' participation to society can be understood within the context of the emerging and related discourses of education for democracy

(Teune 2001) and "universities as sites of citizenship" (Colby *et al.* 2003) and as drivers of socio-economic development. Upon graduation, students join the rest of society in grappling with modern challenges including global warming, religious and ethnic conflict, poverty, decline in citizenship interest and in engagement in political process, increasing ineffectiveness of governments and shift from industrialized to knowledge-based societies. These challenges need quality leaders to tackle them with adaptive and creative solutions (Astin 2000). Further, higher education specifically produces people to work in all sectors of the economy including government, business, law, science, medicine and even the clergy, thus putting the onus on them to produce strong effective leaders. From this perspective, therefore, leadership development in higher education has to go beyond those elected into the student leadership positions in the student government to include the individual students in the general student body. This perception is in line with Astin's (2000) definition of leadership as a process that is ultimately concerned with fostering change. In this regard, a leader is anyone engaged in making a positive change in society, meaning that any student is a potential leader. As a result, universities should empower all students to be effective social change agents by instilling in them leadership attitudes and values. If they expect students to develop the skills and attitudes of effective citizenship, then it is incumbent upon them to exemplify and support these through policies and practices. Otherwise, if students feel that they have little or no influence on decision-making, universities can become sites of negative learning about organizational and civic life (Lizzio and Wilson 2009).

The developmental perspective holds that, depending on its quality, students' participation in decision-making, can provide students with considerable opportunities for learning. There exists a myriad of gains accruing to both student leaders and the general student body. The participation of students in the governance of their universities introduces and socializes them into democratic leadership ideal, values, attitudes and practices (Lee 1987) that come in handy in their future endeavours both in the world of work and their lives in the community where they reside. Essentially, providing space for democratization of students and developing their leadership programmes have been identified as a critical prerequisite to solving the many crises related to governance in higher education and building strong future national leaders (Kamuzora and Mgaya n.d.; Astin 2000). Furthermore, existing research has reported skill development of students in leadership positions, in areas such as teamwork and critical thinking (Cress *et al.* 2001; Kuh 1994; Kuh and Lund 1994). Cress *et al.* (2001) reported significant gains in academic performance by tertiary students in positional student leadership roles engaged in leadership development programmes. In addition, Terenzini, Pascarella and Blimling (1996) demonstrated that extra-curricula activities foster academic and personal development among students.

Furthermore, students implicitly generate their notions and conceptions of leadership from what is taught intentionally and unintentionally across the educational experience. When they engage in campus and student activities and organizations like subject matter clubs, athletics, student government, volunteer activities like community service work, they gain experience that is applicable to employment after college, achieve a greater awareness of community needs and societal issues and create more meaningful relationships with faculty and fellow students (Kamuzora and Magaya n.d.; Astin 2000). Student leaders report that they accrue leadership values and skills including self-awareness, self-esteem, commitment, working collaboratively, authenticity, disagreement with respect and being able to lead constructive change which can be, as well, gained by other students not holding leadership positions but involved in campus activities. Moreover, student leaders have been reported to forge political and administrative careers after using the campus experience as a practicing ground (May 2009; Kamuzora and Mgaya n.d.; Astin 2000).

From the functional perspective, three major benefits to universities can be attributed to students' involvement in governance. First, students are said to have access to experiences and information that can improve the quality, accountability and transparency of decision making (Sabin and Daniels 2001). Student participation is also associated with the enhancement of appropriate consideration of stakeholder views and organizational learning. Evidently, students are full, and perhaps the most important, members of the higher education community, they should also participate in and influence the organization and content of higher education (Luescher-Mamashela 2011; Persson 2003). This perspective is supported by survey results conducted by the Council of Europe Campaign to Combat Violence against Women in 2002 (cited in Persson 2003) which indicated that there is a wide and positive attitude towards increased student influence in higher education based on the fact that they have the right to influence decisions and practices since they are the target group and main stakeholders in higher education. Consequently, students' avenues for formal involvement in governance should be strengthened by increasing the seats reserved for students on the committees at all levels, ensuring stronger rights to vote and speak within these bodies and enjoying regulated rights to participate in evaluation procedures (Persson 2003). 'Students as partners' is another descriptor given to students to define the relationship between students and their time in universities. Usage of the term 'partners' implies the existence of an interactive relationship and mutual respect between students and the other stakeholders in the university community (Menon 2005). In view of the fact that students have the lived experience as students, their wealth of knowledge can be tapped into by universities to solve campus problems in general and conflicts in particular before they begin or spiral out of control, thus engaging them to act as change agents from inside.

Second, the participation of students in governance is considered to have important benefits for the quality of the educational 'product' offered by universities (Lee 1987; Menon 2005). Students' input can facilitate the evaluation of curricula and teaching practices, through the identification of deficiencies in higher education programmes and instruction (Lee 1987). Moreover, students' participation in decision-making plays a role in the creation of an atmosphere of openness and trust, leading to a positive organizational climate (Wood 1993). Such a climate can be expected to reduce the likelihood of conflict between management and students or between management and staff in universities. Obondo (2000), for instance, attributes the management crises at the universities of Nairobi and Kenyatta in Kenya to the failure of administrators to take into account the needs of students and staff members.

Furthermore, student inclusion in university decision-making is essential to avert disruptive strikes and student unrest initiated and organized by student governments. One way through which students articulate their concerns and grievances is student protests and demonstrations (Altbach 2006; Klemenčič 2014; Task Force on Higher Education and Society 2000). As indicated earlier, these are elements of the informal model of students' involvement in governance, representing the application of the unwritten rules of student participation in institutional governance (Task Force on Higher Education and Society 2000). Classic works on student activism (see e.g., Altbach 1991, 1992, 2006) show that students' movements have often disrupted the functioning of higher education institutions, obstructed national and higher education reforms and exerted pressure for social change. In Africa in general, and in Kenya in particular, boycotts remain recognizable features of campus life but the dynamics of student protests vary significantly across space. This means that it would be rather myopic to assume that the existence of unresolved students' grievances and a student government is sufficient to cause a student protest and/ or boycott. In our considered opinion, the quality and integrity of the student leadership is important. Where student leaders are the product of flawed (often rigged) elections, are easily compromised and/or have been co-opted by management, the mobilization necessary for a student strike or protest may be lacking. Furthermore, the level of student apathy could also be a major determinant as to whether or not mobilization for strikes and protests can be effective.

Student protests range from cooperative to confrontational forms. Less confrontational forms have the objective to inform, educate and instigate debate (Luescher-Mamashela 2005). Confrontational forms, normally referred to as 'student unrests', are geared towards, and often result in, the breaking of institutional rules. They assume forms such as mass meetings, rallies, protest marches, street demonstrations and strikes and, class and examination boycotts (Luescher-Mamashela 2005; Maseko 1994; Adu Boahen in UNESCO 1994).

Normally university management will respond to violent protests by inviting the police to intervene, a response that can easily lead to bloodshed and the loss of student lives. Within the African context, student unrests date back to the late 1960s and 1970s, when universities were being established following independence from white rule (Mohamedbhai 2016). With growing student numbers, coupled with declining quality of teaching and learning facilities (lecture halls, laboratories, libraries, student residences, etc.), student unrests on African university campuses have become a common occurrence. Most recently, in February 2016 a wave of student riots swept through South Africa, leading to the closure of the North-West University (NWU) at Mafiking in Potchefstroom, the University of Pretoria (UP) at Hatfield and Groenkloof as well as the University of the Free State (UFS) in Bloemfontein (Azikiwe 2016). The effectiveness of student protests is dependent on the response they receive from within the higher education institution and from the wider society (Luescher-Mamashela 2005). Strikes have also been a common feature of university education since independence (Kiboiy 2013; Mohamedbhai 2016).

Relationship between University and Student Leaderships

Leadership was earlier defined as people who include the leader and the followers working towards a common goal. It is about working together towards a goal and forming a relationship that will foster the right environment to achieve the goals (Rost, 1993). For the purpose of this study, when we speak about university and student leadership we are referring to the relationship between university management and its followers (including students) as well as that between student leaders and the student followers.

Existing evidence tends to suggest that the relationship between university management and the student body has been characterized by frustration and mistrust that in extreme cases has resulted in student riots (Luescher-Mamashela, Kiiru, Mattes, Mwollo-Ntallima, Ng'ethe and Romo 2011; Otieno 2004). Recent evidence also indicates that the practice of student leadership in African universities is a mirror of the political national leadership which in most countries in Sub-Saharan Africa is characterized by allegations of corruption, ethnic inclinations, managerial incompetence and mismanagement of resources (Mapundo 2007). A recent survey on democratic citizenship and universities in Africa conducted in three universities posits that while there was overwhelming student expressing support for students' participation in representative management systems, the existing student unions faced a crisis of legitimacy. According to the study, student leaders were the least trusted people on campus an observation that was made in the light of disputed election results and accusations of corruption (Luescher-Mamashela *et al.* 2011).

With reference to Kenya, Obondo (2000) found that in most cases university senates, faculty and management board and committee structures do not include students, or even when they do, they are integrated as tokens rather than active participants in decision-making. As a result, students constitute one of the most vulnerable and least empowered groups of actors who must be involved in the transformation of Kenyan universities.

According to Obondo (2000), as avenues through which student interests are articulated to the university administration, students' associations remain an important but untapped resource in university efforts to confront the governance crisis. Despite this, the associations are not vibrant in our public universities, which may be a reflection of the quality of leadership they enjoy. He further argued that the lack of adequate involvement of ordinary students in decision-making is normally reflected in the tendency of students to reject and to react negatively toward policy statements from the university authorities and/or decisions by their own leaders. He pointed out that recurrent student unrest and staff disenchantment are reflections of demands for their involvement in campus governance. Therefore, it is imperative that university managements widen the representation and the active participation of students (and staff) in governing bodies and strengthen students' (and staff) associations if they wish to strengthen democratization of university governance. This will in turn increase their propensity to identify with outcomes of the governance processes in these institutions and reduce the incidences of student and/or staff conflict with management.

The Governance of University Education in Kenya

Universities in Kenya are administered through the Ministry of Education in accordance with the Universities Act No. 42 of 2012. Among other roles, the ministry is responsible for improving the quality, relevance, equity and access to higher education and technical training. The government agency mandated to regulate university education in the country, though, was initially the Commission for Higher Education (CHE). The commission was set up by the government in 1985 through an Act of Parliament and mandated to coordinate the development of higher education in the country. Within the context of the public sector, the Commission's responsibilities included the coordination of post-secondary education and training for the purpose of higher education and university admissions; long-term planning, programming, budgeting and financing of universities and other post-secondary institutions; student enrolment; scholarships; staffing and; the recognition of qualifications from other countries. The Commission's administrative mandate was functionally restricted to the regulation of private universities. It presided over matters of the physical development of private universities, quality assurance in private universities and other privately owned institutions of higher education, awarding of letters of interim authority to new private universities and, their eventual confirmation as chartered institutions.

Under the Universities Education Act No. 42 of 2012, which brought the establishing, governance and administration of all universities in Kenya under the same legal framework, CHE's mandate was expanded to include both public and private universities and the Commission was renamed the Commission for University Education (CUE). Among others, the responsibilities of the renamed commission include overseeing the establishment of new universities, the accreditation of all universities, regulation of university education to ensure the maintenance of standards, accreditation of university programmes to guarantee quality and relevance, inspection of universities and the promotion of research and innovation (Commission for University Education 2014; Republic of Kenya 2012).

The second semi-autonomous government agency involved in supporting the University sub-sector in Kenya is the Higher Education Loans Board (HELB) (Ministry of Education 2012). This is a State corporation under the then Ministry of Higher Education, Science and Technology established by an Act of Parliament (Cap 213A) in 1995. Its mandate is to disburse affordable loans, bursaries and scholarship to students pursuing higher education in recognized education institutions in the country. In this regard, HELB's responsibilities include sourcing funds, establishing, managing and, awarding loans bursaries and scholarships to students pursuing higher education in recognized institutions (Ministry of Education 2012; http://www.helb.co.ke/about-helb/history/). Although the Board's mandate initially covered students studying in public institutions only, today that mandate has been expanded to include those in the private sector.

The University Act No. 42 of 2012 delineates the internal administrative structure of universities to include a Chancellor, University Council, a Senate, a Vice Chancellor assisted by a number of Deputy Vice Chancellors, Faculty Boards and Departmental Boards (Republic of Kenya 2012). The Chancellor is the honorary head of the university and, in the name of the university, confers degrees and awards diplomas, certificates and other awards of the university during graduation ceremonies. In public universities, Chancellors are presidential appointees whereas in private universities they are appointed by the Board of Trustees. The Act also authorizes the Chancellor to give any advice considered necessary for the betterment of the University to the University Council. On the other hand, the Vice Chancellor is the Chief Executive of the University. S/he is academic and administrative head of the University with overall responsibility for the direction, organization, administration and programmes of the University.

The Council is the overall administrative body of the university mandated to manage all its resources. It is charged with the responsibility of policy formulation, creation of faculties and departments and, the approval of the appointment of university staff (Republic of Kenya 2012). The University Council has power to determine the method of recruitment, appointment and promotion of all staff of the university; to appoint and determine the terms and conditions of service for all staff of the university; to approve the budget; to determine, after considering the recommendations of the Senate, all fees payable to the university and; to constantly review the viability and financial sustainability of the University. In public universities or their constituent colleges, the University Council is made up of nine members appointed by the Cabinet Secretary in the Ministry of Education. These include a Chairperson, the Principal Secretary in the Ministry responsible for university education, Principal Secretary in the Ministry responsible for university financing, five members appointed by the Cabinet Secretary through an open process and the Vice Chancellor who is an ex-officio member and the Secretary to the Council (Republic of Kenya 2012).

The University Senate is the overall academic authority of the university and is responsible for academic matters, including control of instruction, examination, the award of degrees and, the direction of research (Republic of Kenya 2012). The membership of the Senate include the Vice Chancellor (as Chair), Deputy Vice Chancellors (the Deputy Vice Chancellor in charge of Academic Affairs serve as the secretary to the Senate); Principals of constituent colleges; Deputy Principals; Deans of faculties and Directors of schools, institutes and other academic units; Chairpersons of the teaching departments; all Professors or their representatives and; student representatives, among others. The functions of the Senate are wide and varied (Republic of Kenya 2012). They include: setting the dates of the academic year and determining the schedule of academic programmes within the academic year; approving all syllabi of the university; making regulations governing methods of assessing and examining the academic performance of students; evaluating academic records of both undergraduate and postgraduate candidates for the purpose of admission into the university and; regulating the conduct of examinations. The Senate is also expected to appoint internal and external examiners and recommend to the Council the terms and conditions for their appointment; to approve the award of degrees including the award of honorary degrees and other academic distinctions; promote research and innovation work in the University and; to determine the procedure to be followed in the conferment of the degrees and other awards, among many other responsibilities (Republic of Kenya 2012). Finally, faculty boards and departments are responsible to the Senate, oversee instruction and administer examinations.

In Kenya, initially, the internal governance structures of private universities could differ from those of their public counterparts. However, since the enactment of the Universities Act No. 42 of 2012 with the objective to bring the establishing, governance and administration of all universities in the country under the same legal framework, the internal governance structures of both public and private universities are progressively converging as private universities revise their charters to include all the structures prescribed by the Act. The CUE requires all private universities to adhere to the Act by ensuring that the governance structures include a Chancellor, a University Council, a Senate, a Vice Chancellor assisted by a number of Deputy Vice Chancellors, Faculty Boards and Departmental Boards.

At the realm of governance practices in general and the involvement of students in particular, the existing evidence tends to suggest that the Kenyan situation is not much different from the situation in the rest of the African continent. Although a visionary, creative and inclusive leadership is essential to the success of university education, in Kenya, poor leadership (read poor governance) prevails across most public universities (Mutula 2002; Obondo 2000). In principle students are expected to participate in decision-making at the different levels of university governance. However, in practice the authoritarian paternalistic model of governance (Klemenčič 2014; Leuscher-Mamashela 2013) eclipses the participatory governance model (Johnson and Deem 2003; Klemenčič 2012b; Leuscher-Mamashela 2013), thereby reducing students to unequal partners in decision-making. This is contrary to the expectation that universities should grant students co-decision-making rights.

Kenyan universities have in principle taken some steps to enhance the democratization of decision-making within the university by promoting wider representation of staff and students in key governing bodies and by allowing senior staff a say in the selection of senior university administrators (Mwiria, *et al*, 2007). The shift from government appointed top managers (that is, Vice Chancellor and Deputy Vice Chancellor) to a competitive system of appointing the same, as well as from the Head of State (the President) being the Chancellor of all public universities is a step in this direction. Despite this, much work is needed to actualize shared governance in which stakeholders have co-decision rights. A study conducted by Obondo (2000) found the decentralization of leadership and accountability to be the greatest management challenge to the governance of universities today. The study showed that the management in universities remains largely hierarchical and continues to be portrayed as centralized bureaucracies practicing centralized decision-making. There is absence of mechanisms for consultation, consensus building, open discussions, and the delegation and spread of authority. This is typified by lack of a collaborative, active and widespread participation by stakeholders, including, students, academic staff and support staff (Obondo 2000). The study also revealed that universities lacked proper and established structures for consultation, thereby rendering their management inaccessible except during crises when they make appearances to consult. Based on these findings, Obondo (2000) identified facilitation of greater involvement of stakeholders in university affairs in Kenya as a serious administrative and leadership problem.

One of the indicators of poor governance in higher education in Kenya is political meddling. To streamline governance requires less government meddling in the affairs of universities (Mwiria *et al.* 2007). This calls for greater autonomy for universities, with government providing the regulatory framework and ceasing to be an intervention force. In Kenya, the Universities Act No. 42 of 2012 was a step in this direction. However, higher education in the country, particularly the public sector, continues to be the subject of much political manipulation and intervention (Mwiria, Ngethe, Ngome, Ouma-Odero, Wawire and Wesonga 2007). This undermines the quality of governance in universities. Consequent from the poor governance in universities is indiscipline among students that has pervaded the sector over the years, thus resulting in frequent student strikes, demonstrations and riots from time to time (Kiboiy 2013; Mohamedbhai 2016; Mutula 2002). These in turn lead to closures that prolong the time required to complete degree programmes, thereby disrupting academic life and driving some students and staff to local private and overseas universities.

The intensity and frequency of student strikes in Kenya has increased steadily over the years, as students express their disaffection with the management of the university and the country as a whole and university lecturers and students clamour for academic freedom. These have resulted in frequent closures and, consequently, in prolonging of the minimum period required to graduate; in public universities some students take up to six years to complete what should be a four-year basic degree (Mutula 2002). Between 1969 and 2000, for example, 69 student strikes were recorded in all public universities. Of this total, 31.9 per cent (22) occurred during a span of 20 years, between 1969 and 1989, compared to 68.1 per cent (47) which were recorded between 1990 and 2000 (Kiboiy 2013). During this period one of the most noticeable student unrests occurred in 1982 when students supported and participated in the aborted military coup of August 1, 1982 to express their disaffection with the management of the university and the country as a whole. The coup was staged by some officers in the Kenya air force who attempted to overthrow the government of President Daniel Arap Moi. During 2007/2008, in the wake of the disputed presidential elections, student unrest and rioting, leading to closure of several campuses, occurred in the country (Mohamedbhai 2016). Similar unrests occurred in March 2009 leading to the closure of Kenyatta University, with students protesting over the set deadline for examination registration. The incidents occasioned the death of one student and the serious destruction to university property. In May 2010, the University of Nairobi closed down indefinitely after violent unrest and looting in the streets by students over disputed students' elections. According to Mohamedbhai (2016), the disturbances were allegedly caused by external interference of local politicians in the students' elections. Whereas the genesis of students' unrest are many and varied, lack of involvement of students in decision-making is a leading factor; other factors that include poor living conditions, autocratic administrations, rising cost of education and living and, lack of factual information about the relevant issues, among other causes. In this regard, the double intakes that force cohorts to take long vacations to allow others to be on campus have provided a major catalyst.

Attempts have also been made to strengthen staff and students' associations to enable them play an enhanced role as buffers between staff and students on the one hand and the university administration on the other (Mwiria *et al.* 2007). Staff unions, especially those in the public sector are expected to extend their mandates beyond clamouring for salary increases to include checking the excesses of administration, monitoring the use of resources and, promoting the improved quality of education. Similarly, students' associations are expected to be responsible for ensuring that students are committed to their studies and project a good image in the eyes of the wider public (Mwiria *et al.* 2007). While these are noble steps in the enhancement of the democratization of governance in universities in Kenya, the extent to which the governance climate facilitates their effective implementation remains debatable. To echo Mutula (2002), bureaucratic systems in public universities continue to keep students out of touch with authorities whenever they wish to have discussions to address matters of interest to their studies. Whereas the top managements of universities have in principle embraced the tenet of shared governance, in practice they continue to undermine it by meddling with the activities of staff and students' associations, including stage-managing (or even rigging) elections and the intimidation, compromising or, in some cases, the co-optation of the leadership of staff and student self-governance bodies.

Some scholars have suggested that considerable differences exist between governance models and practices in public and private universities in Kenya (Mutula 2002; Task Force on Higher Education and Society 2000). According to Mutula (2002), for example, private universities have a democratic system of governance, where students are routinely involved in decision-making processes. The institutions are characterized by continuous dialogue among administrators, teaching staff and students, leading to reduced tension that may result in strikes. While this might be true in principle, the practice in many private universities puts to question the extent to which the governance processes are truly democratic. Like in public universities, students in private universities do not enjoy the kind of access to and participation in decision-making structures envisioned by the shared governance principle of good governance in universities.

Research Issues

The preceding historical development of student involvement in university governance presented earlier brings to light several issues that need to be further interrogated and earmarked for research work that will add to the understanding and improvement of students' self-governance in the university setting in Africa. Presented below is a profiling of some of the leading issues.

Policy on Students' Involvement

The area of policy is central because the existence of policies that favour the involvement of students in decision-making affirms the university commitment to the principle of student involvement in governance both in academic and administration matters. Further, explicit laws and guidelines give the university stakeholders an idea of their rights and responsibilities in the governance arrangement ensuring good governance is achieved (Lizzio and Wilson 2009). The importance placed on students' participation in governance and the nature of this participation is usually articulated in university governance policy documents that include university acts at the State level, institutional statutes, vision and mission statements, strategic plans and student handbooks. While evidence suggests that top university policies in the form of acts and statutes support students' involvement in governance, the levels of involvement at the various organizational structures need to be determined and the other support policy structures like strategic plans that are now operational in most African universities need to be cross-examined to determine their status on this subject. For example, it is important to ascertain whether support for the offices of student affairs and dean of students is provided for in the strategic implementation plans.

Further, actual implementation of these policies in terms of the nature of students' involvement in governance at the specific universities, whether private or public, needs to be established to inform future transformations in this area (Mwiria *et al.* 2007). Specifically for Kenya, the gains made in terms of supportive policies for students' participation in governance may have been eroded by ongoing revisions of the institutional statutes of the respective public universities, which process has been alleged to be non-participatory.

Organizational Structures and Nature of Students' Involvement in Governance

The organizational structures are important instruments in university governance because they are instrumental in the attainment of institutional goals. However, effective structures are those which allow the constituent groups to formally and informally dialogue and guarantee a flow of information among them (Mwiria *et al.* 2007; Saint 1992). Universities in Kenya, like others the world over, have similar governance structures that consist of a board of trustees or directors, university councils, chancellors and vice chancellors or rectors and their deputies and the senate. Below this, we have schools or faculties which are headed by deans and departments which are headed by heads of department. Student matters are handled by deans of students (in public universities) and deputy vice chancellors (student affairs) in private universities who work in collaboration with student unions as mediators between students and the administration (Mwiria *et al.*

2007). Research on this issue indicates that decision-making under this structure is committee-based with particularly low engagement of students' representatives at the departmental level in some universities in the European experience, indicating that actual participation of some levels of decision-making and formal involvement as equal partners is not guaranteed (Persson 2003).

The relationship between formal provisions for participation and the actual practice at different levels needs to be investigated further, especially in African contexts where research is currently limited. Further research is also required in terms of which issues students are involved in when decisions are made and whether ordinary students have their issues addressed during these forums. Going by Sifuna's (1998) account of low involvement of staff in the decision-making in faculty and departmental meetings that are held irregularly in the Kenyan context, there are limited possibilities for the participation of students in such forums. Deans and departmental heads set the agenda of these meetings (Sifuna 1998). According to Obondo (2000), reports from Kenya show more influence of student leadership on social and environmental issues and less on issues relating to pedagogical work. The reports also show limited engagement between ordinary students and decision-making mechanisms. Hence, levels of consultation between student leaders and other students and the role of student unions need further scrutiny.

The Role of Student Governance Bodies and their Support Systems

Student unions or governments represent the most efficient way of involving students in university governance given that all students cannot be directly engaged by the administration. However, while 80 per cent of university students in South Africa support the idea that students should be represented at all levels of decision-making, the disjuncture between student demand for representation and the reported lack of trust and faith in student leadership points to inefficiencies in the student leadership (Luescher-Mamasheala 2005). This is further exemplified by data from Kenya where recurrent student riots and unrest in public universities is an indicator of the low levels of communication and interaction between student leaders and the students they represent on the one hand and, on the other hand, university administrations. This is further demonstrated by the tendency of students to reject policies that are developed by universities especially in relation to fees revisions and curriculum changes (Sifuna 2001; Obondo 2000). There is, therefore, need to check the selection processes of the student leaders to determine whether the criteria used are issue, project or popularity based.

Student leaders may be lacking the capacity to adequately represent students on complex matters or translate these issues into projects that address existing problems facing students. One such research should, therefore, check whether the support systems in terms of leadership training are adequate in preparing students to perform their intermediary role between the students and the administration effectively. Based on the experiences of students in Tanzania and Europe respectively, the short period in office for student leaders and low participation in elections by the general student body are other issues that need further exploration in relation to the quality and support systems available to student leaders (Persson 2003; Kamuzora and Mgaya n.d.). Support for student leaders, according to the 2003 Bologna report, should relate to the motivation of these students in terms of compensation for the time used for leadership activities and access to information and knowledge related to their role (Persson 2003).

Inclusiveness of Students' Involvement in Governance

Given the increased diversity of students joining university education as a result of the expanded access opportunities, it is important to ensure that governing arrangements cater for their unique needs. In the Kenyan setting, pointers to the fact that governance conditions, perhaps, do not address students' special needs are inherent in the general poor levels of access to university education and retention of students with disabilities and those from poor and rural backgrounds (Wawire and Elarabi 2010; Obonyo 2013). To enhance retention and quality of education for these groups of students, there is need to ensure that student governments have mechanisms of ensuring that concerns of international students, students with disabilities, students of different academic levels and disciplines, mature students attending evening and weekend classes and those from disadvantaged backgrounds are addressed. This is glaring a gap in the literature that this study aimed to address.

Theoretical Framework

The study utilized the democratic theory to explain students' participation in university governance, zeroing in on how key decisions are made and who makes them. The term democracy, which originates from the Greek words *demos* ('the people') and *kratein* ('to rule'), has been used to refer to 'people rule'. Schumpeter (1950: 269) defined democracy as 'that institutional arrangement for arriving at political decisions in which individuals acquire the power to decide by means of a competitive struggle for the people's vote'. According to Fung (2007:444), democracy is about non-tyranny or the principle that 'no individual or group should decide collective issues regardless of others' interests and preferences'. Underpinning democracy are values such as popular representation; universal suffrage; freedom of speech; assembly; organization and the press (Thierborn, 1977:4); accountability; self-government; reasoned rule; common good, and; self-actualization (Fung 2007), among others. Relative to other forms of governance, democracy is preferable because it renders the leadership accountable to its stakeholders.

Democratic theory is concerned with processes by which ordinary citizens exercise a relatively high degree of control over leaders (Dahl 2006). It examines structures and processes of decision-making from the student perspective to assess whether they are participatory. Democratic theories identify 'democracy' with political equality, popular sovereignty, and rule by majorities. This was clearly illustrated by Aristotle in the *Politics* when he wrote:

> The most pure democracy is that which is so called principally from the equality which prevails in it: for this is what the law in that state directs; that the poor shall be in no greater subjection than the rich; nor that the supreme power shall be lodged with either of these, but that both shall share it. For if liberty and equality, as some persons suppose, are chiefly to be found in a democracy, it must be so by every department of government being alike open to all ; but as the people are in the majority, and what they vote is law, it follows that such a state must be a democracy (cited in Dahl 2006:34).

Similar sentiments have been expressed by many others. For instance, De Tocqueville (2003) in *Democracy in America* wrote that: "The very essence of democratic government consists in the absolute sovereignty of the majority; for there is nothing in democratic states which is capable of resisting it".

Theorizing on democratic practice in society has its roots in Aristotle's work on political theory. In comparing the governing systems of his time, Aristotle singled out democratic rule as the most effective when compared to aristocracy or even monarchy (Rabb and Suleiman 2003). In democratic environments people determine public policy, laws and actions of their state together. Building on Aristotle's political ideas, *participatory democracy* or decision-making was born out of the need to explain how ordinary citizens should be involved more in deciding their collective affairs. Participatory democracy has the advantage of ensuring equity, self-determination, sense of community, acceptability and, relevance of the decisions made by the key stakeholders of the organization. Participation grows transparency by opening up policy formulation and implementation processes to all stakeholders through direct or representative involvement. Through the participatory processes, practical 'people-based' knowledge is shared, debated, combined with technical knowledge and built into the policy process. Participation also increases the bargaining power of stakeholders (Wainwright 2005). This occurs mainly because participation tendens to redistribute power among stakeholders. Participatory democracy enables stakeholders to monitor the work of the executive and other top managers/ administrators. Popular participation lets people, as well as officials, decide the detail on how broad policy commitments are carried out (Wainwright 2005), meaning that how public policy is administered is not value-neutral. The legitimacy of participatory democracy lies in the high degree of activity of what is likely to be a minority through institutions that are transparent, open to all and, based on mutually agreed rules.

According to Wainwright (2005), participatory democracy provides a real alternative, or complement, to elected power: a distinct and organized public sphere in which the demands of the people can be articulated, developed and negotiated between each other, and finally negotiated with the local or other relevant institutions. However, for participatory democracy to be feasible, attain legitimacy, and reinvigorate democratic practices as a whole, certain conditions are required. First, the structures for participation should be open at their foundations to everyone affected by such decisions – even if only a minority participate. As Wainwright (2005) underlined, 'openness is not just a formality; it needs to be worked at'. While not everyone may directly participate, all stakeholders need to be in contact with someone who participates. In the case of this study, this means that while not every student must be involved in decision-making directly, all students need to be connected to someone who is involved; that is student representatives or leadership. Second, participatory democracy requires mutually agreed and openly negotiated rules to regulate the interaction among and behaviour of stakeholders.

The legitimacy of participatory democracy is also pegged on the autonomy of the participatory process from the State (Wainwright 2005), in our case the top managers/ administrators of the university. This is important because participatory institutions have the goal to eventually share decision-making power with government, to exercise some control over the work of State institutions and, to monitor the implementation of government's decisions. Such relationships, though, are contingent on equality, meaning that participatory institutions need to have their own life and dynamism, and to know that the top governance body respects this. A fourth condition for the legitimation of participatory democracy is that there must be genuine sharing of knowledge (Wainwright 2005). In addition, participation must be anchored on real resources that have significance to the lives of the stakeholders. In other words, the consultation must be a process that gets result and not just another consultation exercise leading nowhere (Wainwright 2005). The final condition enhancing the feasibility and legitimacy of the participatory process is the existence of a governance body that believes in it. Referring specifically to the university education environment, the argument here is that for participatory democracy to thrive the top administrator of the university must believe and have faith in this form of governance.

The main contention upon which the key theories of participatory democracy are based is whether citizens should make decisions for themselves through *direct democracy* or let others make decisions on their behalf through *representative (liberal) democracy* (Schmidt 2002). *Direct democracy* is characterized by direct participation of all the stakeholders in the decision-making processes including policy-making and determination of the actions to be taken by the governing body. While this is a practice that gives an opportunity to each group member to exercise control of the direction their lives will take, its applicability has been curtailed by the large membership of most groups, rendering group decision-making inefficient and ineffective. Another criticism levelled against this mode of democracy is that the masses lack the time, wisdom and good judgement to make relevant decisions. James Madison, the late eighteenth and early nineteenth-century American political theorist and statesman, was among those who developed and presented arguments against direct democracy. The opponents of direct democracy argued that the masses should be represented by governing elite groups of people elected to represent their interests in what is known as *representative or liberal democracy* (Baker 1997).

Liberal democracy is a form of government in which representative democracy operates under the principles of liberalism, i.e. protecting the rights of the individual, which are generally enshrined in law. Bollen (1990) defines liberal democracy as 'the extent to which a political system allows political liberties and democratic rule'. The existence of political liberties is reflected in the extent to which people enjoy freedom to voice their political opinions and to form and participate in political groups (Bollen 1993). Democratic rule, on the other hand, exists if the national government is accountable to the general population and individuals have the right to participate in government either directly or through representation (Bollen 1993). In a liberal democracy, among others, there are attempts to defend and increase civil liberties against the encroachment of governments, institutions and powerful forces in society; restrict or regulate government intervention in political, economic and moral matters affecting the citizenry; and, to increase the scope for religious, political and intellectual freedom of citizens (http://australianpolitics.com/democracy/key-terms/liberal-democracy).

Liberal democracy is hinged on the premise that governing power is not exercised directly by the whole body of stakeholders but by representatives elected by members through a voting system. Thus, legislative decision-makers should acquire political authority by means of a competitive but peaceful and legal struggle for the support of a majority of the electorate. Liberal democracy acknowledges the importance of civil society organizations (Wainwright 2005). This is based on the conventional acceptance that a strong civil society keeps elected representatives on their toes. This occurs through organized interest groups pressing their causes on government, sometimes through political parties, sometimes through independent lobbies. This form of democracy is a salient feature of the contemporary world; it has taken root in the Western democratic political systems, such as the United States, Britain, Germany, Japan, Australia, New Zealand, Canada etc., and is being tried in many other countries (Bollen 1993).

We acknowledge that the benefits of both the direct and representative democratic theories can be maximized in organizational governance to enrich participation experiences of key stakeholders. However, for the purpose of this study the liberal (or representative) democracy theoretical framework was utilized to isolate the governance structures, activities and, processes that enabled university students to participate in decision-making either directly or through representation. The study advances the view that, in principle, public and private universities have embraced the democratization of decision-making, in which shared (or participatory) governance is a common feature. In this scheme of things, students, as major stakeholders in universities, are expected to play a major role in policy-formulation and decision-making in these institutions. However, rather than rely on direct democratic governance in which all students are involved in decision-making (or make decisions for themselves), universities have adopted the liberal democratic model in which students participate in policy-formulation and decision -aking through elected (or in some cases appointed) representatives, who are expected to champion the interests of the total student community. Such representation occurs through structures such as student unions, clubs, committee membership and, voting for student leaders (Baker 1997).

4

Research Design and Methodology

This chapter describes the procedures that were used to gather and analyze the data used in the study. It is organized into seven sections. While section one presents the research design elected for the study, section two offers a description of the various study sites. The sample selection procedures, data collection methods, data management and analysis techniques and ethical considerations are presented in sections three through to six, respectively. The final section (seven) focuses on the limitations of the study.

Research Design

A triangulated methodological design blending both quantitative and qualitative approaches to data collection and analysis was employed. Specifically, the survey design was employed. This involved the use of questionnaires, interviews and focus group discussions (FGDs). Generally, it is typical to combine different data collection techniques and procedures in the same study in order to generate appropriate and valid information (Mugenda 2013). The mixed method approach not only allows the researcher to be more confident in the results of the study but also provides a clearer understanding of the phenomenon of the study (Jick 1979; Thurmond 2001; Johnson, Onwuegbuzie and Turner 2007). To illustrate, the researcher is able to use qualitative data as the critical counterpoint to quantitative data and by so doing, the quantitative analysis benefits from the perceptions emanating from the personal experiences and the firsthand observations of the qualitative approaches (Jick 1979). More specifically, by combining the quantitative and qualitative approaches, this study sought to not only bring out the major trends (patterns) and practices in student leadership but also elicit specific voices from students and academic managers and policy-makers. Of course, utilizing mixed methods is not without limitations. For instance, it makes replication exceedingly difficult (Jick 1979; Thurmond 2001).

The Sites of the Study

The study was carried out in Kenya. Kenya lies on the eastern side of Africa. The country is bordered by Ethiopia in the north, Sudan in the northwest, Uganda in the west, Tanzania in the south, and Somalia in the northeast. To the east lies the Indian Ocean. The total area of Kenya is about 583,000 square kilometres. The specific sites for the study were two universities namely, Kenyatta University (KU) and the United States International University, Africa (USIU). Whereas the former is a public university, the latter is a private university. The two institutions are located within the city of Nairobi, and have been in existence for a considerable period of time.

Kenyatta University (KU)

Kenyatta University (KU) is a multi-campus public university. Its main campus is located along Thika Road near the Kahawa barracks in Kiambu County, Ruiru Constituency, Kahawa area. The institution's history can be traced as far back as 1965 when the British Government handed over the Templar barracks in Kahawa to the newly formed Government of Kenya. The barracks were converted into Kenyatta College, a constituent college of University of Nairobi in 1970. It was renamed Kenyatta University College (KUC) and specialized in training teachers at the certificate and diploma levels. It was not until 1972 that KUC admitted its first 200 Bachelor of Education students. In 1978 the faculty of education was moved from University of Nairobi to KUC campus a move aimed at consolidating undergraduate and postgraduate programmes in the country. The college was eventually upgraded into a fully-fledged university following an act of Parliament in 1985.

Since its elevation to the status of a fully-fledged university, KU has birthed and nurtured new colleges into fully-fledged universities. Among these are Jomo Kenyatta University of Agriculture and Technology (JKUAT) and Pwani University. The institution remains a leader in university education. Today, the university comprises 12 campuses spread across the country. These include the Main Campus (which was the locus of our study), Ruiru Campus, Parkland Campus, Kitui Campus, Mombasa Campus, City Centre Campus, Nyeri Campus, Nakuru Campus, Kericho Campus, Dadaab Campus, Embu Campus and Arusha Campus. To remain relevant in the changing higher education market, KU has diversified its programmes and currently boasts of the following 17 Schools: School of Humanities and Social Sciences, School of Visual and Performing Arts, School of Education, School of Pure and Applied Sciences, School of Engineering and Technology, School of Architecture and Spatial Planning, School of Environmental Studies, School of Applied Human Sciences, School of Health Sciences, School of Business, School of Economics, School of Agriculture and Enterprise Development, School of Law, School of Hospitality and Tourism, School of Public Health, Digital School of Virtual and Open Learning and Graduate School.

Kenyatta University is accredited by the Kenya Commission of University Education (CUE), the Inter-University Council for East Africa (IUCEA), the Africa Association of Universities (AAU), the International Association of Universities (IAU) and the Commonwealth Universities. It offers Bachelor's, Master's and Doctoral degrees. From a student population of about 15,000 in 2006, the university has experienced tremendous growth in student numbers; the current enrolment stands at approximately 62,000 students, with female students accounting for 45 per cent of the total. Out of the total student population, 87 per cent are pursuing undergraduate courses, while the rest are studying for postgraduate degrees. The institution boasts of a compliment of 960 academic staff, including 27 professors, 60 associate professors, 120 senior lecturers, 455 lecturers and 298 tutorial fellows.

The overall governing body of the University is the University Council. Among others, this is the body charged with the responsibility to administer the property and funds of the university; provide for the welfare of the students; enter into association with other universities, or other institutions of learning, whether within Kenya or elsewhere; and after consultation with the senate, make regulations governing the conduct and discipline of the students of the university. The Council consists of a Chairman, a vice-Chairman and an Honorary Treasurer; all of whom shall be appointed by the Chancellor; who is normally a government-appointed ceremonial head of the university. Other members of the Council include the Vice Chancellor, Deputy Vice Chancellors, Principals of constituent colleges, Permanent Secretary to the Ministry responsible for University Education, Permanent Secretary to the Ministry of Finance, up to eight members appointed by the President to represent the Government, four persons appointed by the Senate from among its members, two persons appointed by the Convocation from among its members, two members elected by non-Senate members of the academic staff from among themselves, two members elected by the students' organization, one person elected by the non-academic staff from among themselves and not more than two members co-opted to the Council from time to time.

The internal management of the University includes the Vice Chancellor as the chief executive officer. S/he is deputized by four Deputy Vice Chancellors as follows: Deputy Vice Chancellor, Academic Affairs; Deputy Vice Chancellor, Finance and Development; Deputy Vice Chancellor, Administration and Deputy Vice Chancellor, Research and Innovations. Each Deputy Vice Chancellor is assisted by a Registrar. It should be noted that academic matters are normally dealt with by the University Senate. This is a body chaired by the Vice Chancellor and whose membership incorporates Professors, Deans, and Heads of Department.

At Kenyatta University, the Kenyatta University Students Association (KUSA) is the student governing body. KUSA was established in 1970 to represent students' needs and views in the university. However, like other students' organizations, it was banned in the 1990s during the clamour for multiparty democracy in Kenya. The association was reborn in 2004 when the students decided to actively take part in matters affecting them. Since then, the association has been an instrumental part in the governance of the university. The organization is designed to serve the student community in its pursuit of academic excellence, social welfare, peace, competitiveness in the job market, and integrity (Kenyatta University 2014). The aims and objectives of KUSA are to ensure the rights of students in academics, disciplinary actions, administration and health services, catering and accommodation, social welfare services, and security; to deepen the members' sense of duty to our university community, families, and nation; to establish efficient and effective processes and organs for the making and administration of KUSA's policies and; with the approval of the Vice Chancellor, to collaborate with non-political organizations, professional associations, and student groups that share the aims and objectives of KUSA, among many others, (Kenyatta University 2014).

Since KUSA exists to represent all students, any student admitted to Kenyatta University and registered for a course leading to qualification for the award of a diploma or degree of the University becomes an automatic member of KUSA (Kenyatta University 2014). However, a bona fide student is one who has paid university fees and registered on-line during the current semester. Students who have completed a degree programme at Kenyatta University may become affiliate members of KUSA by a written notification to the President of KUSA. KUSA is run by an Executive body and a Congress, made up of elected students through a democratic election that occurs every academic year. The top officials, who normally serve a one-year term, include the President; the Deputy President; the Secretary-General; the Deputy Secretary-General; the Finance Secretary; the Academic Secretary; the Organizing Secretary; the Gender and Social Welfare Secretary; the Special Needs Secretary; the chairpersons of each of the satellite campuses; the Representative for Institution-Based and Open Learning Students and; the Speaker of the Congress as *ex officio* member (Kenyatta University 2014). The governance organs of the association include the Annual General Meeting, also referred to as the AGM; the Special General Meeting, also referred to as the SGM; the Students' Congress, also referred to as the Congress; the Executive Council; and subject to the approval of Congress, any other organ determined by the Executive Council.

The United States International University–Africa (USIU–A)

The United States International University (USIU–A) is a non-profit institution located in the Kasarani area of Nairobi behind Safari Park Hotel, off the Thika Superhighway.

It is the oldest, private secular university in Kenya, having been established in 1969 under the Companies Act, Cap. 486 (now repealed), following an agreement between the trustees of USIU in San Diego, California and the Kenyan Ministry of Education. USIU was part of a multi-campus system of the United States International University based in California. It became regionally accredited in the United States in 1982 as a US entity operating outside of the US. This was the same time it underwent a special review by the Government of Kenya. The university then registered under the Universities Act of 1985 and was inspected by the newly-formed Commission for Higher Education (CHE) in 1987, 1990, 1992, 1992, 1994, 1997, 1998 with a final inspection in 1999 prior to the award of the Charter. The Charter was awarded to USIU on the 10th of December 1999. Officially designated as United States International University–Africa (USIU–Africa), the university is a completely autonomous Kenyan institution governed by the laws of Kenya.

USIU–Africa has undergone considerable changes since receiving its Charter in 1999. Among the most significant developments is the de-linking of USIU in Nairobi from the USIU multi-campus system. USIU–Africa broke away from the USIU San Diego in 2001 to become an independent organization of its own. This was after USIU San Diego merged with California School of Professional Psychology to form Alliant International University. The Commission of Higher Education in Kenya expressed concerns over control of the latter institution. The university hence became independent and sought its accreditation from the Western Association of Schools and Colleges (WASC) which it received in 2005. The university is now an independent university with accreditation in Kenya and the United States, making it the only dually accredited institution in the East African region. Locally, the institution is accredited by the Commission for University Education (CUE). In addition, the university is accredited in the United States of America (USA) by WASC. This status has had significant implications for governance, academic programming and overall accountability.

Currently, the USIU offers courses under four schools, namely: The School of Humanities and Social sciences, the Chandaria School of Business, the School of Science and Technology, and the School of Pharmacy and Health Sciences (United States International University 2015a). The School of Humanities and Social Sciences houses three undergraduate programmes, BA Criminal Justice, BA International Relations and BA Psychology. In addition, the school offers the following postgraduate programmes: MA Clinical Psychology, MA Counselling Psychology, MA International Relations, Doctorate in Clinical Psychology and Doctor of Philosophy (PhD) in International Relations. The Chandaria School of Business is the largest school and offers the following undergraduate programmes: BSc Accounting, BSc Business Administration, BSc Hotel and Restaurant Management, BSc Information Systems and Technology, BSc

International Business Administration and BSc Tourism Management. Graduate programmes offered by the Chandaria School of Business include the Master of Business Administration (MBA), Executive Master of Science in Organizational Development (EMOD), Global Executive Master of Business Administration (GEMBA) and the Doctor of Business Administration (DBA) (United States International University 2015a). The School of Science and Technology, on the other hand, offers BSc. in Applied Computer Technology, BSc. in Information Systems Technology and BA in Journalism at the undergraduate level and two Master's level degrees, that is, MSc. in Information Systems Technology and MA in Communication Studies. Established most recently (Summer 2015), the School of Pharmacy and Health Sciences only offers a single programme, the Bachelor of Pharmacy (United States International University 2015a).

Over the years the USIU has grown to become the largest private institution of higher learning in Kenya, and among the larger of such institutions in the East Africa region. Its current population, as of September 2015, stands at 6,035 students, drawn from 69 countries (United States International University Undated). The international students comprise about 17 per cent of the student body. The current enrolment of 6,035 students represents about 74 per cent growth from the 3,462 students enrolled in the fall of 2006. Of the total students 4,835 (80.1 per cent) are pursuing undergraduate degrees compared to 1,200 (19.9 per cent) who are enrolled in postgraduate courses. In terms of gender composition, 44 per cent of the students are males whereas 56 per cent are females (United States International University, Undated). The university has a compliment of 110 full-time faculty spread across the five schools as follows: School of Humanities and Social Sciences, 48 faculties, Chandaria School of Business (33), School of Science and Technology, 23 and, School of Pharmacy and Health Sciences (6). The university also relies on Adjunct faculty drawn from industry and from public universities.

Based on the revised Charter submitted to the Commission for University Education for approval (the Charter is currently under review to harmonize it with the requirements of the Universities Act No. 42 of 2012), the governance of the USIU-A is vested in the Board of Trustees, the Chancellor, the University Council, the Senate, the Vice-Chancellor, the Management Board and the Student Affairs Council (SAC). The Board of Trustees is vested with 'supreme control' over the university. It adopts the institutions annual plan of financial operation and establishes degrees to be awarded. However, the day-to-day responsibility for administration of the university is delegated by the Board of Trustees to the Vice Chancellor and the Management Board. The Board of Trustees is made up of professional individuals and distinguished scholars drawn from several countries. However, as per the University Charter, a third of them must be Kenyans. The Chancellor is the ceremonial head of the university and confers degrees during graduation ceremonies.

Consistent with the Universities Act No. 42 of 2012, the Council is the overall administrative body of the university mandated to manage all its resources. It is charged with the responsibility of policy formulation, creation of faculties and departments, and approval of the appointment of university staff. The Universality Senate, on the other hand, is the overall academic authority of the university and is responsible for academic matters, including control of the instruction, examination, the award of degrees and, the direction of research. It should be noted that the first University Senate for USIU-A is expected to be inaugurated at the beginning of the 2016/ 2017 academic year. The Management Board, chaired by the Vice Chancellor, provides the Vice Chancellor with decision-making support on matters of day–to–day running of the university. It deliberates on issues affecting the university, reviews and/or proposes recommended policies and priorities which contribute to the university's advancement toward accomplishing strategic initiatives. It also functions as a forum for discussion of pertinent issues affecting the day–to–day running of the university on a weekly basis and therefore the management council meets on a weekly basis. As currently constituted, its membership includes all Deputy Vice-Chancellors, the University Legal Officer and Unit Directors.

The Student Affairs Council (SAC) is a learned, secular, internal, non-political and non-sectarian organization for championing academic and social issues affecting students studying at USIU (United States International University 2015b). It is the official body responsible for students' self-governance, representation, and well-being. The SAC leadership consists of an executive committee, student senate and associated committees, clubs and sports. These are elected yearly and include a Chair, a Vice Chair, an Executive Secretary, a Vice Secretary, a Treasurer and representatives from different academic programmes. The officials are expected to work together to represent the issues affecting students in diverse areas such as academics, sports, club activities, health and other matters pertaining to the students' life in the university. Membership of SAC is open to any student attending the University on a full or part-time basis. All students become members upon registration and payment of an activity fee to the University. Based on the SAC Constitution, SAC shall be the only student organization at USIU and shall have offices solely on university premises. In addition, it shall cooperate and collaborate with both the students and the university management in the dissemination of its objectives (United States International University 2015b). The organization is subject to the policies and regulations of the university. As such, any section of SAC may be suspended or dissolved by the Vice Chancellor where there is evidence that there is mismanagement or engagement in activities affecting the reputation of the university or the wellbeing of the students.

The SAC has the following six objectives (United States International University 2015b):

- to support the University in accomplishing its mission of promoting the discovery and application of knowledge, the acquisition of skills and the development of intellect and character in a manner which prepares students to contribute effectively and ethically as citizens of a changing and increasingly technological world.
- to foster a spirit of cooperation, unity and hard work among the students of the university.
- to provide an effective forum for discussion and negotiation with the university management and any other relevant persons on all matters affecting all aspects of the welfare of the students be they social or academic.
- to provide a forum for the promotion of healthy relationships and mutual progress with other student organizations, institutions or person(s) in consultation with the SAC Advisor/ Designee.
- to facilitate intercultural interactions within the University and with the society in a manner that prepares students to effectively function in a multicultural environment.
- to fulfill any other objective in line with University Mission and Vision.

In pursuance of its aims and objectives, SAC endeavours to embrace good governance practices in its day-to-day administrative and other activities, to develop leadership qualities among the students, and to encourage students to participate in local, national and international students' functions, among others (United States International University 2015b).

Sample Size and Sampling Design

The major source of data for this study was 657 students drawn from Kenyatta University (KU) and the United States International University (USIU) as follows: KU, 456 students and USIU, 201 students. These comprised the primary sample for the study. The selection of the students to be interviewed for the study occurred in three stages. Stage one involved the use of purposive sampling, a non-probability sampling method, to select the universities from which respondents would be drawn. As evident from Table 5.1, Kenya has a total of 39 chartered universities out of which 22 are public institutions and 17 are owned privately. Out of this total, two institutions, Kenyatta University and the United States International University, were purposively selected to participate in the study. Whereas KU represented the public sector, the USIU represented the private sector. The two institutions were purposively selected on account of a number of considerations. The first consideration in the selection of the two universities covered by the study was the length of time they have been in existence. A guiding assumption in this regard was that the longer the institution had been in existence the more established it was in many aspects, including governance structures and their attendant governance culture. Kenyatta University, though the third fully-fledged university to be established in Kenya, after Nairobi and Moi Universities, is the second oldest institution of higher learning in the country. Initially established as a constituent college of the University of Nairobi in 1965, the institution became a fully-fledged university in 1985. Since then, KU has experienced tremendous growth and is today the fastest-growing public university in Kenya. The USIU, on the other hand, is the oldest private and possibly the most established private university in Kenya. As pointed out earlier, the institution was established in 1969 as the first private, secular university to operate in Kenya. Initially it was a satellite African campus of the United States International University of San Diego, California in the United States of America. In 1999, the USIU was awarded a charter by the Kenyan Commission for Higher Education (CHE), granting the University its full accreditation. In 2001, the university broke away from the USIU San Diego to become an independent organization on its own.

Table 4.1: Chartered Public and Private Universities in Kenya by Year of Establishment

Name of Institution	Established
Public Universities	
1 University of Nairobi	1970
2 Moi University	1984
3 Kenyatta University	1985
4 Egerton University	1987
5 Jomo Kenyatta University of Agriculture and Technology (JKUAT)	1994
6 Maseno University	2001
7 Masinde Muliro University of Science and Technology	2007
8 Dedan Kimathi University of Technology	2012
9 Chuka University	2013
10 Technical University of Nairobi	2013
11 Technical University of Mombasa	2013
12 Kisii University	2013
13 Pwani University	2013
14 Maasai Mara University	2013
15 University of Eldoret	2013
16 Laikipia University	2013
17 Jaramogi Oginga Odinga University	2013
18 Meru University of Science and Technology	2013
19 South Eastern Kenya University	2013
20 Karatina University	2013
21 MultiMedia University of Kenya	2013
22 University of Kabianga	2013

Private Universities		
23	University of Eastern Africa, Baraton	1991
24	Catholic University of Eastern Africa (CUEA)	1992
25	Daystar University	1994
26	Scott Christian University	1997
27	United States International University (USIU)	1999
28	Africa Nazarene University	2002
29	Kenya Methodist University	2006
30	St Paul University	2007
31	Pan Africa Christian University	2008
32	Strathmore University	2008
33	Kabarak University	2008
34	Mount Kenya University	2011
35	African International University	2011
36	Kenya Highlands Evangelical University	2011
37	Great Lakes University of Kisumu	2012
38	KCA University	2013
39	Adventist University of Africa	2013

Source: Commission for University Education 2014

Finally, the limited financial resources available for the study did not allow the study to include a large number of institutions. In addition, to cut costs, it was necessary to minimize travel, accommodation and subsistence expenses to be incurred by the researchers. Second, and closely related to the first factor, was the proximity of the two institutions to the areas of residence of the researchers. All the researchers are residents within Nairobi, the very location of KU and the USIU, thereby minimizing the amount of travelling required to complete the study. As a matter of fact, whereas one of the researchers is an employee of KU, the other two work for the USIU. Third, being employees of the selected institutions, the researchers had the undue advantage of enjoying a good rapport with the two universities.

The second and third stages in the selection of the study's primary sample involved the selection of two schools in each university from which the actual respondents were selected; this was followed by the selection of the specific students who served as primary respondents. To select the schools covered by the study, stratified random sampling was employed. From each university covered by the study, two of its existing schools were selected for inclusion in the study. This culminated in the selection of the Schools of Education and Business in Kenyatta University the Schools of Humanities and Social Sciences and of Science and Technology in USIU. For Kenyatta University, being the larger of the two institutions, the target sample was 400 respondents, while for the USIU 200 students were targeted for inclusion in the study. These figures were considered large enough to allow for the statistical manipulation of the data gathered and analyzed for the study.

To select the actual respondents, a combination of non-probability and probability sampling methods was used. The researchers relied on information about teaching timetables in the two institutions to select lecture sessions during which the surveys were administered. This involved the application of a combination of availability (or accidental) sampling, a non-probability sampling technique with simple random sampling, probability method. From each course/ lecture session selected, all students willing to complete the surveys were interviewed for the study. The process continued until the minimum targeted number of respondents in each institution was reached. It culminated with the interviewing of 456 and 201 respondents from KU and the USIU, respectively.

To supplement data collected from the primary respondents, interviews were conducted with key informants and focus group discussions (FGDs) were held with selected students. The key informants were selected purposively and included two top management officials (one from each university) and two student leaders (again one per university). Consistent with the selection of the study's primary respondents, students participating in the FGDs were also selected utilizing a combination of availability and random selection methods as follows:

- Lecture sessions were selected on the basis of availability and from each one of them, focus group discussants were selected randomly.
- In all four focus groups, two from each university spread across the two schools participating in the study, were constituted for the study. The two groups from KU comprised of fourteen members (seven per group), while from USIU, one group was made up of seven members and the other one of six members.

Data Collection Techniques

The study employed a combination of self-administered surveys, key informant interviews and focus group discussions (FGDs) to collect opinions from students and other stakeholders in the governance process in universities in Kenya. The self-administered surveys constituted the primary source of data for this study. Quantitative data were collected from 657 students spread across two universities. The study utilized a pre-coded questionnaire with the response category 'other [specify]' giving it an open-ended feature. The questionnaires gathered information specific to the study objectives and to the demographic and socioeconomic characteristics of the respondents. Utilizing a questionnaire has the advantage of being cheaper (Jankowicz 2000) and the ability of 'yielding a large amount of information about a given population ready for codification and analysis' (Strati 2000:147).

To maximize the trustworthiness of the data and enhance credibility, the research instrument was piloted one month prior to the administration of the surveys utilizing a nonrandom sample of twelve individuals drawn from schools in the study sites that were not to be featured in the study but who reflected the major characteristics of those to be studied. The pre-testing was undertaken as a precautionary measure before the main interviews were conducted to enable the investigators to establish whether the items in the instrument possessed the desired qualities to collect the information/data required for the study and to check on the validity and reliability of the instruments. Through pre-testing the researchers assessed the relevance, accuracy, clarity of question items and the ease of respondents' understanding of the question items. Information from the pilot study enabled the researchers to minimize response bias, ensure that the questions covered exhaustively all aspects of the data sought for the study and to estimate the time needed to administer the questionnaire. The major concern expressed by most of the twelve respondents involved the length of the questionnaire; they found it to be too long. The pre-test, therefore, resulted in a trimming of the questionnaire by eliminating some items from it. In addition, the piloting identified some minor weaknesses in the questionnaire, including spellings and the sequencing of items, meaning that they needed to be corrected before the actual data collection commenced.

To supplement data collected from interviews with students, the study gathered qualitative data from key informants and focus group discussants at each site. From each study site, selected members of upper-level management and members of student leadership were targeted as key informants. The gathering of data from them took the forms of semi-structured interviews, utilizing topics selected in advance and tailored to fit the study. This approach allowed for a chain of probes that yielded richer information relevant to the topic being studied. Other advantages of using semi-structured questions include their ability to provide rich data from the respondents while allowing the conversation to explore new issues emerging in the interview and a possibility of investigating the motives and feelings of the respondents (Mäkelä and Maula 2008). This is unlike close-ended questions which require specific answers from the respondents. The specific topics explored during interviews with key informants included the mainstreaming of student participation in governance in institutional policies and practices, support for students' involvement in governance by university organizational structures, the support systems for enhancing student involvement in university governance, the role of self-governance structures in student participation in governance, the level of inclusivity of student involvement in university governance, as well as the impediments to effective students' participation in governance. The FGDs were conducted with students selected from the same schools of the primary respondents, utilizing similar selection methods (see section 3.3). These were guided by an interview schedule developed for that purpose. The schedule emphasized thematic issues comparable to those keyed on by the in-depth interviews with key informants.

Although the actual data collection did not commence until September 2013, fieldwork began in mid-March the same year. During this initial stage of fieldwork the researchers sought research clearance from the Kenya government through the National Council for Science Technology and Innovations (NACOSTI) and acquainted themselves with the two institutions to be studied. The latter took the form of visitations with the top-level officials to explain the study to them and to file formal requests of consent to execute the survey. Once consent was granted, the next stage of the fieldwork involved visits with the selected (sampled) schools in each university to publicize the study and to book appointments to administer the surveys.

Data were collected during the months of June to November 2013. Whereas the process at Kenyatta University lasted from June to August 2013, at the United States International University it spanned the period September to November 2013. In every case, the process opened with one of the researchers or an assistant explaining the purpose of the study to the respondents before the questionnaire was distributed to them. This was done purposely to further strengthen item accuracy, clarity and ease of respondent completion of the survey. Before enlisting the respondents' co-operation, the researcher or an assistant assured the respondents that their responses would be kept confidential and answered any questions that they might have had. These efforts were supplemented by a letter attached to each questionnaire explaining the purpose of the study, requesting the voluntary co-operation of the respondents and guaranteeing confidentiality of any information given. Interviewees who consented to participate in the study were then issued with a questionnaire and given about 45 minutes to complete it and hand it over to the researcher. As indicated earlier, the surveys were administered during lecture sessions and the cooperation of the specific instructors was essential for the success of the exercise.

Data Management and Analysis

The bulk of the data realized by the study was managed and processed utilizing a computer. The analysis occurred in two stages. The first stage involved the processing of surveys administered to the primary respondents of the study utilizing the SPSS quantitative data analysis software. During this stage, descriptive statistics especially frequency distributions, percentages and, where applicable, means were computed and utilized to display data patterns; that is, to construct a descriptive profile of the study sample and to depict the patterns in the influence of policies and practices targeted by the study. Further statistical treatment of data assumed the form of relational analysis using cross-tabulation. The analysis focused on selected independent variables to assess whether or not they cause variations in perceptions of inclusive governance in higher education institutions. To test for relatedness among variables, the Chi square ($\chi2$) test was applied. The $\chi2$ test statistic depicts association between variables presented in the form of cross-tabulation by examining whether frequencies obtained are different from the frequencies one would attribute to chance variations alone. Where the two frequencies are found to be similar, it is concluded that there is no difference in the two groups under study. On the contrary, where differences are found between the two samples, it shows that, "there is a significant difference in attitudes and/ or perceptions between the two groups under comparison" (Frankel and Wallen 1993: 201).

The second stage in the data management and analysis process involved the transcribing of in-depth interviews and FGDs. These were transcribed and categorized by questions. Patterns from these sources of data constituted a basis for the cross-validation of results (patterns) obtained from the quantitative data. Interpretation was based on themes which emerged from the data and were supported by select quotes.

Ethical Considerations

A major ethical consideration is that the respondents do not come to any harm. The nature of the study did not in any way expose the respondents to any danger. The other consideration is that the respondents' participation is voluntary. This was ensured by informing the respondents of their right to voluntary participation and withdrawal at the beginning of the interview or at any point of the research. The respondents were also informed about the objectives of the study and what the information was to be used for. Every respondent who consented to be interviewed was guaranteed anonymity. Furthermore, no names were required of those interviewed and the information collected from each respondent was to be utilized only in combination with that collected from others rather than individually. According to the regulations governing research activities in Kenya, permission was also sought from the Kenya government through the National Council for Science Technology and Innovations (NACOSTI).

Limitations of the Study

Three factors in particular are likely to have undermined the quality of this study and hence the value of its core findings. First, the study covers only two institutions; KU (public sector) and the USIU (private sector). Net of the consideration of length of time in existence, a single university from each sector is by no means representative of the likely diverse policies and practices with respect to students' involvement in university governance in each sector. This has implications on the extent to which the results of this study can be generalized to universities in the public and the private sectors in Kenya. The gravity of the situation is best captured by taking cognizance of the fact that by 2014 Kenya had a total of 22 public and 17 private chartered universities. As pointed out earlier, the decision to key on only two institutions was for the most part dictated by the financial resources available for the study. Further eroding the generalizability of the study findings is the reliance on the non-probability sampling technique of purposive sampling to select the two institutions keyed on by the study. Reliance on purposive sampling rendered sampled institutions unrepresentative of the 39 chartered universities in the country.

The third factor that may have undermined the quality of this study is the reluctance (disinclination or the lack of eagerness or willingness), especially among top-echelon university managers, to participate in the study as key informants. Such reluctance not only denied the study the opportunity to solicit the ideas of some of major decision-makers in universities but may also have influenced the quality of responses tendered by those who were eventually persuaded to participate as key informants. Nevertheless, the persistent reluctance on the part of top managers in the universities studied must be understood within the context of the sensitivity of the subject of students' involvement in governance. Most universities are still grappling with the question of the extent to which they should democratize the whole process. Some reluctance was also encountered on the part of student leadership. For the most part, the fear among student leaders of victimization by management not only influenced their decision to or not to participate as key informants, but may also have affected the quality of information divulged.

5

Findings

This chapter presents the findings (results) of the study. The chapter is organized into eight major sections. The first section focuses on the socio-economic and demographic characteristics of the study respondents, while the second section presents the profiling of the mainstreaming of students' participation in governance in institutional policies and practices, the third section focuses on the support for students' involvement in governance by university organizational structures. Sections four through six, on the other hand, focus on the support systems for enhancing students' involvement in university governance, the role of self-governance structures in students' participation in governance and the level of inclusivity of students' involvement in university governance, respectively. The impediments to effective student participation in governance are profiled in section seven while the final section (eight) focuses on cross-university variations in policies and practices pertaining to student participation in governance.

Respondents' Socio-Demographic Characteristics

A total of 657 students were interviewed for this study. Of this number, 456 students (69.4 per cent) attended Kenyatta University (KU) while the remainder 201 students (30.6 per cent) were drawn from the United States International University (USIU). Those interviewed included 46.2 per cent (304) males and 53.8 per cent (353) females. The age bracket of the interviewees ranged from under 21 years to those aged 51 and above. As evident from Table 5.1, the overwhelming majority (89.0 per cent) of them were aged 25 and below. Only 4.4 per cent were over 30 years old. Consistent with expectations, 80.8 per cent of the respondents reported being single (never married) compared to 11.3 per cent who reported being married. The remainder included 5.3 per cent who were cohabiting, 1.2 per cent separated, 0.8 per cent divorced and 0.6 per cent who were widowed. Analysis by national origins showed that the majority (90.4 per cent) of the study respondents originated from Kenya. Other parts of the world were represented as follows: Other East African countries (3.6 per cent), the rest of Africa (3.5 per cent), and the rest of the world (2.5 per cent).

The respondents were spread across five schools as follows: Humanities and Social Sciences (17.4 per cent), Business (21.8 per cent), Science and Technology (11.0 per cent), Education (41.2 per cent) and Health Sciences (8.7 per cent). Of the interviewees, 620 (94.4 per cent) were undergraduate students while the remaining 37 (5.6 per cent) were studying for postgraduate level degrees. The undergraduate students were spread across the first to the fourth (final) years of study. Whereas 6.6 per cent were doing their first year, 8.6 per cent were second years and the rest, 37.7 per cent and 47.1 per cent, were third and fourth years, respectively. The respondents included 86.5 per cent full-time students and 13.5 per cent part-time students; the part-timers included those who attended classes during school holidays (school-based students), open learning students as well as evening and/or Saturday students.

Table 5.1: Distribution of Respondents by Age Group

Age bracket	Frequency	Percentage
Below 21 years	94	14.5
21 – 25 years	484	74.5
26 – 30 years	43	6.6
31- 40 years	18	2.8
41 + years	11	1.6
Total	650	100.0

Mainstreaming of Involvement in Governance in Policy Documents, Governance Structures and Practices

The first objective of this study was to determine the extent to which official university policy documents, governance structures and practices mainstream students' involvement in governance and decision-making processes. This was captured through the analysis of university mission and vision statements and the Charters and/ or Acts establishing the various universities, structured interviews administered to 657 students, in-depth interviews with key informants (KIs) and focus group discussions (FGDs) with selected students.

The analysis of documents produced mixed results. Specifically, the results showed the lack of direct connection between university mission and vision statements and students' involvement in governance. On the other hand, the results revealed that, in principle, students are expected to participate in the governance processes in both public and private universities in Kenya. The Charters and/or Acts establishing and or governing universities have sections specifically focusing on students' involvement in governance. For instance/So to speak, article 16 (1) of the Charter granted to the USIU, the private university focused on by this study, states that:

> There shall be a Student Affairs Council of the University which shall consist of all students and other such persons as may be provided by its constitution subject to the approval of the Chancellor and the Board upon recommendation of the Vice-Chancellor.

As for Kenyatta University, the public institution covered by the study, its KU Statutes 2013 and Charter list the institution's students' association as one of the governance structures of the university. The charter even goes further to state that two (2) members elected by the students' association will sit in the University Senate. However, they are not allowed to partake in some discussions. In particular, members of the students' association shall not participate in the deliberation of the senate, which the chairperson considers being confidential or which relates to examinations, grades and such other issues that may pose a conflict of interest.

The survey results for the mainstreaming of students' involvement in governance in institutional strategic/ policy documents and practices are presented in Table 5.2. Overall, the results show that universities recognize students as pertinent members of their governance structures. This was evident from the finding that 69.3 per cent of those interviewed agreed that their university's policy on students' involvement in governance had a constitutional and legal basis; only 18.4 per cent disagreed while 12.3 per cent said they were not aware. However, from the perspective of the interviewees, the practice of mainstreaming students' involvement in institutional strategic/ policy documents and practices may not be as explicit and/ or as widespread as the statements appearing in the charters and in the Acts establishing them would suggest. In this regard, only 54.8 per cent of the combined public-private universities sample interviewed for this study agreed that the statutes governing their university made reference to students' involvement in the governance process; the remainder included 23.3 per cent who disagreed and 21.9 per cent who reported being unaware.

Similarly, 50.5 per cent of students reported that 'student involvement in governance was one of the priority action areas stipulated in their institution's strategic plan, with the rest either disagreeing (27.7 per cent) or not being aware (21.8 per cent). Concerning whether or not students' involvement in the various governance structures and in decision-making was a matter of policy, 46.3 per cent of interviewees replied in the affirmative while 19.4 per cent and 34.3 per cent, respectively, disagreed or indicated that they were not aware. The interviewees were also asked to indicate whether their university has a published policy on students' involvement in governance, with 44.5 per cent agreeing, 23.3 per cent responding negatively and 21.9 per cent saying they were not aware.

Table 5.2: Mainstreaming of Students' Involvement in Governance in Institutional Strategic/ Policy Documents and Practices

	Item	Agree		Disagree		Not Aware		Total	
		No.	%	No.	%	No.	%	No.	%
	Strategic/ Policy Documents								
1	My university's policy on student involvement in governance has a constitutional and legal basis.	455	69.3	121	18.4	81	12.3	657	100.0
2	The statutes governing my university make reference to student involvement in the governance process	358	54.8	152	23.3	143	21.9	653	100.0
3	My university's strategic plan has 'student involvement in governance as one of its priority action areas.	326	50.5	179	27.7	141	21.8	646	100.0
4	In my university student involvement in the various governance structures and in decision making is a matter of policy	301	46.3	126	19.4	223	34.3	650	100.0
5	My university has a published policy on student involvement in governance	286	44.5	169	26.3	187	29.1	642	100.0
	Institutional Practices								
6	My university communicates the importance of student involvement in governance to all members of the university community	315	48.8	169	26.1	162	25.1	646	100.0
7	My university makes necessary amendments and revisions of policies on student involvement in governance	309	47.7	164	25.3	175	27.0	648	100.0
8	My university has put in place mechanisms for the implementation and enforcement of policies on student involvement in governance	293	45.6	220	34.3	129	20.1	642	100.0
9	My university provides opportunities for public debate of matters affecting student involvement in governance	220	33.9	214	33.0	215	33.1	649	100.0

Data from KIs and FGDs yielded results that were consistent with the views expressed above. In both universities student leaders and management officials indicated that there was no direct connection between the mission and vision statements of the two institutions and students' involvement in governance. This was best captured by the top management official interviewed at the USIU who was categorical that:

> Clearly there is no place for governance matters in USIU's vision and mission. Student participation in university governance is not even implied in the institution's mission and vision statements. The USIU vision and mission are really about what the institution wishes to deliver to its stakeholders. The vision expresses what the university wishes to become, *'a premier institution of academic excellence with a global perspective.'* The mission, on the other hand, expresses the pathway the university is to take to achieve its vision. *That is, 'the discovery and application of knowledge, the acquisition of skills and the development of intellect and character in a manner that prepares students to contribute professionally, effectively and ethically as citizens of a changing and increasingly technological world.'*

On the contrary, the KIs and FGDs from both universities confirmed that the universities had mainstreamed students' involvement in governance in important policy documents. And consistent with the findings from document analysis, they revealed that the KU Charter, the KU Statutes 2013 and the KU Students Association (KUSA) constitution as well as the USIU Charter and the USIU Student Affairs Council (SAC) constitution identified students as pertinent members of (some) governance organs. The top management official who served as a KI in USIU was especially emphatic that:

> Student participation in governance is mandated within the USIU Charter. The charter recognizes that students are an important stakeholder who must be involved in policy formulation and decision making at the various levels of the university. The top management of the institutions, therefore, have taken the necessary steps to ensure that such participation is not just mainstreamed into USIU's governance structures, policies and practices but is also protected and encouraged among students studying for various degrees.

Results regarding the extent to which universities mainstreamed student involvement in governance in their practices tended to contradict the message conveyed by the second part of the *verbatim* quote presented above that management not only mainstreamed students' participation in institutional practices but also protected that participation as well as encouraged students to be involved. As evident from Table 5.2, the respondents did not rate their universities any better with respect to the mainstreaming of students' involvement in governance in institutional practices. Less than 50 per cent of the respondents agreed with the statements targeting institutional practices. Specifically, only 48.8 per cent confirmed that their university 'communicates the importance of student involvement in governance to all members of the university community'; 21.6 per cent disagreed while 25.1 per cent reported not being aware. Similarly, 47.7 per cent of the interviewees supported the view that their university 'makes necessary amendments and revisions of policies on student involvement in governance' compared to 25.3 per cent and 27.0 per cent who disagreed or were not aware, respectively. Another practice investigated by the study was whether the university 'has put in place mechanisms for the implementation and enforcement of policies on student involvement in governance'. Whereas 45.6 per cent of the interviewees agreed with it, 34.3 per cent disagreed and 20.1 per cent said they were not aware. Asked whether their 'university provides opportunities for public debate of matters affecting student involvement in governance', only 33.9 per cent responded in the affirmative compared to 33.0 per cent who disagreed and 33.1 per cent who reported being unaware.

The patterns emerging above were consistent with the views of student KIs and FGDs who expressed that they were not aware of the existence of specific institutional practices that seriously promoted the inclusion of students in governance processes in their universities. This was underlined by a member of one of the FGDs conducted at USIU who had the following to say:

> True, the university does make some feeble attempts to encourage us (students) to participate in the governance of the university. The problem though is that the level of patronage is rather high with management literally sending the message that students cannot be trusted to be the custodians of their own affairs. It appears that management believes that students most of the time need the visible hand of a big brother or big sister for them to be make the right choices. And this is where the management comes in to ensure that students are steered in the right direction, which essentially is management's direction or way.

These sentiments were echoed by a student KI interviewed at Kenyatta University who expressed that while the institution has put in place structures and policies to govern students' participation in governance, the practice itself sends the opposite message. According to him/her, that the university did not practice what it preached was evident from the level of management meddling with students' representation in decision-making, whose ultimate goal was to undermine effective involvement of students in the governance process.

Importance Students Attach to Involvement in University Governance

The second objective of this study was to assess the level of importance students in Kenyan universities attach to their involvement in governance structures and decision-making activities. Overall, results from structured interviews with students showed that they considered students' involvement (inclusion) in various governance structures as well as in varied decision-making activities to be important. With specific reference to involvement in governance structures, the results showed that the bulk of the respondents considered students' involvement in governance structures to be of high importance. Based on Table 5.3, of those surveyed, 56.0 per cent, 65.2 per cent and 66.8 per cent, respectively, considered students' representation in University Council/ Board of Trustees, Board of Management/Management Council and/or in Senate to be of high importance. Only 17.4 per cent, 12.7 per cent and 12.3 per cent of the respondents, in the same order, opined that students' involvement in the three structures was not important at all. On the other hand, 73.4 per cent, 71.4 per cent, 74.1 per cent and 71.5 per cent of interviewees, correspondingly, felt that students' involvement in all university-wide committees, deans' committee, school-wide committees and all departmental-/ program-wide committees was of high importance. The proportions of respondents who felt that students' involvement in such structures was not important at all were quite low, standing at 9.1 per cent, 10.0 per cent, 8.6 per cent and 10.7 per cent, respectively.

Table 5.3: Importance Attached to Students' Involvement in University Governance and Decision-making

Item	Level of Low Importance						Total	
	Not at All		Low		High			
	No.	%	No.	%	No.	%	No.	%
Governance Structures								
1 University Council/ Board of Trustees	112	17.4	171	26.6	361	56.0	644	100
2 Board of Management/ Management Council	82	12.7	143	22.1	421	65.2	646	100
3 Senate	80	12.3	136	20.9	434	66.8	650	100
4 All university wide committee	59	9.1	113	17.5	475	73.4	647	100
5 Deans' committee	65	10.0	121	18.6	463	71.4	649	100
6 All faculty-/ School-wide committees	56	8.6	112	17.3	481	74.1	649	100
7 All departmental-/ programs-wide committees	68	10.7	113	17.8	454	71.5	635	100
Decision Making Activities								
1 Formulation of university vision and missions	89	13.7	114	17.5	448	68.8	651	100
2 Strategic planning	78	12.0	131	20.2	441	67.8	650	100
3 Academic planning	69	10.6	87	13.4	494	76.0	650	100
4 Formulation of policies	63	9.7	107	16.4	480	73.9	650	100
5 Admission of new students	126	19.3	143	21.9	383	58.8	652	100
6 Orientation of new students	70	10.8	117	18.0	468	71.2	650	100
7 Curriculum design	85	13.1	128	19.7	436	67.2	649	100
8 Curriculum approvals	70	10.7	134	20.6	448	68.7	652	100
9 Program reviews	66	10.1	128	19.7	458	70.2	652	100

10	Curriculum development	67	10.3	122	18.7	463	71.0	652	100
11	Quality assurance	60	9.2	118	18.2	472	72.6	650	100
12	Student assessment	65	10.0	86	13.2	499	76.8	650	100
13	Student evaluation	70	10.8	86	13.3	492	75.9	648	100
14	Grading policy	92	14.1	67	10.3	492	75.6	651	100
15	Recruitment of faculty and staff	223	34.3	165	25.3	263	40.4	651	100
16	Faculty appraisal and promotions	177	27.3	166	25.6	306	47.1	649	100
17	Dispute resolution	98	15.1	112	17.2	440	67.7	650	100
18	Graduation planning	78	12.0	97	14.9	474	73.1	649	100
19	Disciplinary matters	52	7.9	103	15.8	497	76.3	652	100
20	Student support and advising committees	49	7.5	100	15.4	501	77.1	650	100
21	Procurements	119	18.2	134	20.6	399	61.2	652	100
22	Support services committees (e.g. library, ICT)	58	8.9	110	16.9	481	74.2	649	100
23	Closure and opening of the university	85	13.2	104	16.1	456	70.7	645	100
24	Increment of tuition and other fees	86	13.2	68	10.5	496	76.3	650	100

The respondents were also asked to indicate the level of importance students attached to involvement in various areas of decision-making. In all, 24 areas were analyzed. As evident from Table 5.3, relatively low percentages of those interviewed opined that students' involvement in varied areas of decision-making was not important at all. The overwhelming support for students' involvement in decision-making was evident from the fact that over 50.0 per cent of the interviewees considered students' involvement in all areas of decision-making, save recruitment of faculty and staff (40.4 per cent) and faculty appraisal and promotions (47.1 per cent), to be of high importance. In particular, the results revealed that involvement in the following areas of decision-making was considered to be of high importance by over 70 per cent of those interviewed: academic planning (76.0 per cent), formulation of policies (73.9 per cent), orientation of new students (71.2 per cent), programme reviews (70.2 per cent), curriculum development (71.0 per cent), quality assurance (72.6 per cent), students assessment (76.8 per cent), student evaluation (75.9 per cent), grading policy 75.6 per cent), graduation planning (73.1 per cent), disciplinary matters (76.3 per cent), student support and advising committees (77.1 per cent), support services committees (74.2 per cent), closure and opening of the university (70.7 per cent) and increment of tuition and other fees (76.3 per cent).

The high importance students attached to involvement in governance was also echoed during KI interviews and focus group discussions. A student key informant from Kenyatta University captured the general mood with regard to the subject with the following words:

> The core business of universities revolves around us (students). We are the majority stakeholder in the academic business. Therefore, our participation in policy formulation and implementation and in the making of any other decisions that impact on our lives is very important. Where all students cannot participate directly, then they should be involved through their representatives. Of course, if students are to participate effectively through representation, they must elect strong visionary leaders who cannot be intimidated or easily compromised.

The position expressed above was echoed throughout all focus group discussions and key informant interviews conducted with students at both Kenyatta University and the USIU. In a summative sense, the students were unanimous that their involvement in governance was paramount not just because it was a pertinent element in the democratization of university education, but also because it was one way of ensuring that universities fostered and upheld good governance practices.

Table 5.4: Positive Consequences of Students' Participation in Governance (N= 633)

	Consequences	Frequency	Per cent
1	No positive consequences	18	2.8
2	Improved dispute resolution, stability and peace/ reduced student dissatisfaction and incidences of strikes	285	45.0
3	Facilitates better and more effective protection of students' interests and welfare	275	43.4
4	Better learning environment characterized by streamlined programs and improved performance	228	36.0
5	Better cooperation between students and the university management	223	35.2
6	Opportunity for student to input to decision making	188	29.7
7	Nurtures future leaders/ equips students with leadership, decision making and problem solving skills	185	29.2
8	Good governance	166	26.2
9	Faster feedback to students whenever they have concerns/ streamlines communication between management and students	84	13.3
10	Fairness and equity	73	11.5
11	Better understanding of students' problems	53	8.4
12	Promotes feelings of acceptance and a sense of belonging among students	30	4.7
13	Nurtures a positive attitude towards leadership	11	1.7
14	Enables students to understand issues from university management's perspective and vice versa	10	1.6

Note: Do not total to 100%; respondents selected more than one consequence

Table 5.5 presents the results for negative consequences of student involvement in university governance structures and decision-making processes. Whereas 3.1 per cent of respondents did not consider involvement to have any negative outcomes, the leading negative consequence identified by the interviewees was that it 'grows self-seeking leadership that does not represent students' interests effectively'; it was listed by 28.8 per cent of those surveyed. This was followed by 'it is a waste of time: in reality students have no say on most matters that affect them, management does' (19.5 per cent); 'burdens students leaders thereby undermining their academic performance' 18.1 per cent); 'prolongs and sometimes complicates the decision making process' (17.1 per cent); 'introduces unprofessionalism in decision making' (14.1 per cent); 'provides students with the opportunity to raise non-academic and other disruptive issues that may interfere with learning' (13.6 per cent) and 'increases the opportunity for external political meddling with university programmes and activities' (11.6 per cent). The remaining seven (7) negative consequences of student participation in university governance were supported by less than 10.0 per cent of the study subjects (see Table 5.5 for details).

Table 5.5: Negative Consequences of Students' Participation in Governance (N= 645)

	Consequences	Frequency	Per cent
1	No negative consequences	20	3.1
2	Grows self-seeking leadership that does not represent students' interests effectively	187	28.8
3	It is a waste of time: In reality students have no say on most matters that affect them; management does	126	19.5
4	Burdens students leaders thereby undermining their academic performance	117	18.1
5	Prolongs and sometimes complicates the decision making process	110	17.1
6	Introduces unprofessionalism in decision making	91	14.1
7	Provides students with the opportunity to raise non-academic and other disruptive issues that may interfere with learning	88	13.6
8	Increases the opportunity for external political meddling with university programs and activities	75	11.6
9	Student leadership, even the very best, is rarely appreciated by fellow students	52	8.1
10	Places too much power in students' hands	43	6.7
11	Creates opportunities for corruption	40	6.2
12	Leads to internal rivalry among leaders, e.g. along ethnic and political party lines	30	4.6
13	Increases the opportunity for student-management conflict	23	3.6

| 14 | Victimization of student leadership; e.g., expulsion whenever there is unrest | 19 | 2.9 |
| 15 | Manipulation of student leadership by management, including intimidation in some cases | 15 | 2.3 |

Note: Do not total to 100%; respondents advanced more than one consequence

Respondents who opined that students' participation in governance had negative consequences offered a variety of remedies for those consequences. As evident from Table 5.6, the following emerged as the leading four (4) solutions as recommended by interviewees: 'increase level and breadth of student involvement especially in major decision making; e.g., increasing of fees' (35.2 per cent); 'Set clear limits for student power' (30.6 per cent); 'Cultivate and nurture a more proactive student leadership that is always ready to engage with management' (21.6 per cent) and 'Develop policies against external political interference with overall governance , student leadership and university activities' (17.8 per cent). Other solutions supported by at least 10.0 per cent of the respondents were: 'Develop policies against the intimidation of student leaders' (14.9 per cent); 'improve communication especially with respect to university policies' (14.7 per cent); 'Train students on leadership, democratic decision making and governance matter' (13.6 per cent) and 'Establishment of a body to monitor student governance activities' (13.3 per cent). See Table 5.6 for other solutions supported by less than 10.0 per cent of the respondents.

Table 5.6: Remedies for Negative Consequences of Students' Participation in Governance (N= 625)

	Remedies	Frequency	Per cent
1	Increase level and breadth of student involvement especially in major decision making; e.g., increasing of fees	220	35.2
2	Set clear limits for student power	191	30.6
3	Cultivate and nurture a more proactive student leadership that is always ready to engage with management	133	21.3
4	Develop policies against external political interference with overall governance , student leadership and university activities	111	17.8
5	Develop policies against intimidation of student leaders	93	14.9
6	Improve communication especially with respect to university policies	92	14.7
7	Train students on leadership, democratic decision making and governance matters	85	13.6
8	Establishment of a body to monitor student governance activities	83	13.3

9	Reduce workload for student leaders to enable them to balance leadership roles with academic responsibilities	54	8.6
10	Guarantee and protect transparent and fair engagement between student leadership and management	35	5.6
11	Create an environment in which students feel accepted and respected	28	4.5

Extent, Adequacy of and Satisfaction with Involvement in Governance

All universities in Kenya, whether public or private, are characterized by hierarchical governance structures. However, as illustrated below, minor differences in governance structures exist for the two universities analyzed for this study, and by implications for public and private sector universities:

Kenyatta University	**United States International University**
University Council	Board of Trustees
Board of Management	Management Council
Senate	Faculty/ Staff/ Students Councils
Student Union/staff Union	

Despite the above, the Universities Act No. 42 of 2012 offers a common framework for the governance and regulation of all universities in Kenya. In this regard, private universities, including the USIU, have already set in motion the process of amending their charters to comply with the recommendations of the Act. This means that it is just a matter of time before uniform governance structures characterize both public and private universities in the country. The Act delineates the internal administrative structure of universities to include a Chancellor, University Council, a Senate, the Vice Chancellor assisted by a number of Deputy Vice Chancellors, Faculty Boards and Departmental Boards (Republic of Kenya 2012).

Through its third objective, this study sought to establish the extent, adequacy and level of satisfaction with students' participation in governance and decision-making processes in Kenyan universities. It is to the presentation of the results that we now turn.

The Extent of Students' Involvement in Governance

As a preamble to the extent of students' participation in governance structures and decision making activities, the study sought views about who respondents considered to be the dominant (key) players in university governance and decision-making processes. In all, respondents were provided with a list of eleven possible players and asked to rank them from the most important to the least import. From Table 5.7 it is evident that the top five decision-makers included Vice Chancellor,

Deputy Vice Chancellors, Deans, University Councils and University Senate. These were ranked among the top five players by 81.8 per cent, 76.9 per cent, 73.2 per cent, 65.6 per cent and 48.9 per cent of the respondents, respectively. Other players included Registrars, Government/ State, Department/ Programme heads, students' representatives, regular students and faculty. Whereas Registrars were ranked among the top five decision-makers by 48.6 per cent of the respondents, the Government/ State was so ranked by 40.6 per cent of the study subjects. On the other hand, Department/ Programme heads, regular students, students' representatives, and faculty were ranked among the top five players by 37.5 per cent, 34.8 per cent, 29.9 per cent and 27.4 per cent, in that order. It is instructive to note that, going by its rating among the top five major decision-makers, student representatives ranked ninth out of the eleven players presented to the study subjects. Consistent with expectations, faculty and regular students received the least support.

Table 5.7: Percentage Distribution of Respondents by Ranking of Major 'Players' in University Decision Making [N = 657]

	'Player'	Ranking										
		1	2	3	4	5	6	7	8	9	10	11
1	Vice-Chancellor[1]	47.9	15.1	8.7	7.8	2.3	2.6	3.3	1.7	2.1	3.2	5.3
2	Deputy Vice-chancellors[2]	18.6	24.2	16.7	6.7	10.7	5.0	2.9	3.0	4.3	3.5	4.4
3	Deans[3]	30.9	6.1	11.3	15.2	9.7	7.2	7.0	4.1	3.5	2.3	2.7
4	University Council[4]	19.2	12.0	10.0	11.3	13.1	10.2	5.9	7.5	2.6	2.7	5.5
5	University senate[5]	13.9	7.5	5.5	10.2	11.6	13.2	12.6	9.7	6.7	2.7	6.4
6	Registrars[6]	13.5	5.2	9.4	7.9	12.6	13.5	11.4	7.9	7.8	4.0	6.7
7	Government/ state[7]	19.0	3.7	7.2	4.6	6.1	9.1	4.9	9.0	6.8	12.9	16.7
8	Department/ Program Heads[8]	14.2	3.2	5.8	7.6	6.7	7.2	9.3	11.7	12.9	9.9	11.6
9	Student Representatives[9]	14.0	6.5	5.6	5.5	3.2	3.8	4.1	3.0	4.7	7.5	42.0
10	Regular Students[10]	12.2	6.1	4.9	3.0	3.7	5.3	7.3	11.1	12.6	23.0	10.8
11	Faculty[11]	11.3	3.3	5.2	3.8	3.8	7.6	12.8	14.9	21.2	6.5	9.6

To capture the level of students' involvement in governance, the study focused on the students' overall involvement in governance structures as well as their actual participation in specific areas of decision-making. Concerning the former, the results, as captured in Table 5.8, showed that despite the delineation of students as pertinent members of governance organs by important university policy documents and the high importance students attached to their involvement in the varied governances structures and in decision-making activities (see section 4.2 and 4.3), students' overall participation in governance and decision-making was moderate, sometimes minimal. Based on Table 5.8, only two of the ten items utilized to measure overall involvement were supported by more than 60 per cent of the study subjects. Specifically, 65.8 per cent and 61.1 per cent of them agreed that their university offered sufficient avenues for university-wide communication for students and that in their university students wielded very strong influence on management decision-making, respectively. Whereas 59.8 per cent of the respondents agreed that students in their university were involved in policy implementation, 57.5 per cent, 56.7 per cent, 56.2 per cent and 52.3 per cent concurred that in their university student involvement in governance was mandatory, students were involved in policy formulation, students had a sufficient role in governance and that students wielded very strong influence on management decision-making, respectively. Less than 50 per cent of the interviewees agreed that their university had effective policies on students' participation in decision-making (49.9 per cent), that in their university students have effective mechanisms for providing input into all decisions (44.2 per cent) and that students in their university had a sufficient voice in university policies, planning and budgeting (42.0 per cent).

Table 5.8: Overall Involvement by Students in University Governance

	Item	Agree		Disagree		Total	
		No.	%	No.	%	No.	%
1	My university offers sufficient avenues for university-wide communications for students	428	65.8	222	34.2	650	100
2	In my university students constitute valuable sources of information on decision issues	402	61.6	251	38.4	653	100
3	Students in my university are involved in policy implementation	386	59.8	260	40.2	646	100
4	My university considers students participation in governance is mandatory	374	57.5	276	42.5	650	100
5	Students in my university are involved in policy formulation	368	56.7	281	43.3	649	100
6	Students in my university have sufficient role in university governance	364	56.2	284	43.8	648	100
7	In my university students wield very strong influence on management decision making	342	52.3	312	47.7	654	100
8	In my university, policies for student involvement in the decision making process are effective	323	49.9	324	50.1	647	100
9	In my university students have effective mechanisms for providing input into all decisions	287	44.2	363	55.8	650	100
10	Students in my university exercise a sufficient voice in university policies, planning and budget	273	42.0	377	58.0	650	100

The results for the actual level of students' involvement in the various governance structures and areas of decision-making were consistent with those realized for the overall participation. Based on Table 5.9, the study subjects rated student involvement as moderate. Concerning participation in governance structures only 24.7 per cent, 28.5 per cent and 34.5 per cent of the respondents considered student involvement in University Council/ Board of Trustee, Board of Management/ Management Council and Senate, respectively, to be high. Similarly, 37.8 per cent 41.3 per cent, 39.9 per cent and 37.1 per cent returned a verdict of high students' involvement in all university-wide committees, deans' committee, all school-wide committees and in all departmental/ programme-wide committees, in that order.

Concerning student involvement in specific areas of decision-making, Table 5.9 shows that the proportion of respondents who considered students' involvement to be high ranged from 15.2 per cent for recruitment of faculty and staff to 51.0 per cent for the orientation of new students. Of those surveyed, 45.5 per cent, 41.7 per cent, 39.4 per cent and 36.9 per cent considered students' involvement in student support and advising committees, graduation planning, student assessment and student evaluation, respectively, to be high. On the other hand, students' participation in support services committees (e.g. library and ICT), disciplinary matters, quality assurance, closure and opening of university, dispute resolution and academic planning were rated as high by 38.4 per cent, 36.1 per cent, 34.0 per cent, 33.0 per cent, 32.5 per cent, 32.2 per cent of the study subjects, in that order. The rating of students' involvement in all other areas of decision-making was considered as high by less than 30 per cent of the respondents (see Table 5.9 for details).

Table 5.9: Level of Involvement in Governance Structures and Decision-making Activities

Item	Level of Involvement						Total	
	Not at All		Low		High			
	No.	%	No.	%	No.	%	No.	%
Governance Structures								
1 University Council/ Board of Trustees	222	34.5	263	40.8	159	24.7	644	100
2 Board of Management/ Management Council	201	31.1	262	40.4	184	28.5	647	100
3 Senate	168	26.2	252	39.3	221	34.5	641	100
4 All university wide committee	156	24.2	245	38.0	244	37.8	645	100
5 Deans' committee	135	21.1	241	37.6	265	41.3	641	100
6 All School-wide committees	141	22.0	244	38.1	256	39.9	641	100
7 All departmental-/program-wide committees	146	23.4	247	39.5	232	37.1	625	100

	Decision Making Activities								
1	Formulation of university vision and missions	267	41.3	201	31.1	178	27.6	646	100
2	Strategic planning	229	35.5	241	37.4	175	27.1	645	100
3	Academic planning	209	32.4	229	35.4	208	32.2	646	100
4	Formulation of policies	221	34.3	242	37.5	182	28.2	645	100
5	Admission of new students	280	43.1	182	28.1	187	28.8	649	100
6	Orientation of new students	126	19.4	193	29.6	332	51.0	651	100
7	Curriculum design	297	45.8	186	28.7	166	25.5	649	100
8	Curriculum approvals	309	47.6	180	27.7	160	24.7	649	100
9	Program reviews	267	41.1	204	31.4	179	27.5	650	100
10	Curriculum development	270	41.7	190	29.4	187	28.9	647	100
11	Quality assurance	240	36.9	189	29.1	221	34.0	650	100
12	Student assessment	210	32.4	183	28.2	255	39.4	648	100
13	Student evaluation	225	34.8	183	28.3	239	36.9	647	100
14	Grading policy	340	52.4	147	22.6	162	25.0	649	100
15	Recruitment of faculty and staff	409	62.7	144	22.1	99	15.2	652	100
16	Faculty appraisal and promotions	374	57.4	146	22.4	132	20.2	652	100
17	Dispute resolution	192	29.5	247	38.0	211	32.5	650	100
18	Graduation planning	189	29.0	191	29.3	272	41.7	652	100
19	Disciplinary matters	199	30.5	218	33.4	235	36.1	652	100
20	Student support and advising committees	143	22.0	211	32.5	296	45.5	650	100
21	Procurements	277	42.9	192	29.7	177	27.4	646	100
22	Support services committees (e.g. library, ICT)	186	28.6	215	33.0	250	38.4	651	100
23	Closure and opening of the university	270	41.9	162	25.1	213	33.0	645	100
24	Increment of tuition and other fees	361	55.8	127	19.6	159	24.6	647	100

Results from KI interviews and FGDs were consistent with those presented above; in both cases it was pointed out that, practically, students in universities played minimal roles in governance in general and only influenced decision-making in a small way. The informants were emphatic that students' involvement in university governance processes in both KU and the USIU was mainly anchored on self-governance organizations, including student government associations/ organizations/ unions and other associations, societies and clubs. These are run by the students guided by a constitution. Whereas the Kenyatta University Students Association (KUSA) is the umbrella student self-governance organization in KU, the university has a variety of clubs open to students, ranging from professional or discipline-based clubs, theatre groups, religious clubs (e.g. Christian Union – CU, Catholic Students Association, Seventh Day Adventist Students Association etc.). Operating under the coordination of KUSA, clubs and associations have specific mandates; some promote social interaction among members while others engage in community service. In USIU, on the other hand, the Student Affairs Council (SAC) is the lead student self-governance organ. Operating under SAC's coordination though are of 21 student centred discipline-specific, recreational (sports-related) and social welfare clubs. The clubs are central to the students' involvement in the university; they help students to cultivate leadership skills, to be involved in community service and, for discipline-based clubs, to supplement what is learn in class.

According to the KIs and FGDs, it was the constitutions establishing students' organizations, associations and clubs that clearly spelt out students' mandates in leadership and governance processes. For many students, the constitutions were their basic source of knowledge and understanding of their roles and activities with respect to university governance. In particular, the KIs and FGDs singled out KUSA and the SAC as the major organs through which students visibly exercised leadership roles. They pointed out that, in both universities, it is the elected officials of the two organizations who are mandated to represent students in various organs of governance and decision-making. On the contrary, the KIs and FGDs expressed that students' influence on university-wide policy through clubs and associations was minimal, if not completely lacking. This was best captured by one focus group discussant from USIU as follows:

> Truth be told, we have all these clubs operating under the SAC at USIU. Their activities though center on students' academic and social interests as opposed to the governance of the university. What the clubs are involvement in has nothing to do with the day to day running of the university as a whole. While decisions made by top management such as those touching on finances may affect the running of the clubs, the decisions made by the clubs have no bearing at all on the governance of the university. Not even the SAC has that much influence on the decision making processes in the university. After all the council does not have direct representation in the main decision making organs of the university.

The situation is compounded by the high levels of apathy towards clubs and associations that pervades both KU and the USIU. Based on KI interviews and FGDs, most students did not belong to clubs. At KU, those who belonged to clubs tended to choose ethnic-based and religious-inclined clubs like the Christian Union.

The results of the survey suggested that the level of students involvement tends to increase at lower (committee) level governance structures. This was consistent with data realized from KIs and FGDs which also showed that, overall, students' representation was higher at lower levels of university governance structures. However, the situation is direr at the USIU. Let us stress, once again, that while in principle top university governance structures encouraged the involvement of students, the reality was different. SAC officials (or their representatives) do not sit on both the Board of Trustees and the Management Council, the top decision-making organs of the university. Instead, they are represented by proxy, meaning that matters affecting students are articulated on their behalf by the Deputy Vice Chancellor, Student Affairs. The student KIs and FGDs were quite explicit that the top organs of decision-making are characterized by high levels of patronage and worthy decisions hatched by students are taken over by top management and pursued without further consultation with SAC. The situation was best captured in the words of the SAC Vice Chair who opined that:

> The students are more on the receiving end. In most cases they are simply told what is best for as well as what is expected of them. Even when those in-charge of students' affairs meet with students in the name of collecting their views to take to top management meetings, they tend to come with preconceived ideas of what is best for the USIU students. One would not be exaggerating to dismiss such meetings as serving a political correctness purpose.

In the light of the foregoing, USIU students only enjoy direct representation in lower-level governance structures; that is, the SAC and other students' associations and clubs as well as in school and programme-level committees. According to the KIs and FGDs, at this level, the students' views are valued because they act as checks and balances for the university. As such, they are listened to and their views are conveyed to management. However, based on the sentiments of some of the student KIs and FGDs, the capacity of the students to influence and/ or shape important decisions remains minimal even at the lower level.

On the contrary, KU students are directly represented in both the higher and lower governance structures and wield greater influence on decision-making. Though excluded from the top internal governance organ, the Board of Management, the KUSA President and Secretary General sit in the University Council whereas two KUSA officials – the President and the Organizing Secretary – sit in the Senate, where they have the responsibility to present students' concerns directly to management and give feedback to the student body. What may cast doubts though is the extent and quality of participation by students' representatives in governance, as reflected through attendance of management meetings, articulation of students' issues, voting power and capacity to influence decisions, contribution of solutions to students' problems and the provision of feedback to their constituents. At the lower level, students' representatives sit in various structures, including school-wide and programme-wide committees. Bears testimony to that is the fact that, students are represented in disciplinary committees, bursary awarding committees, the quality assurance board, and tuck shop suppliers' oversight committee, among others. They are also directly involved in the setting of semester dates, making decisions about the closure and opening of the university, the recruitment and evaluation of lecturers and in the recruitment of staff in deans' offices, as well as serving as school, departmental and class representatives.

The results from KI interviews and FGDs also suggested that the practice of operationalizing students' involvement in governance as stipulated in charters and/or Acts, Statutes, and constitutions governing students' associations differed across the sectors. For instance, in USIU, representing the private sector, students' involvement is not legally binding. Students operate mainly through the SAC which, unlike students' organizations in public universities, is not registered by the Registrar of Societies. As such, the council is not a legally recognized and binding entity. To quote the top official interviewed at USIU, 'SAC is only recognized within the USIU.' It would not be farfetched to describe the SAC as a tokenism organization whose goal is to make the institution appear to be politically correct with respect to integrating students in its governance process. While students elect their officials to represent their interests in the governance and decision-making process, those officials do not exercise any real power and rather than participate directly in decision-making they do so by proxy by channelling their concerns and contributions to management council through the Deputy Vice Chancellor, Student Affairs who articulates them on their behalf. On the contrary, the KUSA is a legal and binding entity. It is registered with the Registrar of Societies and, therefore, is recognized beyond Kenyatta University. It can employ the trade union model in championing the welfare of the students. However, it is the level and effectiveness of the organization's representatives in governance that remains a moot issue.

Furthermore, the study revealed an apparent lack of awareness among most students of how they are involved in governance beyond students associations – the KUSA and the SAC – whose officials are voted in office to represent them within the university. To illustrate how deep-seated this problem is, one student in an FGD at KU expressed that s/he was hearing about the KUSA constitution for the first time during the focus group discussions. By way of explaining this state of affairs another FGD participant from KU had the following to say:

> Students have many issues, other than governance, preoccupying them including, security, fees, bus fare in the shuttle services (too high need to be reduced), availability of space in the hostels (many building are coming up yet accommodation continues to be a major issue in KU) and long queues at the health unit.

Adequacy of Students' Involvement in Governance and Decision-making

The respondents were also asked to rate the adequacy of students' involvement in the governance and decision-making processes utilizing a number of seven select indicators, at is: attendance in meetings, input/ contributions during meetings, representation of student issues, voting power, ability to influence decision-making, capacity to contribute solutions to problems faced by students, and feedback to students. As evident from Table 5.10, the bulk of those interviewed rated students' representation either as lacking at all or inadequate. Only 39.4 per cent, 34.6 per cent, 34.4 per cent and 45.8 per cent of respondents considered student leadership's attendance of meetings, input/ contributions during meetings, representation of students' issues and voting power, respectively, to be adequate. Similarly, 24.7 per cent, 30.1 per cent and 32.2 per cent of interviewees concurred that student representatives' ability to influence decision-making, their capacity to contribute solutions to problems faced by students and the provision of feedback to students, in that order, were adequate.

Table 5.10: Adequacy of Involvement in Governance and Decision-making

Activity	Adequacy of Involvement						Total	
	Not at All		Inadequate		Adequate			
	No.	%	No.	%	No.	%	No.	%
1 Attendance in meetings	86	13.2	309	47.4	257	39.4	652	100
2 Input/ Contribution during meetings	99	15.2	327	50.2	226	34.6	652	100
3 Representation of students' issues	96	14.8	324	49.8	230	34.4	650	100
4 Voting power	81	12.4	272	41.8	298	45.8	651	100
5 Ability to influence decision making	165	25.3	326	50.0	161	24.7	652	100
6 Capacity to contribute to solution student problems	126	19.3	330	50.6	196	30.1	652	100
7 Feedback to students	140	21.5	302	46.3	210	32.2	652	100

The inadequacy of students' involvement in governance and decision-making documented above was supported by qualitative data gathered for the study. Based on FGDs held with KU students, despite student representation at both the upper the lower levels of management, the focus group discussants felt that such representation was not effective. This was evident from the fact that 'issues took too long to be addressed, thereby discouraging students from airing their grievances. At the same time, attendance of meetings (e.g. departmental meetings) and consultative forums among student representatives was very poor, in some cases totally lacking. According to these informants, student leaders were mainly preoccupied with gratifying their personal and management's needs as opposed to being effective representatives of the student body.

In USIU, on the other hand, students were less concerned about the effectiveness of their leaders. The institution is characterized by the lack of student interest in being involved in governance. This was evident through the rampant apathy among regular students that translated in to a lack of enthusiasm about participation in governance and, consequently, to limited or no competition for prospective leadership positions; the students seemed to be attracted by extra-curricular activities and entertainment, rather than by matters touching on their welfare. One of the focus group discussants summed up the situation using the following words:

> Students are not interested in the SAC positions because there are no incentives to attract them. Most officials go in unopposed, thereby making the SAC a moribund institution. As a result, in the eyes of many students, SAC Suks!

The rampant apathy among students was also reflected in the fact that, despite the provision for a public *baraza* (forum) once every semester for students to meet with their leaders to air their views on issues affecting them, the meetings tended to be poorly attended. To quote the Vice Chair of SAC, 'Students don't turn up, which I think boils down to lack of interest.' From the perspective of some of the KIs and FGDs, the rampant apathy (or lack of interest) that characterized USIU students could partly be explained in terms of the fear of expulsion from the university due to activism. To quote one KI participant: 'Most students say "I'm paying (money) for my education and, therefore, I cannot risk being sent away".' Another possible explanation of the rampant apathy could be the top-down management style practiced by the institution. However, a top management official interviewed for this study suggested that lack of student interest may be due to the fact that they (students) are contented with the services they receive from the university.

Another measure of adequacy of students' involvement in decision-making analyzed by this study was the extent of inclusiveness of students' representation in self-governance and in the overall university governance structures. The study focused on 10 criteria of inclusivity. At the broad level we focus on the existence of a diversity policy and the observance of that policy during elections.

On the other hand, at the more specific level we focused on age, gender, disability, sexual orientation, ethnicity, nationality, study programme and year of study representation during elections. The results are presented in Table 5.11. Based on the Table, in principle universities have diverse policies governing student representation in the governance process. Of the interviewees, 64.5 per cent affirmed the existence of such a policy. A comparable proportion (60.8 per cent) of respondents concurred that the election of student representatives to university governance structures catered for the diversity of the student body.

At the more specific level, the study showed that only criteria such as year of study, mode of study, and gender were major considerations in student representation in university-wide governance structures and in student self-governance structures. Of those interviewed, 57.1 per cent, 53.9 per cent and 53.7 per cent, correspondingly, agreed that these must be observed in such representation. All other factors analyzed were supported by less than 50 per cent of the respondents with the following receiving support from between 40.0 and 49.9 per cent of the interviewees: Age (47.6 per cent), nationality (46.9 per cent), study programme (46.9 per cent) and disability (40.8 per cent).

Results from KI interviews and FGDs showed that KU had formal structures for catering for divergent needs, including gender, disability, and non-traditional students, among other social categories. The KUSA constitution has provision for electing representatives for gender, disability, faith groups (catholic, SDA, protestant), school-based, graduates, hostels (congress man / congress woman), school and class representatives. For instance, students with disabilities are represented in KUSA by the special needs secretary (a position that is voted by all students) and by a nominated member to congress. Whereas KU also has a centre for students with disabilities, such students are given a tuck shop to do business, given hostel accommodation on the ground floor and have access to other services. Similarly, the KUSA board has established positions for both postgraduate and school-based students.

Table 5.11: Extent of Inclusivity of Students' Involvement in University Governance

	Area of Influence	Agree No	Agree %	Disagree No	Disagree %	Total No	Total %
1	It is university policy to observe diversity in representation of students in various governance structures	403	64.5	222	35.5	625	100
2	The election of student representatives to university governance structures caters for the diversity of the student body	381	60.8	246	39.2	627	100
3	Year of study must be observed in the representation of students in overall university governance and student self-governance structures	356	57.1	278	42.9	624	100
4	Mode of study must be observed in the representation of students in overall university governance and student self-governance structures	338	53.9	289	46.1	627	100
5	Gender must be observed in the representation of students in overall university governance and student self-governance structures	333	53.7	287	46.3	620	100
6	Age must be observed in the representation of students in overall university governance and student self-governance structures	300	47.6	330	52.4	630	100
7	Nationality must be observed in the representation of students in overall university governance and student self-governance structures	291	46.9	329	53.1	620	100

8	Study program must be observed in the representation of students in overall university governance and student self-governance structures	293	46.9	332	53.1	625	100
9	Disability must be observed in the representation of students in overall university governance and student self-governance structures	243	40.8	353	59.2	596	100
10	Ethnicity must be observed in the representation of students in overall university governance and student self-governance structures	236	38.0	385	62.0	621	100
11	Sexual orientation must be observed in the representation of students in overall university governance and student self-governance structures	213	35.8	382	64.2	595	100

On the contrary, the USIU does not have specific structures to ensure inclusivity in SAC participation. According to the KI interviews, no gender, age, ethnicity or disability considerations are provided, meaning that no special seats are reserved based on gender, age, disability, special needs or any other social characteristics. However, at the club, association or society level such needs may be accommodated, depending on the mandate of the group. However, the university encourages every student to vie for SAC seats irrespective of nationality, ethnic background, gender, social status etc. This explains why females tend to dominate SAC leadership.

Satisfaction with Involvement in Governance Structures and Decision-making

With respect to satisfaction with students' involvement in governance, only 36.4 per cent (215) of the interviewees expressed overall satisfaction with students' involvement in the same, as compared to the 63.6 per cent who said that they were dissatisfied. To further demonstrate the level of satisfaction or its lack thereof, the study further analyzed different manifestations (or indicators) of students' representation in governance as well as their (students') involvement in different governance structures and decision-making activities. Concerning the former, the results were not that much different from those for overall satisfaction. As evident from Table 5.12, 49.9 per cent were satisfied with student leadership's attendance of meetings, 47.6 per cent with input/contributions during meetings, 45.3 per cent with the representation of students' issues and 56.5 per cent the leadership's voting power. On the other hand, 36.6 per cent expressed their satisfaction with the ability of student representatives to influence decision-making, 40.6 per cent with their capacity to contribute to the solution of problems faced by students and 44.2 per cent said they were satisfied with student representatives provision of feedback to the general student body.

Table 5.12: Satisfaction with Students' Involvement in University Governance Processes

Item	Satisfied		Dissatisfied		Total	
	No.	%	No.	%	No.	%
1 Attendance in meetings	324	49.9	325	50.1	649	100
2 Input/ contributions during meetings	309	47.6	340	52.4	649	100
3 Representation of student issues	295	45.3	356	54.7	651	100
4 Voting power	367	56.5	282	43.5	649	100
5 Ability to influence decision making	237	36.6	411	63.4	648	100
6 Capacity to contribute to the solution of problems faced by students	264	40.6	387	59.4	651	100
7 Feedback to students	287	44.2	362	55.8	649	100

The results for the level of satisfaction with students' involvement in different governance structures and in different areas of decision-making are presented in Table 5.13. From the Table, it is evident that, like for both overall satisfaction and satisfaction with different manifestations of involvement, the levels were generally moderate, falling in the 40/50 in percentage. With reference to students' involvement in various governance structures, only 44.4 per cent of the interviewees reported being satisfied with students' participation in the University Council/ Board of Trustees while 45.3 per cent were satisfied with involvement in the Management Council and 50.8 per cent expressed satisfaction with involvement in the Senate. Whereas 48.8 per cent said they were satisfied with participation in all university-wide committees, 52.9 per cent, 52.0 per cent and 53.2 per cent expressed their satisfaction with students' participation in the Deans' committee, all faculty-/ school-wide committees and with all departmental-/ programme-wide committees, respectively. These results mirror those for levels of involvement that tended to suggest that students' participation was higher in lower-level structures.

The findings for satisfaction with involvement in various areas of decision-making were not that much different – again the bulk of them lay between the 40s and 50 per cent bracket. Based on Table 5.13, satisfaction levels ranged from 38.4 per cent for increment of tuition and other fees to 62.5 per cent for 'orientation of new students'. Satisfaction with orientation of new students was followed by satisfaction with participation with graduation planning (57.6 per cent), student support and advising services (55.8 per cent), student evaluation (54.9 per cent), recruitment of new faculty (54.9 per cent), closure and opening of the university (54.5 per cent), admission of new students (54.3 per cent), dispute resolution (54.3 per cent) and faculty appraisals and promotions (54.2 per cent). Other areas of students' involvement in decision-making with which over 50.0 per cent of the respondents expressed satisfaction included disciplinary matter (53.8 per

Findings 119

cent), student assessment (52.6 per cent) and formulation of university vision and mission (51.9 per cent). The proportion of respondents satisfied with students' participation in the remaining 11 of the 24 areas of decision-making focused on by the study stood at less than 50.0 per cent (see Table 5.13 for details).

Table 5.13: Satisfaction with Involvement in Governance Structures and Decision-making Activities

	Item	Satisfied		Dissatisfied		Total	
		No.	%	No.	%	No.	%
	Governance Structures						
1	University Council/ Board of trustees	287	44.4	360	55.6	647	100
2	Management Council	292	45.3	353	54.7	645	100
3	Senate	329	50.8	319	49.2	648	100
4	All university wide committee	315	48.8	330	51.2	645	100
5	Deans' committee	343	52.9	305	47.1	648	100
6	All School-wide committees	336	52.0	309	48.0	645	100
7	All departmental-/ programs-wide committees	336	53.2	296	46.8	632	100
	Decision-making Activities						
1	Formulation of university vision and missions	334	51.9	309	48.1	643	100
2	Strategic planning	306	47.2	342	52.8	648	100
3	Academic planning	303	46.8	344	53.2	647	100
4	Formulation of academic and other university-wide policies	281	43.4	366	56.6	647	100
5	Admission of new students	352	54.3	296	45.7	648	100
6	Orientation of new students	405	62.5	243	37.5	648	100
7	Curriculum design	318	49.2	329	50.8	647	100
8	Curriculum approvals	316	48.8	331	51.2	647	100
9	Program reviews	308	47.6	339	52.4	647	100
10	Curriculum development	313	48.5	333	51.5	646	100
11	Quality assurance	318	49.0	330	51.0	648	100
12	Student assessment	341	52.6	308	47.4	649	100
13	Student evaluation	357	54.9	293	45.1	650	100
14	Grading policy	278	42.7	372	57.3	650	100
15	Recruitment of faculty and staff	356	54.9	292	45.1	648	100
16	Faculty appraisal and promotions	352	54.2	297	45.8	649	100
17	Dispute resolution	353	54.3	297	45.7	650	100
18	Graduation planning	373	57.6	275	42.4	648	100
19	Disciplinary matters	348	53.8	299	46.2	647	100
20	Student support and advising committees	361	55.8	286	44.2	647	100

21	Procurements	301	46.5	346	53.5	647	100
22	Support services committees (e.g. library, ICT)	343	52.7	307	47.3	650	100
23	Closure and opening of the university	353	54.5	295	45.5	648	100
24	Increment of tuition and other fees	249	38.4	400	61.6	649	100

Results realized from KI interviews and FGDs supported the finding presented above. Overall, both categories of informants felt that students' involvement in the governance of their universities was not effective. According to them, attendance of policy and decision-making meetings by student representatives tended to be characterized by tardiness and even when the representatives attended such meetings, for the most part they served as silent observes rather than as active debaters. The informants also opined that student participants in decision-making meetings appeared not to have the capacity to articulate students' issues. The KI and FGDs from Kenyatta University, where students had direct representation in top organs of decision-making, were especially categorical that their representatives did a shoddy job. As one FGD participant put it:

> The colleagues we have elected to represent us especially in top organs of decision making, like the Senate, appear to lose their voices during deliberations. They do not articulate students' issues as expected and their ability to influence decisions is minimal if not totally lacking. Matters are not made any easier by the fact that they have no voting power. More often than not, their inability to input into solutions to problems facing students is heightened by the tendency for management to compromise some of them right from the time of electing them and also to intimidate those who appear to be firm. Are we surprised that the representatives rarely give us any meaningful feedback? The answer is a categorical no!

The situation was not much different at the USIU where students are represented by proxy in the major organs of decision-making, with students only allowed direct representation in lower levels (school, and departmental/ programme levels) of decision-making. Even at the lower levels, the KIs and FGDs felt that their representatives were not assertive enough. Furthermore, most student representatives were habitually absent from key meetings that deliberated on important matters affecting students. In this regard, a student key informant at the USIU had the following to say:

> The university allows us to elect representatives to most of the school-wide and program-wide committees. Those we elect though do not appear to understand their roles and responsibilities and tend to take them very lightly. Absenteeism is the norm and even when present, our representatives tend to give up the co-decision rights they are supposed to enjoy. The general trend is one where decisions end up being made with hardly any input from students.

Incentives for Enhancing Students' Involvement in Governance

This study had as its third specific objective to document existing structural and material (reward) incentives utilized by universities to nurture and entrench students' involvement in governance. The results are captured in Table 5.14. Consistent with earlier findings, student self-governance structures, including student government councils/ associations/unions, clubs and associations, emerged as one of the structural incentives relied on by both KU and the USIU, and by implication by public and private universities in Kenya. A total 77.7 per cent of the survey respondents indicated these structures were available either sometimes or often/ always. It will also be remembered that earlier in this study, KIs and FGDs stressed that students' involvement in university governance processes in both KU and the USIU was mainly anchored on self-governance organizations, particularly student government councils/ associations/unions – that is, the Kenyatta University Students Association (KUSA) and Students Affairs Council (SAC) at USIU, respectively. This qualifies such structures to be a key avenue for students' participation in university governance and decision-making. At the realm of clubs, both KU and the USIU boast a wide variety of academic and extra-curricular clubs and societies (e.g., academic discipline, sporting/ recreational and social welfare-related clubs, associations and/or societies).

Self-governance structures perform a number of functions (or mandates) for students. These include representation of students in top organs of governance, moderation of top management and other high-level organs of decision-making, catering for students' welfare, tackling academic concerns (issues), ensuring quality assurance of student programmes and services, participation in the recruitment of faculty and staff and budgeting and finance. Membership to student self-governance organizations as well as to clubs is mainly voluntary. However, for professional/ subject-related (academic) clubs, sporting clubs, national associations, recreational associations and ethnic associations certain predetermined qualities (e.g., area of study, nationality, ethnic background and disability, among others) hold sway. To become an official in most student self-governance structures is contingent upon a number of factors: being popularly (democratically) elected, programme of study (for discipline-specific clubs), ethnic and national background (for ethnic and national associations), in some cases academic standing and disability and minority status (more so in KU). Despite the proliferation of self-governance structures and the important role they play in student representation in governance and decision making, data from KIs and FGDs suggested that the bulk of students were not active members of or showed no interest in such structures. Further, it was the considered opinion of the two categories of respondents that other than student government councils/ associations, clubs, other associations and societies played a peripheral role, if at all, in overall university governance and decision-making.

As evident from Table 5.14, other structural support mechanisms used by universities to grow and entrench students' participation in governance and decision-making that the survey respondents said were available either sometimes or often/always included the following: a special office for coordinating students' involvement in governance (90.0 per cent), formal appeal and complaint structures (88.9 per cent), periodic democratic elections (88.8 per cent), motivational guest speakers (86.3 per cent) and public addresses or symposiums (86.9 per cent). Also making the list of structural incentives were institutionalized channels of communication at all levels (85.7 per cent), retreats (79.9 per cent), office space (85.0 per cent), legal/policy frameworks governing students' involvement in governance (80.5 per cent), leadership training (74.6 per cent), short and long refresher courses (66.5 per cent) and mainstreaming of governance issues in the curriculum and other activities (66.5 per cent). On the other hand, the list of material incentives included free transport (30.9 per cent), monetary allowances (62.5 per cent), tuition waivers (55.5 per cent), free meals (44.5 per cent) and free accommodation (40.6 per cent).

Data from KIs and FGDs supported the existence of varied incentives for motivating student participation in governance and decision-making. The qualitative data also suggested that, in both KU and the USIU, support systems have a major bearing on the level and quality of students' participation in governance among students as a whole and particularly among student leaders. The qualitative data also pointed to the existence of public-private university differences in terms of incentives for enhancing students' involvement in governance. While structural incentives were shown to be common (universal) to the two universities studied, of course in varying qualities and proportions, material incentives – such as free food, free accommodation, sitting allowance, monthly monetary allowances, opportunity for international travel, and a direct budget controlled by the student leadership – were mainly confined to KU. This most probably explains the result that, while student KIs and FGDs from KU expressed satisfaction with the incentives available for promoting students' involvement in governance, their counterparts in USIU were quite dissatisfied with the same. Furthermore, it can be deduced that it is the combination of a wide variety of both structural and material incentives available to KU students that is responsible for the high competition for nomination and election to positions of student leadership that was recorded by this study. On the contrary, the study found that 'it is a job' trying to fill vacant student leadership positions at USIU.

Table 5.14: Incentives for Enhancing Students' Involvement in University Governance

	Support Services	Level of Availability						Total	
		Not at all		Sometimes		Often/ Always			
		No.	%	No.	%	No.	%	No.	%
	Structural Incentives								
1	Existence of student self-governance structures	144	22.3	198	30.7	303	47.0	645	100
2	Special office to coordinate student involvement in governance	64	10.0	208	32.4	369	57.6	641	100
3	Formal appeal and complaints structures	71	11.1	207	32.2	364	56.7	642	100
4	Periodic democratic elections	108	11.2	218	34.0	352	54.8	642	100
5	Reliance on motivational guest speakers	86	13.7	222	35.2	322	51.1	589	100
6	Public addresses/symposiums	82	13.1	231	36.8	315	50.1	628	100
7	Institutionalized channels of communication at all levels	92	14.3	252	39.3	298	46.4	642	100
8	Retreats	128	20.1	234	36.7	275	43.2	637	100
9	Provision of facilities (e.g. office space)	96	15.0	279	43.6	265	41.4	640	100
10	Legal/ policy frameworks	125	19.5	289	45.1	227	35.4	641	100
11	Leadership training	162	25.4	261	41.0	214	33.6	637	100
12	Short and long refresher courses	213	33.5	224	35.2	199	31.3	636	100
13	Mainstreaming of governance issues in the curriculum and other activities	210	33.2	244	38.5	179	28.3	633	100
	Material Incentives/ Rewards								
14	Free transport	209	32.6	234	36.5	198	30.9	641	100
15	Monetary allowances	241	37.5	209	32.5	193	30.0	643	100
16	Tuition waivers	286	44.5	183	28.5	173	27.0	642	100
17	Free meals	356	55.5	145	22.6	141	21.9	642	100
18	Free accommodation	381	59.4	124	19.3	136	21.3	641	100

Note: Do not total to 100%; each respondent identified multiple incentives

Level of Influence of National Politics on Students' Self-governance Processes

The fifth specific objective of this study was to gauge the extent of national political influence on students' governance processes in Kenyan universities today. Overall, the survey results showed that national politics and political parties wielded tremendous influence on students' self-governance structures and processes. This is particularly so for students' government councils/ associations/ unions. As evident from Table 5.15, overwhelming proportions of the respondents affirmed that all of the 11 possible areas of influence analyzed by the study were greatly impacted on by national politics and political parties. As expected, the influence was stronger on students' campaigns for elections, with 78.7 per cent of the interviewees supporting the existence of such influence sometimes or often/ always. This was followed by actual elections (75.4 per cent), set-up of governance structures (75.2 per cent), the choice of guests invited to students' government activities and functions (75.2 per cent), social activities organized by students' government (73.8 per cent), nomination process for elections (73.4 per cent), clubs/ societies/ associations meetings and activities (73.0 per cent), agenda for public discussion, debates and forums (72.9 per cent) and students' *barazas/ kamukunjis* (72.1per cent). Other areas of influence identified by the study subjects were formulation of constitutions and other legal frameworks (66.7 per cent) and the representation of students' grievances (66.0 per cent).

Qualitative data obtained from in-depth interviews and focus group discussions substantiated the trends manifested through the survey results. In particular, both categories of respondents concurred that national politics had trickled down, especially to the public universities, where the agenda and dynamics of student politics coalesced along the lines of the major political parties; with the dominant national political parties – most recently The National Alliance (TNA) party, the United Republican Party (URP) and the Orange Democratic Movement (ODM) – wielding the greatest influence. As a result, students' electioneering and governance processes tend to reflect the trends in national politics, currently dominated by two political alliances: the Jubilee Alliance and the Coalition for Reform and Democracy (CORD). The situation was best summed up by one of the key informants as follows:

> Universities have become another battle ground for our major political parties and political alliances. These not only front the candidates who contest leadership seats but also fund the electioneering process, provide the campaign agenda, influence the outcome of the elections as well as mentor the leadership that is elected. As a result, what happens within student governments tends to be a microcosm (or mirror image) of our national politics.

To illustrate, Kenya held its national elections in March 4, 2013. The elections were hotly contested by CORD and the Jubilee Alliance. Although the final declared results gave the Jubilee Alliance the win, CORD challenged the outcome declaring that the results had been manipulated in favour of their rival contestant. This led to a court drama that culminated with a confirmation of the Jubilee Alliance's victory. This plot was to be replicated during the University of Nairobi students' government elections held in Mid-April 2013. Consistent with the

March 4, 2013 national elections, the contestation was between CORD-allied and Jubilee Alliance-allied students. The outcome also mirrored what happened at the national level with Jubilee Alliance-allied students carrying the day. Like their counterparts in national politics, the CORD-allied students cried foul, declaring that the elections were rigged in favour of Jubilee Alliance-allied contestants.

Table 5.15: Influence of National Politics on Students' Self-Governance Processes

	Area of Influence	Level of influence						Total	
		Not at all		Sometimes		Often/ Always			
		No.	%	No.	%	No.	%	No.	%
1	Campaign for elections	141	22.1	168	26.3	330	51.6	639	100
2	Actual elections	157	24.6	161	25.2	320	50.2	638	100
3	Student barazas/ kamukunjis	178	27.9	178	27.9	281	44.2	637	100
4	Nomination process for elections	169	26.6	186	29.3	280	44.1	635	100
5	Set up of governance structures	158	24.8	205	32.2	274	43.0	637	100
6	Choice of guests invited to student government activities and functions	156	24.8	223	35.4	251	39.8	630	100
7	Social activities	166	26.2	224	35.3	244	38.5	634	100
8	Clubs/ societies/ associations meetings and activities	172	27.0	234	36.7	231	36.3	637	100
9	Agenda for public discussion, debates and fora	171	27.1	234	37.0	227	35.9	632	100
10	Representation of student grievances	216	34.0	222	35.0	197	31.0	635	100
11	Formulation of constitutions and other legal frameworks	213	33.3	257	40.2	169	26.5	639	100

Impediments to Effective Students' Participation in Governance

The final objective of this study was to identify the impediments to effective students' involvement in University governance from the perspective of different stakeholders. The study showed that these were many and varied. Table 5.16 reveals, among the leading impediments to effective students' involvement that of the 24 impediments identified by the survey respondents, the following ranked among the top five: 'Mistrust of student leaders among students leading to apathy' (73.8 per cent), 'lack of adequate recognition of students' role in university governance' (65.7 per cent), 'limited power and authority among student leaders' (62.7 per cent), 'fear of victimization by management among student leaders' (59.0 per cent) and 'lack of transparency and a consultative democratic process in university governance' (54.8 per cent). These were followed by impediments such as 'compromising of students leaders by management' (48.2 per cent), 'lack of financial, physical and other supportive resources' (43.7 per cent), 'inadequate grievance and appeal structures' (41.1 per cent), 'management's tendency to impose decisions while ignoring students' inputs' (39.4 per cent) and 'lack of leadership capacity among students' (36.5 per cent).

Other impediments to effective students' participation in university governance that were listed by at least 25.0 per cent of the interviewees were as follows: 'intimidation of student leaders by management' (35.6 per cent), 'management's lack of awareness of and/or insensitivity to students' needs' (35.4 per cent), 'poor communication between students' leaders and the general student body' (34.4 per cent), 'inadequate constitutional/legal basis to facilitate student participation in governance' (31.4 per cent), 'representation of individual rather than the group's interests by student leadership' (27.9 per cent), 'poor implementation of students' involvement policies and strategies' (26.7 per cent) and 'external interference especially by politicians and political parties' 26.0 per cent). For other less popular impediments to students' involvement in leadership listed by the study respondents, see Table 5.16.

The qualitative data gathered from key informant interviews and focus group discussions supported the trends identified from the quantitative data. However, the KIs and the FGDs also identified other challenges undermining students' involvement in governance and decision-making processes. Ranking highly in this regard was apathy among students, as manifested through poor attendance of meetings. Indifference to governance process makes it difficult for student leaders to gather issues from different students and give feedback to the students, among others. The KIs and FGDs also singled out the one-year term students in elective offices served as another stumbling block to effective representation. According to them, 'one year is too short to make a difference'. Further, the KIs and FGDs identified the feeling among students that their opinions are not consequential as an additional impediment to student involvement in governance. For instance, , in USIU, it was expressed that student leadership was always on the receiving end of management and had no business investing time in decision-making structures and processes. In the words of the vice Chair of SAC, 'students' leaders are KYMs (*kanda ya mikono*), literally translated to mean manual labourers. Other impediments unique to the KIs and FGDs included:

- Lack of interest in leadership roles among students in general and commitment to leadership among students of student leaders.
- Balancing between academic work and leadership roles: student leaders often find it hard to attain such a balance.
- Lack of true democracy: despite the mainstreaming of students' involvement in governance in important university policy documents, students enjoy dwindling freedom to assemble and to voice their concerns. In KU, for example, some students lamented that 'kamukunjis (student open forums) do not exist anymore. If caught holding one you are expelled.'

- Constitutional rigidity: in KU example, FGDs indicated that the KUSA constitution was very rigid and tended to alienate the students. According to them, the university uses the constitution to kill student motivation for involvement in governance matters.

The results from KIs and FGDs suggested that some of the impediments to effective students' participation in governance were specific to either KU or the USIU; signifying some public-private sector differences. In particular, the challenge of a large student population that made it impossible to mobilize and represent everyone's needs was unique to KU. Closely related to this was the large diversity of students' views and needs, which rendered it difficult to harmonize and represent them effectively. In addition, political meddling is especially rife in public universities, in this case KU. Based on the KIs and the FGDs, although politicians are only involved when invited as speakers, some sponsor the students' campaigns as evidenced by the expensive posters that students make. Some of the aspirants meet with politicians in town. Earlier (see section 5.6), some of the KIs and FGDs were captured lamenting about trickling down of national politics to the especially public universities where the agenda and dynamics of student politics coalesced along the lines of the major political parties: which contrasts with the situation at USIU where political meddling with students electioneering activities is minimal, if not totally non-existent, because it is against the SAC constitution.

Table 5.16: Impediments to Effective Students' Participation in Governance (N= 630)

	Impediments	Frequency	Per cent
1	Mistrust of student leaders among students	465	73.8
2	Lack of adequate recognition of students' role in university governance	414	65.7
3	Limited power and authority among student leaders	395	62.7
4	Fear of victimization by management among student leaders	372	59.0
5	Lack of transparency and a consultative democratic process in university governance	345	54.8
6	The tendency for student leaders to be compromised by management	304	48.2
7	Lack of financial, physical and other supportive resources	275	43.7
8	Inadequate grievance and appeal structures	261	41.4
9	Management's tendency to impose decisions while ignoring students' inputs	248	39.4
10	Lack of leadership capacity among students	230	36.5
11	Intimidation of student leaders by management	224	35.6

12	Management's lack of awareness of and/or insensitivity to students' needs	223	35.4
13	Poor communication between students leaders and the general student body	217	34.4
14	Inadequate constitutional/legal basis for to facilitate student participation in governance	198	31.4
15	Representation of individual rather than the group's interests by student leadership	176	27.9
16	Poor implementation of students' involvement policies and strategies	168	26.7
17	External interference especially by politicians and political parties, often leading to the balkanization of student bodies into parallel camps	164	26.0
18	Excessive bureaucracy	157	24.9
19	Inadequate feedback mechanisms to student leaders	156	24.8
20	Internal manipulation of student leadership by management	147	23.3
21	Lack of adequate information about the importance of student participation in university governance	114	18.1
22	Poor enforcement of students' involvement policies and strategies	104	16.5
23	Failure by university to honor most agreements reached with students	82	13.0
24	Lack of regular amendments/ revision of policies governing students involvement in governance to make them current	68	10.8

Note: Do not total to 100%; each respondent selected multiple impediments

Similarly, in USIU despite the Charter elucidating that students should be involved in governance, one of the major impediments to their active participation is that SAC is not registered with the Registrar of Societies and therefore lacks (legal) recognition beyond the university. This is unlike KUSA, and other public sector university students' governance organizations/ unions or associations which, being registered entities, operate like trade unions and, hence, have the capacity to aggressively champion students' interests and welfare. Another impediment to effective participation that applies only to USIU is the lack of direct student representation in all top structures of governance and decision-making, i.e., the Board of Trustees and the Management Council. As pointed out earlier, unlike their KU counterparts whose representatives sit in the University Council and the Senate, students at USIU have no direct representation in any of the two top governance structures. Another challenge affecting students' involvement in governance in USIU was inadequate support systems (or incentives). In particular, the data showed that USIU lacked especially material rewards for motivating students to take on leadership positions and to play the roles associated with them with commitment and zeal.

The survey respondents proffered a variety of remedies for overcoming the impediments to effective student participation in university management. As evident from Table 5.17, in all, 12 remedies were tendered. Topping the list was recommendation to 'nurture and entrench a culture of student involvement in governance and decision making'; it was offered by 65.1 per cent of the study subjects. This was followed by suggestions to 'improve management communication of policies and other issues affecting students' (49.0 per cent), 'reward student leaders who have excelled in their duties to nurture greater interest in leadership among students' (39.8 per cent), 'create external structures for students to appeal management decisions' (37.5 per cent) and 'guard against manipulation and intimidation of student leadership by university managements' (37.4 per cent). Completing the list of top 10 remedies were the following: 'greater autonomy, respect for and recognition of student leadership organizations' (34.0 per cent), 'reduce bureaucracy where necessary to improve efficiency' (32.7 per cent), 'greater management honesty, openness, transparency and receptivity when dealing with student leaders' (32.4 per cent), 'increase university physical and financial support to student leadership bodies' (31.7 per cent) and 'organize frequent training sessions for student leadership' (30.9 per cent. The remaining two remedies were supported by at least 20.0 per cent of the respondents (see Table 5.17 for details).

Table 5.17: Overcoming Challenges to Effective Students' Involvement in Governance (N= 621)

	Remedies	Frequency	Per cent
1	Nurture and entrench a culture of student involvement in governance and decision making	404	65.1
2	Improve management communication of policies and other issues affecting students	304	49.0
3	Reward student leaders who have excelled in their duties to nurture greater interest in leadership among students	247	39.8
4	Create external structures for students to appeal management decisions	233	37.5
5	Guard against manipulation and intimidation of student leadership by university managements	232	37.4
6	Greater autonomy, respect for and recognition of student leadership organizations	211	34.0
7	Reduce bureaucracy where necessary to improve efficiency	203	32.7
8	Greater management honesty, openness, transparency and receptivity when dealing with student leaders	201	32.4

9	Increase university physical and financial support to student leadership bodies	197	31.7
10	Organize frequent training sessions for student leadership	192	30.9
11	More effective implementation of policy decisions emanating from student-management cooperation	171	27.5
12	Educate students, especially freshmen, on the importance and relevance of student involvement in governance	126	20.3

Note: Do not total to 100%; each respondent provided multiple solutions

Testing for Cross-University Differences

Given its focus on both the public and the private sectors of University education in Kenya, this study considered it prudent to assess the following: cross-sector differences in policies and practices on students' involvement in governance; opportunity for and level of student involvement in governance; importance attached to, adequacy of and satisfaction with involvement in governance; support services for enhancing student involvement in governance and for differences in external political influence. In this regard, further analyses were carried out using the Chi square ($\chi 2$) as the test statistic. In all cases the assessment of significance utilized a 2-tailed test. Table 5.18 summarizes the significant cross-university (or cross-sector) variations obtained from the cross-tabulation analyses. The detailed results are presented in Appendix II, Tables A21 to A29.

Policies and Practices on Students' Involvement in Governance

The examination of cross-university differences in policies and practices focused on five strategic/policy documents and four institutional practices (see Table 5.2). The aim was to establish the extent to which the KU students differed from their USIU counterparts in terms of the extent to which they felt that strategic/policy documents and institutional practices mainstreamed students' involvement in governance. As evident from Table 5.18, significant differences were noted in four of the five policies and in all four of the practices analysed. Specifically, relative to their USIU counterparts, KU students were found to be more agreeable that their university's policy on students' involvement in governance had a legal basis; their university's strategic plan had students' involvement in governance as one of its priority areas of action; in their university students involvement in governance structures and decision-making was a matter of policy; and that, their university had a published policy on students' involvement in governance. On the contrary, USIU students were more likely to disagree with and/or not to be aware of their institution's mainstreaming of students' participation in governance in strategic/policy documents.

Findings

The regarding practices were not different from those about policies. The said results showed that, relative to their USIU counterparts, KU students were more likely to support the views that their university communicated the importance of students' involvement in governance to all members of the university community; made the necessary amendments and revisions to policies on students' involvement in governance; had put in place mechanisms for the implementation and enforcement of policies on students' involvement in governance; and that, the university provided opportunities for public debate/ discussion of matters affecting students' participation in the institution's governance process.

Table 5.18: Significant Cross-University Differences in Policies, Practices and Students' Involvement in Decision-making

Policy/ Practice/ Activity	χ^2 Value	d.f.	p-value
Policies and Practices on Students' Involvement in Governance			
My university's policy on student involvement in governance has a constitutional and legal basis.	27.197	2	.000
My university's strategic plan has 'student involvement in governance as one of its priority action areas.	8.637	2	.013
In my university student involvement in the various governance structures and in decision making is a matter of policy	25.936	2	.000
My university has a published policy on student involvement in governance	8.083	2	.018
My university communicates the importance of student involvement in governance to all members of the university community	7.092	2	.029
My university makes necessary amendments and revisions of policies on student involvement in governance	5.971	2	050
My university has put in place mechanisms for the implementation and enforcement of policies on student involvement in governance	22.913	2	.000
My university provides opportunities for public debate of matters affecting student involvement in governance	12.408	2	.002
Opportunity for Involvement in Governance and Decision-making			
My university offers sufficient avenues for university-wide communications for students	12.978	3	.005
Students in my university are involved in policy formulation	21.941	3	.000
Level of Students' Involvement in Governance Structures and Decision-making			
Orientation of new students	33.638	3	.000

Student assessment	10.364	3	.016
Faculty appraisal and promotions	15.430	3	.001
Graduation planning	29.636	3	.000
Student support and advising committees	9.491	3	.023
Support services committees (e.g. library, ICT)	19.262	3	.000
Importance Attached to Involvement in Governance Structures and in Decision-making			
Governance Structures			
Senate	7.823	3	.050
All departmental-/ program-wide committees	7.872	3	.049
Decision Making Activities			
Formulation of university vision and missions	11.503	3	.009
Strategic planning	12.690	3	.005
Academic planning	15.033	3	.002
Orientation of new students	8.462	3	.037
Curriculum development	11.171	3	.011
Recruitment of faculty and staff	11.785	3	.008
Faculty appraisal and promotions	9.430	3	.024
Dispute resolution	13.228	3	.004
Disciplinary matters	10.947	3	.012
Student support and advising committees	10.042	3	.018
Closure and opening of the university	14.530	3	.002
Adequacy of Student Involvement in Decision Making Activities			
Input /contributions during meetings	13.094	2	001
Representation of student issues	9.788	2	.007
Satisfaction with Participation in Decision-making			
Governance Structures			
University Council/ Board of trustees	12.413	3	.006
Senate	8.667	3	.034
All departmental-/ program-wide committees	8.196	3	.042
Decision Making Activities			
Admission of new students	7.896	3	.048
Orientation of new students	9.018	3	.029
Graduation planning	20.882	3	.000
Disciplinary matters	9.555	3	.023
Student support and advising committees	11.766	3	.008
Procurements	9.966	3	.019
Support services committees (e.g. library, ICT)	23.431	3	.000
Closure and opening of the university	13.932	3	.003

Support Services for Enhancing Students' Involvement in Governance			
Special office to coordinate student involvement in governance	13.404	3	.004
Periodic democratic elections	11.331	3	.010
Institutionalized channels of communication at all levels	12.555	3	.006
Existence of student self-governance structures; i.e. clubs and associations	74.548	3	.000
Tuition waivers	40.026	3	.000
Free meals	18.390	3	.000
Free transport	14.123	3	.003
Leadership training	19.362	3	.000
Public addresses/symposiums	8.669	3	.034
Invited guest speakers	12.205	3	007
External Political Influence			
Clubs/societies/associations meetings and activities	8.087	3	.044
Nomination process for elections	25.937	3	.000
Campaign for elections	41.771	3	.000
Actual elections	27.525	3	.000
Set up of governance structure	25.195	3	.000
Student barazas/kamukunjis	19.746	3	.000
Agenda for public discussion, debates and for a	14.399	3	.002
Social activities	8.423	3	.038
Personal matters	9.859	3	.020

The above results mirror the earlier finding that USIU students are mainly represented in governance through proxy whereas at KU there is a strong element of direct representation of students in the university's governance structures. They are also consistent with the high levels of student apathy to the governance process identified at the USIU. As a matter of fact, that apathy it is which is, most probably responsible for the high proportions of USIU students who either disagreed or were not aware of the existence of policies and practices in their university that mainstreamed students' involvement in governance structures and processes.

Opportunity for and Level of Students' Involvement in Governance

Chi-square tests were also conducted to assess for cross-university differences in opportunities for students' participation in governance and decision-making as well as in the actual involvement in governance structures and decision-making. In all 10 opportunities, seven governance structures and 24 decision-making activities were analysed. The results revealed significant differences only in two of the 10 opportunities focused on. That is, relative to KU students, USIU students were shown to be more likely to agree with the view that their university offered sufficient avenues for university-wide communication for students. This finding is consistent with the fact that the university operates based on an open-door policy that allows students to file their grievances with any office. On the contrary, KU students were found to be more likely to be involved in policy formulation compared to their USIU counterparts. As pointed out earlier, this is a reflection of the more direct representation of KU students in the governance structures of their university.

Concerning students' actual involvement in governance structures and in decision-making activities at the various levels of governance, the chi-square tests did not reveal the existence of cross-university differences in students' involvement in the seven governance structures spotlighted. However, differences were observed in six of the 24 decision-making activities analysed. In particular, USIU students were shown to be more likely to participate in decision making related to the following: orientation of new students, student assessment, faculty appraisals and promotions, graduation planning, student support and advising and support services (e.g. library and ICT). A closer look at these areas of decision-making reveals that they are at the lower echelons of the governance structure of the university; in other words, they are lower level decision-making activities. As such, the results support the earlier findings that USIU students enjoy proxy representation at the upper tier of governance and decision-making but are directly represented at the lower levels (that is, school and departmental/ programme levels) of decision-making.

Importance Attached to Students' Involvement in Governance and Decision-making

The analysis of the "importance" criteria spanned both the governance structures and specific decision-making areas focused on by this study. In all, seven structures and 24 areas of decision-making were analyzed. The results revealed cross-university differences in two structures and 11 areas of decision-making (see Table 5.18). In terms of structures, KU students were shown to attach greater importance to students' participation in the Senate, relative to their USIU counterparts. On the contrary, USIU students appeared to attach more importance to their involvement in all departmental/ programme-wide committees. These findings echo those documented earlier that whereas KU students have direct representation in upper structures of governance and decision-making, USIU students only enjoy direct representation at the lower levels of governance and decision-making.

Concerning the importance attached to students' participation in specific decision-making areas, the chi-square analysis revealed that KU students were more likely to attach great importance to involvement in formulation of the university vision and missions, strategic planning, curriculum development, dispute resolution, disciplinary matters and closure and opening of the university, a compared to USIU students. A closer look at these findings suggests that most of the decision-making ambits concerned touch on the upper echelons of the university's governance structures. With specific reference to dispute resolution, disciplinary matters and closure and opening of the university, it could also be argued that the importance KU students attach to them is a manifestation of the reliance of a union model of students' self-governance, the ever-recurring conflict between students and management and the consequent closures of the university, respectively. On the other hand, USIU students were found to attach greater importance than KU students to students' participation in academic planning, orientation of new students, recruitment of faculty and staff, faculty appraisals and promotions and student support and advising committees. Again, as underlined earlier, these are all lower-level areas of decision-making in which USIU students enjoy direct representation.

Adequacy of and Satisfaction with Students' Involvement in Governance

Differences in the adequacy of students' involvement in decision-making was measured utilizing seven items as follows: attendance in meetings, input / contributions during meetings, representation of student issues, voting power, ability to influence decision-making, capacity to contribute to the solution of problems faced by students and feedback to students. Cross-university differences were observed only in input/ contributions during meetings and representation of students' issues. Specifically, USIU students were found to consider their leadership representation in these two areas to be adequate relative to their KU equivalents. Otherwise, just like their KU counterparts, they did not evaluate their leadership's attendance in meetings, voting power, ability to influence decision-making, capacity to contribute to the solution of problems faced by students and feedback to students to be adequate.

The level of satisfaction with students' involvement in governance and decisions making was examined at two realms; at the overall (global) realm and the realm of students' involvement in specific structures and decision-making ambits. At the global level, the results showed that KU and USIU students were equally dissatisfied with the overall students' involvement in the governance of their university, $\chi 2$ Value = 5.885; d.f. = 3; P-value = .117. Whereas 63.7 per cent of KU students expressed dissatisfaction with the level of students' involvement in governance, 61.7 per cent of their USIU counterparts did the same.

With respect to cross-university differences in the level of satisfaction with students' participation in specific governance structures and areas of decision-making, the chi-square analysis revealed significant differences in three of the seven governance structures and in eight of the 24 areas of decision-making analyzed.

At the level of governance structures, it was found that USIU students were more likely to express satisfaction with students' involvement in the University Council/ Board of Trustees, the Senate and in all departmental-/ programme-wide committees, as compared to their KU counterparts. Concerning the University Council and the Senate, the findings are rather baffling since students at USIU do not enjoy direct representation in the two bodies. However, they could also manifest a pass of confidence in the proxy participation that they enjoy. Results for participation in specific areas of decision-making showed that, relative to KU students, USIU students were more likely to be satisfied with students' involvement in the following areas: all departmental/ programme-wide committees, admission of new students, orientation of new students, graduation planning, disciplinary matters, student support and advising committees, procurements, support services committees and closure and opening of the university. Once again, the bulk of these are lower-level areas of decision-making in which USIU students enjoy direct representation.

Support Services for Enhancing Students' Involvement in Governance

The study also assessed for cross-university differences in support services available for the enhancement of students' involvement in governance and decision-making. Differences were examined for a total of 18 support services. As evident from Table 5.18, significant differences were obtained in 10 of the 18 support services analysed. Specifically, the study found that, relative to KU, USIU was more likely to rely on the following support services by way of motivating students to get involved in governance and decision-making: provision of offices and persons responsible to coordinate students involvement, periodic democratic elections, institutionalized channels of communication at all levels, students' self-governance structures, tuition waivers, free meals, leadership training, and invited guest speakers. The finding about periodic democratic elections and institutionalized channels of communication at all levels, may be interpreted within the context of the rampant management meddling with students' elections in public universities and the existence of an open-door policy at USIU, respectively. On the contrary, it was revealed that KU was more likely to rely on free transport and public addresses or symposia to increase students' interest in governance and decision-making.

External Political Influence

The final area of cross-university differences analyzed by the study was external political influence. As evident from Table 5.18, significant differences were acknowledged in nine of 12 areas of possible external political meddling as follows: Clubs/ societies/ associations' meetings and activities; nomination process for students' elections; campaign for elections; set-up of governance structures; student *kamukunjis/ barazas;* agenda for public discussion; debates and forums; social activities and personal matters. In all cases, the results showed that external political meddling was more likely to occur at KU in comparison to the situation at USIU. The findings support the view advanced earlier in this study that being a private university, USIU is more insulated from external political interference. As a result, the students are less politicized and mainly concentrate on completing their studies.

Notes

1. Ranked among top five by 81.8 per cent of respondents.
2. Ranked among top five 76.9 per cent of respondents.
3. Ranked among top five 73.2 per cent of respondents.
4. Ranked among top five 65.6 per cent of respondents.
5. Ranked among top five 48.7 per cent of respondents.
6. Ranked among top five 48.6 per cent of respondents.
7. Ranked among top five 40.6 per cent of respondents.
8. Ranked among top five 37.5 per cent of respondents.
9. Ranked among top five 34.8 per cent of respondents.
10. Ranked among top five 29.9 per cent of respondents
11. Ranked among top five 27.4 per cent of respondents

6

Summary, Discussion, Conclusions and Recommendations

The overall aim of this study was to investigate the subject of students' involvement in the democratic governance of universities in Kenya. Specifically, the study aimed to: a) identify the extent to which students' participation in governance and decision-making processes are mainstreamed in important university policy documents and in governance structures and practices; b) assess the importance students attach to their involvement in governance and decision-making processes; and; c) establish the extent, adequacy and level of satisfaction with students' participation in governance and decision-making processes. In addition, the study sought to: d) document existing structural and material (rewards) incentives used by universities to nurture and entrench students' involvement in university governance and decision-making; e) gauge the extent of national political influence on student self-governance processes and to identify the impediments to effective students' involvement in university governance, from the perspective of different stakeholders. This chapter summarizes the major findings of the study, discusses them and presents the key conclusions drawn from them and recommendations offered.

Summary of Findings

Three categories of respondents contributed to this study. The first, made up of 657 students distributed as follows: 456 from Kenyatta University (KU) and 201 from the United States International University, Africa (USIU) –A, and who comprised the primary sample. These included 46.2 per cent (304) males and 53.8 per cent (353) females. They ranged in age from under 21 years to those aged 51 and above and were spread across four schools as follows: Education (44.3 per cent), Business (25.1 per cent), Humanities and Social Sciences (19.8 per cent) and Science and Technology (10.8 per cent). Whereas 94.4 per cent of them were undergraduate students, the remaining 5.6 per cent were postgraduate students. The majority of the primary respondents (90.4 per cent) were Kenyan nationals; the rest originated from other East African countries (3.6 per cent), the rest of Africa (3.5 per cent), and the rest of the world (2.5 per cent). Data from the primary sample were supplemented with interviews conducted with four key informants (KIs) – two top management officials and two student leaders – spread evenly across the institutions covered by the study and from 27 student focus group discussants divided into four discussion groups, again spread evenly across the two universities. Whereas the KIs included three males and one female, the focus group discussants comprised 14 males and 13 females. The summary of findings in relation to the study objectives is presented below.

Mainstreaming of Involvement in Policy Documents, Governance Structures and Practices

To capture the mainstreaming of students' involvement in official university policy documents, governance structures and practices and in decision-making processes, the study analyzed the contents of university mission and vision statements, Charters and/ or Acts and student government constitutions; administered structured interviews to 657 students; conducted in-depth interviews with four KIs and held four focus group discussions with selected students. The results showed that, in principle, students were expected to participate in university governance. Whereas there was no direct connection between university mission and vision statements and students involvement in governance in the two institutions, the KU Charter, the KU Statutes 2013 and the KU Students Association (KUSA) constitution as well as the USIU Charter and the USIU Student Affairs Council (SAC) constitution identified students as pertinent members of (some) governance organs. However, in practice, the situation varied from institution to institution. Whereas student representatives at KU sat directly in the Council and the Senate but were excluded from the Board of Management (the main internal governance structure), their counterparts at USIU were excluded from the Board of Trustees and only represented by proxy in the Management Council, the top internal decision-making organ.

Consistent with the overall picture obtained from the analysis of documents, the survey results showed that universities recognize students as pertinent members of their governance structures. Of the 657 respondents 69.3 per cent agreed that their university's policy on students' involvement in governance had a constitutional and legal basis. The respondents, nevertheless, pointed out that the practice of mainstreaming students' involvement in institutional strategic/ policy documents and practices may not be as explicit and/ or as widespread as the statements appearing in the charters and in the Acts establishing them would suggest. To illustrate, only 54.8 per cent of the respondents agreed that the statutes governing their university made reference to students' involvement in the governance process and 46.3 per cent felt that, in their university, students' involvement in the various governance structures and in decision-making was a matter of policy. These sentiments were corroborated by the data from KIs and FGDs which confirmed that both universities had mainstreamed students' involvement in governance in important policy documents, especially those listed above.

The results for the mainstreaming of students' involvement in governance in institutional practices presented a moderate picture, with less than 50 per cent of the survey respondents agreeing with any of the statements used to capture it. To illustrate, only 48.8 per cent confirmed that their university 'communicates the importance of students' involvement in governance to all members of the university community, 47.7 per cent supported the view that their university 'makes necessary amendments and revisions of policies on students' involvement in governance' and 45.6 per cent agreed that their university 'has put in place mechanisms for the implementation and enforcement of policies on student involvement in governance', among others. These patterns were consistent with the views of student KIs and FGDs according to whom they were not aware of the existence of specific institutional practices that seriously promoted the inclusion of students in governance processes in their universities.

Importance Students Attach to Involvement

On the whole, the results of the structured interviews showed that students attached high importance to their inclusion in various governance structures and in varied decision-making activities. With reference to governance structures, 56.0 per cent, 65.2 per cent and 66.8 per cent, respectively, considered student representation in the University Council/ Board of Trustees, Board of Management/Management Council and/or in Senate to be of high importance. Turning to lower level structures, 73.4 per cent, 71.4 per cent, 74.1 per cent and 71.5 per cent of interviewees, correspondingly, felt that involvement in all university-wide committees, deans' committees, school-wide committees and all departmental-/ program-wide committees was of high importance. Similar trends were observed for decision-making activities, with relatively low percentages of the respondents feeling that student involvement was not important at all. Out of the 24 areas of decision-making analyzed, students' involvement in 21 of them was considered to be of high importance by over 60 per cent of the respondents. Only in the two areas of recruitment of faculty and staff and faculty appraisal and promotions did the proportion of students who considered involvement in them to be of high importance stand at less than 50 per cent.

The primary respondents considered the benefits of students' participation in governance and decision-making to outweigh the negative consequences; only 2.8 per cent considered involvement not to have positive consequences. The top three positive consequences of participation as identified by the study subjects included: 'improved dispute resolution, stability and peace/ reduced student dissatisfaction and incidences of strikes'; facilitates better and more effective protection of students' interests and facilitates better and more effective protection of students' interests and welfare'. The top three negative consequences of involvement identified by the study subjects included that it: 'grows self-seeking leadership that does not represent students' interests effectively'; 'it is a waste of time: in reality students have no say on most matters that affect them, management does'; and it 'burdens students' leaders thereby undermining their academic performance'. In every case, the proportion of students supporting each consequence fell below the 30 per cent mark. The respondents offered a variety of remedies for the negative consequences of students' involvement in governance and decision-making. The top four of them included: 'increase level and breadth of student involvement especially in major decision making'; 'set clear limits for student power'; 'cultivate and nurture a more proactive student leadership that is always ready to engage with management' and 'develop policies against external political interference with overall governance, student leadership and university activities'.

Extent and Adequacy of and Satisfaction with Involvement

Asked to identify the top five decision-makers in Kenyan universities, the primary respondents listed the following: Vice Chancellor, Deputy Vice Chancellors, Deans, University Councils and University Senate. Out of a list of 11 decision-makers, students' representatives were 9th, regular students 10th and faculty 11th. With specific reference to the extent of overall involvement in governance structures and decision-making activities, the results showed that it ranged from moderate to minimal. This was despite the delineation of students as pertinent members of governance organs by important university policy documents and the high importance students attached to their involvement in the various governances structures and in decision-making activities. Only two of the ten items utilized to measure overall involvement were supported by more than 60 per cent of the study subjects. Similar results were obtained for the actual level of students' involvement in the various governance structures and areas of decision-making.

The results from KIs and FGDs were not different; they showed that students in universities played minimal roles in governance in general and only influenced decision-making in a small way. The situation is direr at the USIU, where students do not sit on neither the Board of Trustees nor the Management Council, the top decision=making organs of the university. The informants reported that students' involvement in university governance processes in both KU and the USIU occurred mainly through self-governance organizations, especially students' government associations/ organizations/ unions, in this case the KUSA and SAC. In both universities, elected officials of the two organizations are mandated to represent students in various organs of governance and decision-making. The minimal participation of students in governance and decision-making is compounded by the high levels of apathy towards students' government organizations, clubs and associations that pervades universities. However, it was evident from the survey, as well as KIs and FGDs results that the level of students' involvement tends to increase at lower (committee) level governance structures.

The ratings for the adequacy of students' involvement in the governance and decision-making processes supported the minimal involvement of students realized by this study. Utilizing seven indicators of involvement – that is, attendance in meetings, input/ contributions during meetings, representation of student issues, voting power, ability to influence decision-making, capacity to contribute solutions to problems faced by students, and feedback to students – the bulk of the primary respondents rated students' representation ether as lacking or inadequate. These results were echoed by the KIs and the FGDs; in both universities which felt that, despite student representation at both the upper and lower levels of management, such representation was not effective. Concerning inclusivity, the study found that only KU had formal structures for catering for divergent needs, including gender, disability, and non-traditional students, among other social categories.

The results for satisfaction with students' participation in governance and decision-making revealed low levels of the same. Only 36.4 per cent of the primary interviewees expressed overall satisfaction compared to 63.6 per cent who reported being dissatisfied. The results for the analysis of different manifestations (or indicators) of student representation in governance and their involvement in different governance structures and decision-making activities were not that much different. Nevertheless, consistent with the outcome that students' involvement seemed to intensify as one descended to lower levels and structures of decision-making, the level of satisfaction tended to improve with lower-level decision-making activities.

Structural and Material Incentives for Nurturing Students' Involvement

The study documented the existence of a raft of structural and material incentives utilized by universities to nurture and entrench students' involvement in governance. These included student self-governance structures, especially students government councils/ associations/unions, clubs and associations. However, it was felt that these played a peripheral role, if at all, in overall university governance and decision-making. Other structural incentives included a special office for coordinating students' involvement in governance, formal appeal and complaint structures, periodic democratic elections, motivational guest speakers, public addresses or symposia, institutionalized channels of communication at all levels, retreats, leadership training and office space, among others. At the tail end were material incentives, such as free transport, monetary allowances, tuition waivers, free meals and free accommodation.

Results for KIs and FGDS supported the existence of varied incentives for motivating students' participation in governance and decision-making. The data also pointed to the existence of KU-USIU differences, with the outcome that structural incentives were common (universal) to the two universities studied whereas material incentives were mainly confined to KU. Also, while student KIs and FGDs from KU expressed satisfaction with the incentives available for promoting students' involvement in governance, their counterparts in USIU were quite dissatisfied with the same. The informants suggested that the combination of a wide variety of both structural and material incentives available to KU students was responsible for the high competition for nomination and election to positions of student leadership while the lack of the same, especially reward incentives may be responsible for the apathy characteristic of the USIU.

Level of National Political Influence on Students' Self-governance Processes

Results of the survey showed that, overall, national politics and political parties wielded tremendous influence on students' self-governance structures and processes, working especially through students' government councils/ associations/ unions. All of the 11 possible areas of influence analyzed by the study were greatly impacted on by national politics and political parties. The influence was greatest on student campaigns for elections, actual elections, set-up of governance structures, the choice of guests invited to student government activities and functions, social activities organized by student government, nomination process for elections, clubs/ societies/ associations meetings and activities, agenda for public discussion, debates and forums and student barazas/ kamukunjis. These results were consistent with those from KIs and FGDs. The informants concurred that national politics had trickled down especially to the public universities where the agenda and dynamics of student politics coalesced along the lines of the major political parties.

Impediments to Effective Students' Involvement in University Governance

The study identified many and varied impediments to students' involvement in governance and in decision-making. For the primary respondents, the following are the top five: 'Mistrust of student leaders among students leading to apathy', 'lack of adequate recognition of students' role in university governance', 'limited power and authority among student leaders', 'fear of victimization by management among student leaders' and 'lack of transparency and a consultative democratic process in university governance. The qualitative data collected for the study were consistent with or the quantitative data. However, the KIs and FGDs also identified other challenges undermining students' involvement in governance and decision-making processes, including apathy among students, the one-year term served by students in elective offices, the feeling among students that their opinions are not consequential, lack of interest in leadership roles among students in general and commitment to leadership among student leaders, balancing between academic work and leadership roles, lack of true democracy and constitutional rigidity. Based on the KIs and FGDs, some impediments were specific to either KU or the USIU; signifying some public-private sector differences. To illustrate, the large student population, large diversity of students' views and needs and high levels of political meddling were specific to KU. On the other hand, the failure to register with the Registrar of Societies in the country is specific to USIU. Those interviewed for the study suggested a variety of interventions that could be harnessed to address the challenges identified by the study.

Cross-University Differences

Further analysis using the Chi Square ($\chi 2$) as a test statistic, revealed the existence of significant differences in some of the areas focused on by this study. In terms of the extent to which students considered strategic/policy documents and institutional practices to mainstream student involvement in governance, significant differences were noted in both policies and practices. Within the context of policies, KU and USIU students differed significantly in their perceptions in all four areas analyzed; that is: policy having a legal basis; university's strategic plan prioritizing students' involvement, students' involvement being a matter of policy and; university having a published policy on students' involvement in governance. Relative to their USIU counterparts, KU were found to be more agreeable concerning the four policy areas analyzed. Similar results were obtained with respect to the practices brought under scrutiny, with KU students being more likely to support the views expressed. A look at cross-university differences in opportunities for students' participation in governance and decision making revealed significant differences only in two of the 10 opportunities focused on. USIU students were more likely to agree with the view that their university offered sufficient avenue for university-wide communication for students while their KU counterparts are more likely to be involved in policy formulation. With respect to actual involvement in governance, no significant differences were obtained between KU and USIU students. However, differences were observed in six of the 24 decision-making activities analyzed. USIU students were more likely to participate in decision-making related to orientation of new students, student assessment, faculty appraisals and promotions, graduation planning, student support and advising and support services.

Chi Square test results for importance attached to participation revealed that KU students attached greater importance to students' participation in the Senate, while USIU students attached greater premium to involvement in all departmental-wide committees. Concerning participation in specific decision-making areas, the results showed that KU students valued more involvement in formulation of university vision and missions, strategic planning, curriculum development, dispute resolution, disciplinary matters and closure and opening of the university. On the contrary, USIU students attached greater importance to students' participation in academic planning, orientation of new students, recruitment of faculty and staff, faculty appraisals and promotions and student support and advising committees. The fourth area of cross-university comparisons was the adequacy of and satisfaction in involvement. Cross-university differences were observed only in input/ contributions during meetings and representation of students' issues; USIU students considered their leadership representation in these two areas to be adequate relative to their KU colleagues. Concerning satisfaction, the analysis revealed that KU and USIU students were equally dissatisfied with the overall students' involvement in the governance of their university. At the level of participation in governance structures, USIU students were more likely to be satisfied with involvement in University Council/ Board of Trustees, the Senate and in all departmental-/ programme-wide committees. Results for participation in specific areas of decision-making showed that USIU students were more likely to be satisfied with students' involvement in all programme-wide committees, admission of new students, orientation of new students, graduation planning, disciplinary matters, student support and advising committees, procurements, support service committees and closure and opening of the university.

Cross-university differences in inducements for enhancing involvement and in external political influence were also assessed. Concerning the former, significant differences were obtained in 10 of 18 motivators. Relative to KU, USIU was more likely to rely on provision of offices and persons responsible to coordinate students' involvement, periodic democratic elections, institutionalized channels of communication, students' self-governance structures, tuition waivers, free meals, leadership training and, invited guest speakers to motivate students to get involved in governance. On the contrary, KU was more likely to motivate students using free transport and public addresses or symposia. Turning to political influence, significant differences were obtained in nine of 12 areas of possible external political meddling, with external political meddling being more likely to occur at KU relative to USIU.

Discussion of Findings

This study had as its first objective to determine the extent to which official university policy documents as well as governance structures and practices or mainstream students' participation in governance and decision-making processes. The results established that, indeed, students' participation in the governance of their universities was the subject matter of important university documents, especially Charters and/or Acts, Statutes and constitutions governing students' association. These documents identified students as important stakeholders who should be incorporated in institutional decision-making structures and processes. Paradoxically though, no substantial evidence was colleagues by the study supporting the underlining of such involvement by other important university policy documents (such as strategic plans) or the mainstreaming of it into university governance practices. This can be interpreted to be an indictment on the commitment of the top management of universities to actively involve students in governance. It could also be viewed as a pointer to tokenistic and political correctness approaches embraced by top management in dealing with the important subject of students involvement in governance.

Based on the results of this study, 69.3 per cent of the students interviewed supported the view that their university's policy on students' involvement in governance had a constitutional and legal basis. This not only underlined the fact that universities, both public and private, recognize students as pertinent members of their governance structures but also echoed the finding that charters establishing universities have sections specifically focusing on students' involvement in governance. The finding might also signify that those interviewed were familiar with the contents of the Universities Act No. 42 of 2012 which delineates the Students' Council as one of the elements of the internal governance (administrative) structure of universities in the country. According to the Act, other elements of that structure include a Chancellor, University Council, the Senate, the Vice Chancellor assisted by a number of Deputy Vice Chancellors, Management Boards, Faculty Boards, and Departmental Boards (Republic of Kenya 2012).

Overall, the results of this study showed that students considered it important to be involved in the various governance structures in their university. However, the greater premium appears to have been attached to involvement in committees at the various levels (Deans, university-wide, school-wide/ faculty-wide and departmental-wide/ programm-wide) relative to top-level structures, that is, University Council/ Board of Trustees, Management Councils and Senate (see Table 5.3 for details). This could be interpreted to suggest that it is in such structures (committees) that students felt they made real impact as compared to high-level governance structures. This is consistent with the finding from in-depth interviews with key informants and focus group discussants that, especially in private universities, students' representatives in governance and decision-making processes do not exercise any real power. It can also be argued that students attached greater premium to committees because it is at this level that important academic decisions that affect them directly are made. The results could also be considered to be the affirmation of the position taken by Zuo and Ratsoy (1999) that student representation on departmental committees appears to be the most strategic and potentially useful participative mechanism, because it aids problem solving at a local level, on issues that have an immediate impact on students, while offering the greatest potential for building a sense of community and social capital between staff and students.

That students should be involved in governance is not a moot issue. After all students are full-time and possibly the most important stakeholders in the higher education community; meaning that they should participate in and wield considerable influence on institutional governance procedures, processes and activities (Persson 2003; Luescher 2011). Despite this, the results of this study revealed that both public and private universities tend to be characterized by lukewarm (or pseudo) participation of students in governance. In both KU and the USIU, for example, students were not directly represented in the core internal decision-making organs, that is, the Management Board and the Management Council, respectively. Yet in all probability, these two organs make the most important decisions that affect the student body directly. The decision by the two institutions to exclude students from direct representation in the internal organs of governance is a serious indictment to the institutions' commitment to the democratization of the governance process in general and to entrenching students' involvement in that process in particular. It forces one to question the seriousness of the two universities studied in ensuring greater democratization of the governance process and in guaranteeing effective students. Involvement in the governance process. Consistent with Oggawa and Bossetrt (1995), we argue that for students to be considered as properly involved in the governance processes in their institutions, their (students') leadership should not only be involved in some matters and/ or some levels of governance. Rather, it should be adequately involved in major decision-making and at all levels of decision-making. In addition, and very important, the universities must allocate students adequate material and non-material resources needed for effective participation in governance.

That students were more visible in lower levels of decision-making testifies to the fact that public and private universities in Kenya in principle encourage the democratic governance while in practice they lean toward the authoritative paternalistic model of governance. This is an approach in which students are integrated into the institutional governance structure but given limited discretion for involvement on issues strictly concerning them (e.g., student services and teaching quality) and only in an advisory role rather than in a co-decision capacity. The approach manifests a 'management-controlled participation' as opposed to the open participatory process, thereby relegating students to the status of junior members of the academic community who are not capable of contributing to decisions on an equal level as academics and administrators (Leuscher-Mamashela 2013). This failure by universities to practice what they preach has previously been observed by Johnson and Deem (2003) who argued that more often than not, incongruence between espoused and practical participation characterizes university institutions. Whereas university policy may emphasize student-centerdness, its practical implementation often focuses on 'managing the student body' more than responding to the experiences of the students. Argyris and Schon (1978) considered this to be an enduring aspect of social and organizational life.

The decision by universities to confine students' direct representation to lower levels of decision-making points to a university administration that might be well versed with the many arguments that have been advanced to rationalize why students should be excluded from decision-making. For instance, the transient nature of studentship, rapid turnaround of elected student officials (most serve a one-year term) (Klemenčič 2014; Task Force on Higher Education and Society 2000) and, the belief among management that students may not have the competence to provide constructive input in many areas of decision-making have been used to bequeath faculty and administrators authority over students in important areas of decision-making, leaving them to make major contribution only in areas affecting their lives in which they have the competence to provide constructive input. In this regard, a top management official who served as a key informant in USIU advanced the view that students did not merit direct representation in top-level organs of decision-making because 'they do not make much contribution.' Where administrators have authority over students in decision-making, their status as equal partners in the governance and decision-making processes of their institutions is weakened considerably. The explanations presented above, though, should not eclipse the fact that the total exclusion or feeble involvement of students in university governance in Kenya mainly manifests the failure of a democratic culture to take root in universities. This is rather paradoxical given that universities are the cradle of knowledge and, therefore, should be the best expression and practitioners of democratic principles. University administrators are drawn from the best academicians and presumably have the best understanding of democratic governance. In conformity with this, they are best placed to express (practice) democratic governance which should inherently include the inclusion of students on a co-decision basis.

Among the principles of good governance in universities is shared governance; others being academic freedom, clear rights and responsibilities, meritocratic selection, financial stability and accountability (Kauffeldt 2009). Also termed cooperative governance, it entails giving various groups of people a share in the decision-making process. In a university setting, the existence of shared governance denotes the involvement of all stakeholders, administrators, faculty and students in the making of critical decisions affecting the institution (Kauffeldt 2009; Task Force on Higher Education and Society 2000). These are accorded a meaningful voice in policy formulation and in decision-making in general. The study results suggested that university administrators in both the public and private sectors do not take students' involvement in governance very seriously. In the two universities studied, the data suggested that the important principle of shared governance was not being accorded the seriousness it merits for the true democratization of decision-making to take root. Among others, this was evident from the tokenistic representation of students in important internal organs of policy and decision-making, which denied them the co-decision rights (see Klemenčič 2014) central to shared governance. The absence of shared governance in the institutions covered by this study is consistent with the findings of previous studies (see e.g., Kauffeldt 2009; Obondo 2000). Kauffeldt (2009) found the lack of cooperation in institutional governance to be rampant in many universities. Similarly, Obondo (2000) showed that in most cases university senates, faculty and management boards and committee structures do not include students; or even when they do, they are integrated as tokens rather than active participants in decision-making. As a result, students constitute one of the most vulnerable and least empowered groups of actors who must be involved in the transformation of Kenyan universities.

The results of this study provided no strong evidence that the exercise of power in students' self-governance as well as in overall university governance structures was shared among all stakeholders, with the leadership holding shared values, standards and ideals; delegating duties; learning from others and, most important, being change drivers (Basham 2010). Rather, they pointed to the existence of a conservative leadership that seeks to monopolize power and to be the source of most of the decisions that affect the stakeholders. The study also showed that both student leadership and the official university managers tended to achieve things alone instead of bringing on board all stakeholders, thereby defeating the very conception of participative leadership. This is consistent with Obondo (2000) who pointed out that, when it comes to governance, universities in Kenya tend to be characterized by individuals with vested interests who may hinder participation at different levels. The institutions, more so the top management, also tend to lack a culture of openness and frequent dialogue on issues, thereby disenfranchising some members of the decision-making organs. This renders it hard for the institutions to embrace change even when it is beneficial and necessary.

According to Mutula (2002) private universities have a democratic system of governance, where students are routinely involved in decision-making processes. These institutions are characterized by continuous dialogue among administrators, teaching staff and students, leading to reduced tension that may result in strikes. The results obtained from the USIU appear to contradict Mutula's (2002) position. Indeed, than confirm the existence of a deep-rooted democratic culture, the study revealed that, like their counterparts in the public sector, USIU students' contribution to the governance of the institution was minimal. This was evident in a number of ways. First, students are not directly (actively) represented in top internal organs of decision making, that is, the Board of Trustees and the University Senate. Instead they enjoy proxy representation. Second, while students appear to be more active in lower levels of decision making, there is a general lack of interest among them in general and among their leadership, thereby watering down the extent of democratization of the decision-making processes. The study results also suggested that private universities are not completely immune from the meddling by management with student and staff organizations, including their self-governance processes, functions and their activities. As a matter of fact, the respondents from private universities suggested that it is the payment of fees and not the active representation of students in governance structures coupled with continuous dialogue between management and students that is mainly responsible for the absence of student strikes, demonstrations and riots that have become the hallmark of public universities.

One factor that obviously renders inadequate the representation of students in governance in USIU is the proxy representation students enjoy in top governance organs; the Board of Trustees and the Management Council. Although a top management official rationalized the absence of students' representatives in top governance structures by arguing that the students 'don't make much contribution', student interviewees as KIs and FG discussants felt that representation by proxy was very ineffective. The following voice from one of the focus group discussants summed up this ineffectiveness as follows:

> It is very hard to channel ones grievances through someone else. Yes, student *barazas* are held and SAC representatives periodically meet with the dean of students and the DVC, (Student affairs to raise issues affecting students for onward transmission to management council but at the end of it all not much is done to tackle the issues until they get out of hand.

We acknowledge that physical presence does not guarantee effective representation of students. Even proxy representation if actualized well can address students' concerns that bear on their capacity to achieve what brought them to the university. However, this calls for holding the proxy representatives of students accountable to ensure that they deliver the messages that are given to them by students and do so without contaminating them. As articulated by the students during in-depth interviews and focus group discussions, the proxy representatives of students in top-level management forums tend to do so selectively. As such, they decide on their own whether or not to convey students' concerns to top-level management, or when they do, what particular aspects of the students' voices they should pass to top management. One way to hold proxy representatives accountable is to do a report-back of discussions on matters touching on students' academic and social welfare. More specifically, the proxies could transmit minutes of items covering non-censored students' matters to their constituencies for deliberations. Furthermore, for proxy representation to be effective, it calls for structures and systems for holding the proxy representatives accountable. Unfortunately, such structures and systems did not exist in any of the two universities covered by this study.

In USIU, the tighter control of students could be understood in terms of the business model that underpins the institution and, by implication, private universities in the country. These institutions while not necessarily driven by profit, do, nonetheless, operate along a business model. This means that intense student activism anchored on the trade union model, as exists in public universities would be disruptive and, therefore, "not good for business". This argument makes even more sense when viewed within the uniqueness of the education market. Unlike regular markets where buyers demand from sellers the best quality of goods that their money can fetch, in the education market both the buyer and the seller must work collaboratively to determine the quality of the final product delivered to the buyer. As a matter of fact, the very quality of the final product rests overwhelmingly with the buyer. Thus, the fact that students must work hard to ensure that they get value for their money (the fees they pay), bolsters the view held by students at USIU that student activism would not serve them well. As pointed out earlier, the majority of the students held the view that, "I am paying money for my education and, therefore, cannot risk being sent away".

Despite the fact that, on the one side, students are officially delineated as pertinent members of top-level decision-making organs in both public and private universities and, on the other side, the importance students attached to their inclusion in governance and decision making, the study results suggest that, in reality, students play minimal roles in the governance process. The results of this study suggest the existence of too much tokenism coupled with the tendency toward political correctness in the nurturing of students' participation in the governance processes in both the public and the private institutions studied. In addition, the corruption, lack of transparency and mismanagement that are the hallmark of Kenya's national psyche appear to have permeated university governance processes. Student leaders appear to be ready to be compromised by top management and to serve their own interests instead of the interests of their constituents. The above results support the findings of a study conducted by Menon (2005) focusing on the views of students regarding the extent of their participation in the management of their university and their satisfaction with the degree of this participation. The study revealed that students believed that their involvement in the management of their institution was very limited. This applied to both high and low levels of decision-making, with their input being greater in less important decisions. The perceived limited involvement resulted in feelings of frustration and dissatisfaction among students, with the majority of respondents demanding a higher level of participation.

One of the practices that are recommended for universities to achieve good governance is data driven decision-making (see Task Force for University Education and Society 2000). It is argued that decisions anchored on adequate data are more objective, balanced and likely to be acceptable to the stakeholders concerned. Despite the exclusion of students from important decision-making university organs, universities continue to make decisions affecting students without scientific evidence or data collected from students focusing on their needs, desires, likes and dislikes. Yet any policy that is not anchored on authentic scientific research findings is likely to fall short or not address the situation adequately. It is often the case that exclusion is a basis for injustice and sometimes bitterness. Thus, decision making that excludes students is likely to trigger experiences of distributive injustice among students. As a consequence, the students may engage in justice-restoring behaviours such as go-slows, demonstrations and riots or violent confrontations, which have become a hallmark of many public universities not only in Kenya but also in other African countries (see e.g., Azikiwe 2016; Kiboiy 2013; Luescher-Mamashela 2005; Mohamedbhai 2016; Mutula 2002; Mwiria *et al.* 2007).

A visible feature of higher education in Africa as a whole and in Kenya in particular today is the transformation that university education has undergone, including the rising number of universities, expansion in enrolments and declining public funding, among others (see e.g., Gudo *et al.* 2011; Kaburu and Embeywa 2014; Kinuthia 2009; Munene 2016; Mutula 2002; Nganga 2014; Nyangau 2014; Odhiambo 2011; Okioga, Onsongo and Nyaboga 2014). These transformations ignite the need for universities to re-examine their governance systems to ensure effectiveness. In particular, stakeholder participation in governance must be accommodative of all institutional members, including students. This is imperative considering that stakeholder involvement in decision-making is one of the key principles in the practice of good governance (OCED 2003; Eurydice 2008). Involvement is the hallmark of shared governance; a process which gives various groups the opportunity to get involved in the management of the affairs of their organization either directly or through elected representation. Whereas many universities including those in Kenya, have expressed the desire to depart from the traditional models of governance in which one supreme leader exercised power in decision-making (Parrish n.d.), the capacity of these institutions to embrace truly representative (democratic) governance remains elusive (or a pipe dream). This was evident from the results of this study which showed that in both public and private universities the lack of transparency, accountability and commitment in the management of students' participation in university governance is reflected through varied practices by top management as well as student behaviour and attitudes toward their involvement in governance. The following examples are quite illustrative, in this regard:

- The failure to grant students direct representation in the umbrella internal organs of decision-making, the Management Board at KU and the Management Council at USIU, instead electing by proxy representation.
- The manipulation of student government elections in both public and private universities by management to ensure that candidates of their choice occupy especially the strategic positions of president/ chairperson and secretary general. This could take forms such as the imposition (or handpicking) of candidates or the outright rigging of elections. Concerning the rigging of elections, one FGD at Kenyatta University had the following to say:

> You will never guess the length management is willing to go to ensure that compliant student officials are elected to lead KUSA. Management will handpick and promote the election of particular (read favorite) students especially for the positions of President and the Secretary as well as dangle goodies to compromise strong candidates who have massive support from the student body. In extreme cases, should management sense defeat, it will not hesitate preside over the rigging of the election by managing the printing and stuffing of ballots. In this regard, tales of management orchestrated printing of ballots for student elections in suspicious printing presses located in the industrial area of Nairobi abound.

Other factors that may hamper students' full and effective involvement into democratic governance processes and activities in both public and private universities, may include the following:

- The censorship or vetting of decisions made by student leaders despite the freedom of expression guaranteed by the constitutions underpinning student self-governance bodies.
- The high levels of apathy or the lack of interest in student mobilization that was evident in both KU and the USIU.
- Reliance on social networks that guarantee anonymity instead of speaking in open student forums to air grievances and matters affecting student welfare.
- The high levels of mistrust and lack of confidence that characterize the relationship between students and top management as well as student leaders and their constituents. Because of the mistrust students have of management, dialogue between students and management, though an essential and critical element of the governance process, remains a very delicate balancing act, if not altogether elusive.

- In the USIU, the failure by management to register SAC with the Registrar of Societies thereby denying it national recognition as well as the powers (or opportunity) to act like a union.

The study reveals that there exists general mistrust of student leaders and management by the general student body in both the public and the private universities in Kenya. This tends to undermine the confidence students have in their leaders, as well as it casts doubts about the credibility and effectiveness of students' participation in governance processes. In particular, it renders impotent the mobilization of the student community, through student self-governance bodies (in this case the KUSA and SAC) for governance purposes; it also compounds the apathy that students have towards involvement in decision-making. The existence of mistrust in the relationship between students and their leaders is supported by the results of a survey on democratic citizenship and universities in Africa conducted in three universities which showed that, while there was overwhelming student support for students' participation in representative management systems, the existing student unions faced a crisis of legitimacy. According to the study, student leaders were the least trusted people on campus, an observation that was made in the light of disputed election results and accusations of corruption (Luescher-Mamashela *et al.* 2011).

Our universities constitute a core pillar in the training of future leadership for the different sectors of the economy and society. Their actions negative behavior/behavior and tendencies as recorded in the course of this study, may play a major role in the entrenchment of non-democratic non-transparent, corrupt and non-accountable leadership at the national level. But like the saying goes, 'one can only defecate what one has eaten'. In this regard, and consistent with Astin (2000) and May (2009), the leadership produced by institutions of higher learning are the product of the general governance practices that the students are exposed to. Based on the results of this study, students in universities in Kenya are not exposed to progressive governance cultures that inculcate in them democratic and transformative principles engendering effective participative (or stakeholder involvement in) decision-making. This was evident from students' experiences with self-governance structures as well as with the umbrella organs of decision making in their universities. This situation is a disservice to the country and, it may be concluded, does not augur very well for future quality leadership in the different sectors of the society, especially for the entrenchment of democratic ideals.

To reiterate, the study results suggested that students are not active participants in the governance processes in their universities even when they are directly represented in major decision-making organs. Rather, they are, for the most part, participant observers whose opinions are either silent or simply overlooked by top management. This was evident from the sentiments expressed by some of the respondents that students' voices and/or opinions counted for very little, if at all, with respect to major governance matters including those affecting the social welfare of students directly. We argue that, while the lack of a democratic culture is the major factor affecting the level of students' participation in governance processes in Kenyan universities, extensive apathy or the lack of student interest in involvement in governance has a role to play. The study documented the existence of high levels of apathy regarding student mobilization for governance purposes in the two institutions that were covered by this study. This was reflected through the lack of interest in governance matters among the larger student community, the poor leadership demonstrated by students' representatives, the tendency for students' representatives to serve their own selfish interests as opposed to the interests of their constituents and the tendency for management to capture and compromise student leaders. The existence of apathy among students in Kenyan universities supports the views expressed by Klemenčič (2014: 399) that despite the significant legitimate power conferred on student governments as key university stakeholders through legislation and institutional rules and the significant coercive power of students' movements, the "majority of students rarely get politically engaged in student government, even though this involves only casting a vote in student elections" (Klemenčič 2014: 399). The apathy factor tends to be compounded by the tendency for student leadership to prioritize selfish interests over the interests of the larger student community and by the co-optation (or compromising) of student leadership by management that tends to prevail in many universities.

A major factor undermining students' interests and effective participation in governance was the lack of incentives to act as motivators. The situation though appeared to be worse in the private sector. The study showed that at the USIU the only incentive directly beneficial to the individual student leader was a certificate awarded at the end of one's term of office. On the contrary, at Kenyatta University students leaders enjoyed a wide range of benefits. In addition to adequately funding KUSA activities, the university provided a KUSA vehicle, a meeting hall, monthly allowances for officials and, imprest when officials go out for trips. Once elected, student leaders are treated to a one-week training session in a three-star hotel at the coast (North Coast Hotel) and to in-between retreats, during which they are schooled on governance and leadership.

As suggested above, the study revealed that students' elections in both universities studied were infiltrated by management to ensure a captured and co-opted student leadership. In both public and private universities, management infiltration of students' elections aims to produce a pro-management line-up and, more often than not, it culminates in rigged elections and the perpetuation of injustice among students. This snowballs into justice-restoring behaviours such as student militancy, demonstrations, and/or riots, thereby undermining the peace and security necessary for a conducive learning environment. Alternatively, students, especially those in the private universities, may display apathy with regard to (lack of interest for) and commitment to student leadership. In public universities, the situation is compounded further by external interference from national political parties that desire to have a student leadership that furthers their political agenda within university campuses. The aim is to transport external interests, some of them coated with a personal/ selfish agenda, to the universities. Furthermore, political infiltration engenders control and manipulation, interference, confusion, contestation and disorganization.

Student elections, it should be underlined, are a democratic governance issue and a measure of the extent to which our universities are nurturing a democratic or participative culture. As such, any management interference with student election process through the imposition of candidates or the manipulation of outcomes is an indictment on management's commitment to the very democratization of university governance. It is our considered opinion that universities should be the champions of merit-based systems. In this regard, we consider the meddling in students' self-governance processes by university management to be both retrogressive as well as defeatist of the agenda of effective students' participation in the governance process in institutions of higher learning. Clearly, students' self-governance organs such as KUSA and SAC are the seed-beds for the entrenchment of a democratic culture among students in our universities. This being the case, management interference with the processes and activities (or functions) of such organs, e.g., by hand-picking candidates for various offices, aiding the rigging of elections, buying off (compromising) office-bearers and by intimidating (even harassing) non-conformist office holders, as was documented by this study, is tantamount to management sabotaging its very agenda of ensuring greater students' involvement in the governance process. As such, unless top management in our universities embrace a true democratic culture – a culture of real/ actual students' participation as opposed to shadow (or pseudo) involvement – the agenda of effective students' involvement in governance will remain a pipe dream. Stated differently, for students to take interest in and desire to be involved in the governance process in their universities, tokenism must be weeded out; meaning that their representatives should not only be seen to be part of the decision-making process; students should also actively contribute to shaping the agendas and debates focusing on matters affecting them and their universities at large.

Going by the USIU example, this study revealed that students' self-governance organizations in private universities lack the legal status necessary for them to gain national recognition and to embrace the trade union model in their activities like their public sector counterparts. The organizations, though anchored in negotiated constitutions, are not officially registered with the Registrar of Societies in the country; thus their operations remain confined and regulated at the level of the institution. In lieu of this, it can be concluded that private universities in Kenya have resisted actualizing students' involvement in governance as stipulated in the Universities Act No. 42 of 2012. By implication, the university is flouting the same Act it has initiated revisions of its Charter to comply with, which is rather contradictory.

One of the critical offices in universities dealing with students' welfare, including their relationship with top management is the Dean of Students Office. This office is critical to university peace and security as well as to harmonious relationships between students and top management. Despite this, the study found that such offices are not only ill equipped to deal with student challenges of today but also that deans of students are excluded from the top management organs of the two universities covered by the study. Furthermore, the office of the Dean of Students lacks the significant autonomy necessary for it to have the kind of teeth to adequately address issues affecting students. In the light of the fact that deans of students are the frontline managers of students' affairs and social welfare – they are the first port of call for students, possibly more accessible to individual students than student government representatives – these are misnomers that call for urgent rectification. This position gains more credence when viewed within the context of the student apathy toward or lack of interest in self-governance processes and activities as well as the eroded student confidence in their leadership as recorded by this study.

Based on the findings of this study, university students and, by implications, their involvement in governance processes are a macrocosm of the larger Kenyan society. Despite the fact that most universities tend to discourage tribal associations and groupings, Kenyan universities, particularly those in the public sector, are characterized by both tribalism and diminished nationalistic sentiments. The situation is compounded by the infiltration of national party politics into the universities. Kenyan political parties have mainly fermented along ethnic lines. As such, their influence on and meddling with student mobilization for governance in universities has resulted in contestations for ethnic supremacy (dominance) in university decision-making structures. It is such ethnic competitions, coupled with the failure by most university managers to listen to and treat student voices with seriousness that has been responsible for violent tendencies in (public) universities, which has also been responsible for recurring closures of Kenyan universities. Furthermore, consistent with the national psyche, corruption appears to have permeated student politics in our universities, with funding from external networks partially influencing the outcome of student elections. The situation is compounded further by the lack of transparency and fairness in such elections as management strategies aim at ensuring that a leadership of its choice takes office. In some cases this has led to manipulation, including outright rigging of student elections. The trends depicted by the study concur with the existing empirical evidence which suggests that the practice of student leadership in African universities is a mirror of the national political leadership, which in most countries is characterized by allegations of corruption, ethnic inclinations, managerial incompetence and mismanagement of recourses (Mapundo 2007).

Clearly, effective students' involvement in the governance process calls for a university leadership that is both transparent, accountable and democratic. Only this way will the leadership be integrative and representative of all stakeholders, including students. Furthermore all leaders will be able to actively drive the decision-making process and all members of the university community will come to know their roles and responsibilities and to execute them well for the attainment of the institutional goals (Brownlee n.d.). The results of this study suggest that the leadership practiced by both management and student leaders in our universities did not meet these criteria. As pointed out earlier (see Literature Review), a transformational leader is one who motivates others through a shared vision of where they want to go and what they want to achieve, shares power with others, learns from others, identifies with needs of others, responds to change quickly and is able to inspire others to also achieve and grow (see e.g., Parrish n.d; Gous 2003; Basham 2010). On the other hand, participative leadership engages everyone (all stakeholders) at the decision-making level (Diamond 2006; Obondo 2000). The leadership in students' self-governance structures and in the major organs of university decision-making did not meet these thresholds.

The study utilized the democratic theory to explain students' participation in university governance zeroing in on how key decisions are made and who makes them. The results showed that the governance of universities occurs within the ambit of liberal democracy. This is one aspect of participatory democracy, the other being direct democracy. As indicated in Chapter Three, in direct democracy stakeholders participate directly in the decision-making processes, whereas in liberal (or representative) democracy governing power is exercised by representatives elected by members through a voting system. Clearly, this study did not reveal any direct participation by the total student body in decision-making in the two universities where the study took place. This is understandable given that students constitute the mass of stakeholders in universities and any attempt to include each one of them in decision-making would render the whole process chaotic if not totally dysfunctional. In lieu of this fact, one would understand the decision by universities to lean towards liberal democratic practices in their attempts to democratize the governance process. While there is nothing wrong with the decision by universities to rely on the liberal (or representative) democratic model, it is the way this is exercised that makes it ineffective as well as it denies the institutions the opportunity to nurture a truly democratic culture that has been the goal of the democratization of university governance.

As evident from the results of this study, the practice of liberal democracy in universities in Kenya denies students the co-decision rights essential for a truly democratic culture to prevail. Through this study it became evident that the top administrations of universities are not committed to true democratization of decision-making. Rather than nurture equal partnership among all stakeholders, including students, they continue to rely on some form of pseudo representation of students in which the latter are excluded from some of the top organs of decision-making and only feature in lower levels of decision-making. Even when allowed to be involved, the evidence suggests that their voices are not taken seriously. Furthermore, it was found that management has continued to meddle in the governance activities of students including students' self-governance bodies. This takes many forms such as the manipulation of student elections and in some extreme cases the rigging of the same, the compromising of student leaders and, the intimidation of those who desire to stand firm. All these are detrimental to the permeation of a democratic culture in university governance.

Conclusions

Based on the findings of this study and guided by its very objectives, a number of conclusions can be drawn. First, overall, universities in Kenya recognize, both in principle and practice, the importance of students' involvement in governance processes. In this regard, policies, structures and support systems exist for the enhancement of students' involvement in governance of both public and private universities. Second, the nature and level of involvement of students in the governance processes in universities in Kenya varies by category of university, whether public or private. The variations occur in terms of institutional policies and practices, level of students' involvement in various governance structures (including the level at which students are allowed direct representation), the nature of the representation (whether direct or indirect), the support systems that are in place to act as motivators to students, student perceptions of those support systems, and the effect of support systems on students' involvement.

A third conclusion emanating from the results of this study is that students are practically excluded from high-level organs of decision-making in universities in Kenya. In many cases they are not directly represented in such organs, and where direct representation takes place, the voices of student leaders are dimmed by top administrators. This relegates students' involvement in decision-making to lower levels of decision-making such as the school/faculty and departmental/ programme levels. Closely related to this is the conclusion that students' participation in university governance and in the making of key decisions that affect their academic and social welfare mainly occurs through students' self-governance councils/ unions as well as through students' participation in different committees (e.g. university-wide, school/ faculty and programme/departmental committees).

However, there are other avenues such as clubs, associations and societies that may also present them with opportunities to influence the governance process.

The fifth conclusion emanating from the results of this study is that despite attempts by universities to involve students in governance, Vice Chancellor, Deputy Vice Chancellors, Deans, University Councils and University Senate remain the dominant players in the governance of institutions of higher learning in Kenya. Although students constitute the majority stakeholders in universities and despite the fact that both students and university administrators recognize the need for students' participation in self-governance and in the overall university governance structures, yet students continue to be alienated from the making of the bulk of the decisions that affect them and the functioning of their universities. While policies on inclusivity (participatory democracy) exist in many universities, the practice at the level of breach exceeds its observance.

Based on the findings of this study, it may also be concluded that students value their overall involvement in governance of their universities, including involvement in the various structures of governance and in the making of specific decisions that affect their academic and social welfare. In this regard, students have a good understanding of the positive and negative consequences of their integration into the governance process through their leadership/ elected representatives. They are also aware of the major impediments standing in the way of effective students' participation in the governance of universities. Another conclusion that derives from the results of this study is that there exists general mistrust of management and student leaders by the general student body in both the public and the private universities. Concerning the latter, the mistrust emanates from the belief among the larger student community that leaders are mainly serving their own interests as opposed to the interests of their constituents. This tends to undermine the confidence students have in their leaders; it also casts doubts about the credibility and effectiveness of students' participation in governance processes.

The eighth conclusion that can be drawn by this study is that student's participation in self-governance and in the governance of the university as a whole is not immune from the influence of national politics and political parties. If anything, universities in Kenya, more so those in the public sector, provide political parties with another arena for political contestation. Finally, on based the results of this study, particularly those focusing on the behaviours and actions of top university management, it may be concluded that top university management is not interested in the real and active students' participation in governance. What they are looking for is a captured/ co-opted/ domesticated student leadership whose involvement in governance is mainly tokenistic but gives the institution an image of political correctness. As a result, our universities are dotted with what for the lack of a better term, one may classify as "management-controlled participation" of students in the governance process.

Recommendations

Based on the findings of this study, a number of recommendations are offered by way of growing and entrenching a truly democratic culture in the governance of Kenyan universities in general and in the involvement of students in particular. These include the following:

1. A paradigm shift must occur in our universities, both public and private, concerning the handling of students' involvement in the governance process. In particular, well calculated and deliberate steps must be taken to end the cultures of tokenism and political correctness that currently pervade our universities' handling of students' involvement in the governance process. For this to be judged to have taken root, management must elevate students, through their representatives, to the status of equal partners in the decision making processes. Only in this way will universities stem the apathy, lack of interest and the all too visible malaise characterizing both members of the student leadership and the larger student body in universities today with respect to participation in governance.

2. Universities, both public and private, must evolve specific strategies for the nurturing and entrenching of a democratic and participative culture among students as well as among all cadre of management staff. This should entail the development of well-structured courses focusing on the development of leadership skills among students to complement the current practices of teaching leadership skills to student leaders through induction retreats and experiences through extra-curricular involvements. These should form part of the common courses and the general education courses offered by public and private universities respectively and should be compulsory for (or required of) all students, regardless of their major. The courses should teach students leadership skills; enlighten them about the importance of leadership attributes such as transparency, accountability, integrity, participation and teamwork, among others; whilst enhancing the students' understanding regarding their leadership identity, ability, and willingness to lead. This will, certainly improve both student participation in the governance processes of universities and the quality of the leadership offered by those bequeathed the mantle to represent the student body in varied capacities of leadership. Further importance of the courses lies in the fact that higher education is expected to educate individuals so they can become leaders in their chosen profession and in society. The leadership courses should, therefore, supplement rather than replace the leadership retreats that the universities conduct for newly-elected members of students' self-governance bodies, which in the eyes of many students have been turned into a form of reward for accepting to be a student leader as opposed to being opportunities for sharpening leadership skills.

3. In the light of students' apathy towards involvement in governance, there is a need to review university policies on this subject matter to ensure that they truly actualize and nurture student participation in various levels of decision-making. This must be done in such a way that students are guaranteed that their voices count with respect to the making of major decisions affecting the running and operations of universities, as opposed to being participant observers as is currently the case.

4. To change the negative attitude students have toward involvement in university governance, universities should institutionalize teaching faculty, by way of encouraging faculty to discuss governance imperatives, including the advantages of effective students' representation, during their interactions with students in class. Similarly, the universities should impress on faculty who patron clubs to use the clubs as avenues for spreading the governance gospel to students. The mentoring of student leadership should also be encouraged at the lower levels of management especially at the departmental and faculty/ school levels. In this regard, deans, heads of department, and chairs of lower-level committees should be encouraged to accord student representation greater voices in decision-making.

5. An appropriate curriculum dedicated to inducting students into leadership roles should be developed and implemented in all universities, both public and private. All students who desire to join students' self-governance structures and/ or to represent fellow students in overall university governance structures should be required to have successfully completed that curriculum. The curriculum should not only teach leadership skills but also impart other important virtues of governance such as transparency, core values and ethics.

6. It is important to create incentives to motivate students to get involved in governance in universities. Given that both public and private universities in Kenya offer common courses and/ or general education courses, one way to reward those who participate in leadership is to create a leadership course at that level whose requirements can also be met through involvement in student leadership. Institutions, especially those in the private sector, should also consider introducing a monetary package and other non-monetary rewards to motivate interest in leadership positions among students.

7. Where it is absolutely necessary for universities to make decisions without involving students or their representatives, this should be done guided by adequate scientific evidence or data collected from students focusing on their needs, desires, likes and dislikes. Only in this way will the situation in question be addressed effectively, and will the propensity for violent conflict between management and students be averted.

8. Closely related to the above, where proxy representation must be used, it requires the development of structures and systems for holding the proxy representatives accountable. Such structures and systems did not exist in any of the two universities studied.
9. To guarantee effective students' involvement and the involvement of all other stakeholders in governance processes in our universities, the leadership of students' self-governance structures as well as those who sit in the top organs of decision-making bodies embrace a transformative as well as a truly participative form of leadership. This calls for active training and skilling in the two forms of leadership. In this regard, universities should be required to develop guiding manuals as well as provide the necessary training that would equip the leadership at all levels with the necessary competences to combine and practice the two forms of leadership effectively.
10. Finally, consistent with Obondo (2000), this study recommends that university management speeds up the widening of the representation and the active participation of students (and staff) in governing bodies, and strengthens student (and staff) associations if it wishes to strengthen democratization of university governance. This will in turn increase their propensity to identify with outcomes of the governance processes in these institutions and reduce the incidences of student and/or staff conflict with management.

References

Aina, T., 2010, 'Beyond Reforms: The Politics of Higher Education Transformation in Africa', *African Studies Review*,Vol. 53, No. 1 (April 2010), pp. 21-40.

Akinwumi, F. S., 2010, 'Proliferation of Higher Education in Nigeria: Implications for Quality Education', *Kenya Journal of Education Planning Economic Management*, Vol. 2, pp 45-51.

Altbach, P. G., 2006, 'Student Politics: Activism and Culture', *International Handbook of Higher Education*, J.J.F. Forest and P.G. Altbach, 329–45. Dordrecht, Springer

Altbach, P. G., 1992, 'Student Movements and Associations', *The Encyclopaedia of Higher Education*, B. Clark and G. Neave, eds, pp1740–49, Oxford, Pergamon.

Altbach, P. G., 1991, 'Student Political Activism', *International Higher Education: An Encyclopedia*, Altbach. P. G., ed., pp 247–60. New York, Garland.

Anderson, D. and Johnson, R., 2006, 'Ideas of Leadership underpinning Proposals to the Carrick Institute: A Review of Proposals from the "Leadership for Excellence in Teaching and Learning Program"', Carrick Institute Leadership Forum, Sydney, Australia

Anyang' Nyong'O, P., 1989, 'State and Society in Kenya: The Disintegration of the Nationalist Coalitions and the Rise of Presidential Authoritarianism, 1963–1978', *African Affairs* 88 (35) pp. 229–51.

Appiagyei-Atual, K., 2015, 'Time for an African Charter on Academic Freedom' (http://www.universityworldnews.com/article.php?story=20150717165536327). August 22, 2016.

Argyris, C. and Schon, D., 1978, *Organizational Learning: A Theory of Action Perspective*. New York: McGraw-Hill.

Assie-Lumumba, N'Dri T., 2006, *Higher Education in Africa: Crises, Reforms and Transformation*, Working Papers Series, Dakar: CODESRIA.

Astin, A.W., 1997, 'Liberal Education and Democracy: The Case for Pragmatism', in Orill, R. ed., *Education and Democracy: Re-imagining Liberal Learning in America*, New York: College Entrance Examination Board, pp. 207-223.

Astin, A. W. and Astin, H., 2000, *Leadership Reconsidered: Engaging Higher Education in Social Change*, Kellogg Foundation.

Azikiwe, A., 2016, *Three South African Universities Closed Due to Student Unrest*. (http://www.globalresearch.ca/three-south-african-universities-closed-due-to-student-unrest-anc-charges-regime-change-strategy-implicating-us/5511168). July 28,2016.

Badat, M. S., 1999, *Black Student Politics, Higher Education and Apartheid: From SASO to SANSCO, 1968-1990*, Pretoria: Human Sciences Research Council.

Bailey, T., Cloete, N., and Pillay, P., 2013, *Universities and Economic Development in Africa – Case Study: Kenya and University of Nairobi*, Wynberg: The Centre for Higher Education Transformation (CHET).

Baker, J., 1997, *What is Participatory Democracy?* London: Community Workers Cooperative.

Barr, J. Y. and Duke, K., 2004, 'What Do We Know About Teacher Leadership? Findings from the Two Decades of Scholarship', *Review of Educational Research*, 74 (3), pp. 225-316.

Basham, L. M., 2010, 'Transformational and transactional leaders in higher education', *International Review of Business Research Papers*, 6 (6), pp. 141-152.

Bloom, D. and Ahmad, K., 2000, *Higher Education in Developing Countries: Peril and Promise*, Washington DC: The World Bank.

Bloom, D., Canning, D. and Chan, K., 2006, *Higher Education and Economic Development in Africa*, Washington DC: The World Bank.

Boahen, A., 1994,'The Role of African Student Movements in the Political and Social Evolution of Africa from 1900 to 1975', in *UNESCO General History of Africa* ,Vol. 2, Paris, UNESCO Publishing.

Boit, J. M. and Kipkoech, L. C., 2012, 'Liberalization of Higher Education in Kenya: Challenges and Prospects', *International Journal of Academic Research in Progressive Educationand Development*, 1(2), pp. 33-41

Bolden, R., Petrov, G. and Gosling, J., 2008, 'Developing Collective Leadership in Higher Education', in H. Goreham, ed., *Research and Development Series*, London Leadership Foundation for Higher Education.

Bollen, K., 1993, 'Liberal Democracy: Validity and Method Factors in Cross-National Measures', *American Journal of Political Science*, Vol. 37: 1207-1230.

Bollen, K., 1990, 'Political Democracy: Conceptual and Measurement Traps', *Studies in Comparative International Development*, vol. 25, pp. 7-24.

Bolman, L. and Deal, T., 1995, *Leading with Soul*, San Francisco, CA: Jossey-Bass.

Brookes, S., 2006, 'Out with the Old, In with the New: Why Excellent Public Leadership Makes a Difference to Partnership Working', *The British Journal of Leadership in Public Services*, Vol. 2 (1), pp. 52–64.

Brownlee, P. P., n.d, 'Effecting Transformational Institutional Change', (http://www.thenationalacademy.org/readings/effecting.html) March 20, 2015.

Brungardt, C. L., n.d., *The New Face of Leadership: Implications For Higher Education*, (http://www.nwlink.com/~donclark/leader/lead_edu.html

Bryman, A., 2007, 'Effective Leadership in Higher Education', *Research and Development Series*, 1-38, London: Leadership Foundation for Higher Education.

Carnoy, M., Castells, M., Cohen, S. S. and Cardoso, F. H., 1993, *The New Global Economy in the Information Age: Reflections on our Changing World*, University Park: Pennsylvania State University Press.

Castells, M., 1991, *The University System: Engine of Development in the New World Economy*, Washington DC: The World Bank.

Chacha, N. C., 2004, 'Reforming Higher Education in Kenya: Challenges, Lessons and Opportunities', Paper presented at the State University of New York workshop with the Parliamentary Committee on Education, Science and Technology held at Naivasha, Kenya, August 2004.

Chege, M., 2009, 'Post-Moi era Discourse Patterns in Kenyan Universities: A Nation crying for Organic Intellectuals', *Kenya Studies Review*: 1 (1), pp. 31-53.

Cheng, Y. C. and Tam, W. M., 1997,'Multi-models of quality in education', *Quality Assurance in Education*, 5(1), pp 22-31 (http://dx.doi.org/10.1108/09684889710156558).

Cloete, N., Bailey, T., Pillay, P. Bunting, I. and Maassen, P., 2011, *Universities and Economic Development in Africa*, Wynberg: The Centre for Higher Education Transformation (CHET).

Coleman, A., 2006, *Lessons from Extended Schools*, Nottingham: NCSL.

Commission for University Education, n.d.(a), *University Education in Kenya; A Brief History,* (http://www.cue.or.ke/old/history.html) August 1, 2016.

Commission for University Education, n.d. (b), *Standards and Guidelines for University Academic Programmes,* (http://www.cue.or.ke/) August 12, 2016.

Commission for University Education, 2014, *Universities Authorized to Operate in Kenya*, (http://www.education.go.ke/home/images/cppmu/) September 6, 2015.

Commission for University Education, 2016, *The Status of Universities (Universities Authorized to Operate in Kenya*, (http://www.cue.or.ke/) August 2, 2016.

Craig, J., 2005, *Taking the Wide View: the New Leadership of Extended Schools*, London: Demos.

Cress, C.M., Astin, H.S., Zimmerman, B., Oster, K. and Burkhardt, J. C., 2001, 'Developmental Outcomes of College Students' Involvement in Leadership Activities', *Journal of College Student Development,* 1, pp.15–29.

Dahl, R.A., 2006, *Preface to Democratic Theory*, Chicago: The University of Chicago Press.

Damtew, T. and Altbach, P.G., 2004, 'African Higher Education: Challenges for the 21st Century', *Higher Education*, vol 47, pp. 21-50.

Davis, J., 2003, *Learning to Lead*, Westport, CT.: American Council of Education/Praeger.

Day, M., 2012, 'Dubious Causes of No Interest to Students?: The Development of National Union of Students in the United Kingdom', *European Journal of Higher Education*, vol 2 (1), pp. 32-46.

Department for Education and Skills, 2006, *Championing Children: A Shared Set of Skills, Knowledge and Behaviors for Those Leading and Managing Integrated Children's Services. Non-Statutory Guidance*, London: Department for Education and Skills.

De Tocqueville, A., 2003, *Democracy in America*, New York: Penguin Classics (First published 1835).

Dobbins, M., Knill, C., & Vogtle, M. E., 2011, 'An analytical framework for the cross-country comparison of higher education governance', *The International Journal of higher education research, 62* (5): 665-683.

Duderstadt, J. J., 2002, *The Future of Higher Education in the Knowledge-driven Global Economy of the 21st Century,* Paper presented during the 175th Anniversary Symposium of the University of Toronto, Toronto: Canada.

EDULINK, n.d., 'CCAU – Catalyzing Change in African Universities', (http://www.acp-edulink.eu/content/ccau-catalysing-change-african-universities), November 19, 2011.

Effah, P., 2003, 'Ghana', in D. Teferra, and P.G. Altbach, eds, *African Higher Education: An International Reference Handbook*, Bloomington: Indiana University Press, pp. 563-573.

Eisemon, T. O., 1992, 'Private Initiatives in Higher Education in Kenya', *Higher Education*, vol. 24, pp.157-175.

Eurydice, *Higher Education Governance in Europe.Policies, Structures, Funding and AcademicStaff.* Brussels: Eurydice, 2008

Fearn, H., 2011, *Plagiarism Software Can Be Beaten by Simple Tech Tricks,* (https://www.timeshighereducation.com/news/plagiarism-software-can-be-beaten-by-simple-tech-tricks/414881.article), August 16, 2016.

Fieden, J., 2008, *Global Trends in University Education*, Education Working Paper Series No 9, World Bank.

Freeman, J. P. and Goldin, A., 2008, 'The increasing importance of student leadership development programs in higher education', *NASPA net results.*

Fung, A., 2007, 'Democratic Theory and Political Science: A Pragmatic Method of Constructive Engagement', *American Political Science Review*, Vol. 101 (3): 443-458.

Gardiner, L. F., 2005, 'Transforming the enviroment for learning :A crisis of quality', in S. C. Blossey, ed., *To Improve the Academy:Resources for Faculty, Instructional and Organizational Development*, Bolton, MA: Anker Publishing Company, pp. 3-15.

Gibbs, G. Knapper, C. and Picinnin, S., 2009, 'Departmental Leadership for Quality Teaching in Research-Intensive Environments, *Research and Development Series*, London Leadership Foundation for Higher Education.

Gibbs, G., Knapper, C. and Picinnin, S., 2006, 'Departmental Leadership for Quality Teaching - An International Comparative Study of Effective Practice', (http://www.lfhe.ac.uk/research/projects/ggexcel.doc/) November 18, 2011.

Gogo, J. O., 2010, 'The Development of University Education in Kenya: The Problem of Human Resource in Private Universities', A paper presented at EMSK conference at Kabarak University, Kenya on 26th to 28th August 2010 on the theme: Resources for Quality Education Development in Kenya.

Goleman, A., 2000, 'Leadership that Gets Results', *Harvard Business Review*, 78 (2), 78-90.

Goleman, D., 2000, 'Intelligent Leadership/, *Executive excellence*, 17 (4), 17.

Gous, M., 2003, 'Leadership in support of learning for the unknown future', Paper presented at the HERTSDA 2003 conference. (http://surveys.cantebury.ac.nz/herdsa03/pdfsnon/N1071.pdf). March 26, 2005.

Government of Kenya, 2011, *University Bill 2011*, Government Printers.

Government of Kenya, 1981, *Second University: Report of Presidential Working Party (Mackey Report)*. Nairobi: Government Printer.

Granam, A. and Stella, A., 1999, 'Emerging Trends in Higher Education and their Application for the Future', *Journal of Education Planning and Administration*, Vol.13 No.2.

Gudo, C. O., Olel, M. A. and Oanda, I. O., 2011, 'University Expansion in Kenya and Issues of Quality Education: Challenges and Opportunities', *International Journal of Business and Social Science,* Vol. 2, No. 20, pp. 203-214.

Harker, R. M., Dobel-Ober, D., Berridge, D. and Sinclair, R., 2004, 'More than the Sum of Its parts? Inter-professional Working groupe in the Education of Looked after Children', *Children and Society*, Vol. 18 (3), pp. 179–193.

Harvey, L. and Green, D., 1993, 'Defining quality', *Assessment and Evaluation in Higher Education* vol. 18(1), pp .1-35.

Healey, J. and Robinson, M., 1994, *Democracy, Governance and Economic Policy: Sub-Saharan Africa in Comparative Perspective*, London: Overseas Development Institute.

Heather, J. A., 2010, 'Turnitoff: Identifying and Fixing a Hole in Current Plagiarism Detection Software', *Journal of Assessment and Evaluation in Higher Education*, 35 (6), pp. 647-660.

Her Majesty's Government, 2005, 'Statutory Guidance on Inter-Agency Co-Operation to Improve the Wellbeing of Children: Children's Trusts', London: Department for

Education and Skills. (http://publications.teachernet.gov.uk/eOrdering) August 19, 2016.

Holm, J. D., 2010, 'When Family Ties Bind African Universities', Commentary Published in *The Chronicle for Higher Education*, August 2010.

ICEF Monitor, 2016, 'Kenyan students staying home in greater numbers but quality concerns persist', (http://monitor.icef.com/2016/02/kenyan-students-staying-home-in-greater-numbers-but-quality-concerns-persist/) August 4, 2016.

ICEF Monitor, 2015, *Governments and Educators in Kenya Struggling to Keep Pace with Demand for Higher Education*, (http://monitor.icef.com/2015/06/governments-and-educators-in-kenya-struggling-to-keep-pace-with-demand-for-higher-education/) August 2, 2016.

Institute on Governance, 2016, *Defining Governance*, (http://iog.ca/defining-governance/) August 18, 2016.

Jick, T. D., 1979, 'Mixing Qualitative and Quantitative Methods: Triangulation in Action', *Administrative Science Quarterly*, vol. 24, pp. 602-611.

Johnson, R., 2002, 'Learning to manage the university: tales of training and experience', *Higher Education Quarterly*, vol. 56, pp. 33-51.

Johnson, R.N., and Deem, R., 2003, 'Talking of Students: Tensions and Contradictions for the Manager-academic and the University in Contemporary Higher Education', *Higher Education*, vol. 46, pp. 289–314.

Johnson, R. B., Onwuegbuzie, A. J. and Turner, L. A., 2007, 'Towards a Definition of Mixed Methods Research', *Journal of Mixed Methods Research*, Vol. 1, Number 2, pp. 112-133.

Johnstone, B. D.; Arora, A. and Experton, W., 1998, 'The Financing and Management of Higher Education: A Status Report on Worldwide Reforms', paper supported by the World Bank, Presented at the UNESCO World Conference on Higher Education in Paris, France, October 5-9, 1998. (http://www.worldbank.org/html/extdr/educ/postbasc.htm) August 1, 2016.

Jones, A., 2011, Faculty Involvement in Institutional Governance: A Literature Review, *Journal of Professoriate*, vol. 6 (1), pp. 117-135.

Jowi, J., 2003, 'Governing Higher Education in the Stakeholder Society: Rethinking the Role of the State in Kenya's Higher Education', paper presented at the CHEPS Summer School, June 29 – July 4, 2003, University of Maribor, Slovenia.

Kaburu, J. and Embeywa, E. H., 2014, 'An Evaluation of Quality of University Education in Kenya during this Massification Era', *Mediterranean Journal of Social Sciences*, Vol. 5 No 5, pp. 345-349.

Kalai, J. M., 2010, 'Expansion of University Education in Kenya: Reflections on the Twin Challenge of Balancing Access and Quality' a paper presented at EMSK Conference at Migori Teacher's College Kenya on 12th to 14th April 2010 on the theme "Providing Quality Secondary Education in Kenya".

Kamara, A. and Nyende, L., 2007, 'Growing a Knowledge-Based Economy: Public Expenditure on Education in Africa', *Economic Research Working Paper*, No. 88. Tunisia: African Development Bank.

Kamuzora, F. and Mgaya, Y., n. d., 'Students Own Governance and Leadership Development in Democratisation of Universities: Case Studies of University of Dar es Salaam and Mzumbe University'.

Kauffeldt, J. K., 2009, 'The Commission for Higher Education in Kenya: A Case Study Regarding The Establishment, Role and Operations of an Intermediary Body in the Higher Education System of a Developing Nation', an unpublished Thesis submitted in conformity with the requirements for the Degree Doctor of Education, Ontario Institute for Studies in Education (Theory and Policy Studies), University of Toronto, Canada

Kaufmann, D., Kraay, A. and Zoido-Lobaton, P., 1999, *Governance Matters,* Policy Research Working Paper 2196, October, Washington: The World Bank.

Kelly, M. J., 2001, *Challenging the Challenger: Understanding and Expanding the Response of Universities in Africa to HIV/AIDS*, Lusaka, Zambia: University of Zambia.

Kendall, S., Lamont, E., Wilkin, A. and Kinder, K., 2007, *Every Child Matters: How School Leaders in Extended Schools Respond to Local Needs*, Nottingham: NCSL. (http://www.ncsl.org.uk/media/AFB/86/ECM-how-school-leaders-respond) August 14,

Kenya National Bureau of Statistics, 2014, *Economic Survey 2014,* Nairobi: Government Printers.

Kenyatta University, 2014, 'The Constitution of Kenyatta University Student Association (KUSA*)*', Nairobi: Kenyatta University.

Kiboiy, K. L., 2013, 'The Dynamics of Student Unrests in Kenya's Public Higher Education: The Case of Moi University', an unpublished thesis presented as Partial Fulfillment of the Requirements for the Degree of Doctor of Philosophy in Education Management and Policy, University of Cape Town, Cape Town, South Africa.

Kihara, J., 2005, 'New Departure in Provision of Higher Education', *University Journal,* a publication of the *Daily Nation* Newspaper, July 28th 3, Nairobi: Nation Media Group.

Kinuthia, W., 2009, 'Educational Development in Kenya and the Role of Information and Communication Technology', *International Journal of Education and Development Using ICT*, Vol. 5, No. 2. (http://ijedict.dec.uwi.edu/viewarticle.php?id=740&layout=html). July 28, 2016.

Klemenčič, M., 2014, 'Student Power in a Global Perspective and Contemporary Trends in Student Organizing', *Studies in Higher Education*, Vol. 39, Issue. No 3, pp. 396-411.

Klemenčič, M. 2012a. "Student Representation in Western Europe: Introduction to the Special Issue." *European Journal of Higher Education* vol. 2 (1), pp. 2–19.

Klemenčič, M., 2012b, 'The Changing Conceptions of Student Participation in HE Governance in the EHEA', *European Higher Education at the Crossroads: Between the Bologna Process and National Reforms*, Adrian Curaj, Peter Scott, Lazăr Vlasceanu and Lesley Wilson, eds, pp. 631–53, Heidelberg: Springer.

Kouzes, J. and Posner, B., 2002, *The leadership challenge,* 3rd ed., San Fransisco: Jossey-Bass.

Kouzes, J. and Posner, B., 1995, *The Leadership Challenge: How to Keep Getting Extraordinary Things Done in Organizations*, San Francisco, CA: Jossey-Bass.

Kuh, G. D., 1994, *Student Learning Outside the Classroom: Transcending Artificial Boundaries,* Washington, DC: Office of Educational Research and Improvement.

Kuh, G. D. and Lund, J. P., 1994, 'What Students Gain from Participating in Student Government', *New Directions for Student Services* vol. 66, pp. 5–17.

Kulati, T., 2000, 'Governance, Leadership and Institutional Change in South African Higher Education: Grappling with Instability', *Tertiary Education and Management,* vol. 6, pp. 177–92.

Layfield, D. K., Radhakrishna, R. B., University, C., Andreasan, R. J., & University, S. M., n.d., Self-perceived leadership skills of students in a leadership programs in Agricultural course. 62-68.

Lee, H., 1987, 'The Nature and Scope of Student Participation in Policy-Making in Academic Government', Proceedings of the 6th International Seminar on Current Issues in University Education of Korea and Japan, Seoul, Korea: Korean Council for University Education.

Lizzio, A. and Wilson, K., 2009, 'Student Participation in University Governance: The Role Conceptions and Sense of Efficacy of Student Representatives on Departmental Committees', *Studies in Higher Education*, vol. 34 (1), pp. 69-84.

Lodge, C., 2005, 'From Hearing Voices to Engaging in Dialogue: Problematizing Student Participation in School Improvement', *Journal of Educational Change*, vol 6, pp 125–46.

Lord, P., Martin, K. and Atkinson, M., 2009, *Narrowing the Gap in outcomes: What is the relationship between leadership and governance?* Slough: NFER.

Lownsborough, H. and O'Leary, D., 2005, *The Leadership Imperative: Reforming Children's Services from the Ground Up*, London: Demos.

Luescher-Mamashela, T.M., 2013, 'Student Representation in University Decision Making: Good Reasons, a New Lens?', *Studies in Higher Education*, vol. 38 (10), pp. 1442–56.

Luescher-Mamashela, T. M., 2005, *Student Governance in Africa: Thematic Summary of Key Literature, prepared for the Center for Higher Education Transformation*, Wynberg (South Africa): Centre for Higher Education Transformation (CHET).

Luescher-Mamashela, T. and Mugume, T., 2014, 'Student Representation and Multiparty Politics in African Higher Education', *Studies in Higher Education*, vol. 39 (3), pp. 500-515.

Luescher-Mamashela, T. M., Kiiru, S., Mattes, R., Mwollo-Ntallima, A. M. Ng'ethe, N.and Romo, M., 2011, *The University in Africa and Democratic Citizenship: Hothouse or Training Ground? Report on Student Surveys conducted at the University of Nairobi, Kenya, the University of Cape Town, South Africa, and the University of Dar es Salaam, Tanzania*, Wynberg (South Africa): Centre for Higher education Transformation (CHET).

MacGregor, K., 2009, 'Africa: Call for Higher Education Support Fund', *University World News*, (http://www.universityworldnews.com/article.php?story=20090322082237425), 22 July 2009.

Mäkelä, M. M. and Maula, M. V., 2008, 'Attracting Cross-Border Venture Capital: The Role of a Local Investor', *Entrepreneurship and Regional Development, vol. 20* (3), pp. 237-257.

Mamdani, M., 2007, *Scholars in the Marketplace: The Dilemmas of Neo-Liberal Reform at Makerere University, 1989–2005*, Kampala: Fountain Publishers.

Manyasi, B., 2010, 'OL & DE as a Means of Increasing Access to Higher Learning in Kenya', *Journal of the KIM School of Management*, Vol. 1, pp. 123 – 130.

Martin, K., Lord, P., White, R., Mitchell, H. and Atkinson, M., 2009, *Narrowing the Gap in outcomes: Leadership*, Slough: NFER.

Martin, E., Trigwell, K., Prosser, M. and Ramsden, P., 2003, 'Variation in the Experience of Leadership of Teaching in Higher Education', *Studies in Higher Education*, 28 (3), pp. 247-259.

Maseko, S. S., 1994, 'Student Power, Action and Problems: A Case Study of UWC SRC, 1981-1992', *Transformation*, 24, pp. 70-90.

Maxwell, J., 2005, *Developing the Leader Within You*, Nashville, TN: Nelson Business.

May, W. P., 2009, 'Student Governance: A Qualitative Study of Leadership in a Student Government Association', *Educational Policy Studies Dissertations,* Paper 36.

Menon, M. E., 2005, 'Students' Views Regarding their Participation in University Governance: Implications for Distributed Leadership in Higher Education', *Tertiary Education and Management*, 11, pp. 167-182.

Merriam-Webster, 1986, *Webster's Third New International Dictionary*, Merriam-Webster, Inc.

Middlehurst, R. Goreham, H. and Woodfield, S., 2009, 'Why Research Leadership in Higher Education? Exploring Contributions from the UK's Leadership Foundation for Higher Education', *Leadership*, 5 (30), pp. 311 – 329.

Ministry of Education (MoE), 2012, *Towards a Globally Competitive Quality Education for Sustainable Development*, Nairobi: Government Printers.

Mohamedbhai, G., 2016, 'Student Unrest on African Campuses', *The World View: A blog from the Center for International Higher Education*, July 18, 2016, (https://www.insidehighered.com/blogs/the_world_view/student_unrest_on_African_campuses). July 28, 2016.

Mosha, H. J., 1986, 'The Role of African Universities in National Developments: A Critical Analysis', *Higher Education*. 15 (1), pp. 113-134.

Munene, I., 2016, 'Kenya's universities are in the grip of a quality crisis', *The Conversation: Africa Pilot*, (http://theconversation.com/kenyas-universities-are-in-the-grip-of-a-quality-crisis-54664) July 28, 2016.

Munene, I., 2003, 'Student Activism in African Higher Education', in D. Teferra and P.G. Altbach, eds, *African Higher Education: An International Reference Handbook*. Bloomington IN: Indiana University Press.

Musisi, N. B. and Muwanga, N., 2003, *Makerere University in Transition, 1993-2000: Opportunities and Challenges*, Oxford: James Currey; Kampala: Fountain Publishers.

Mutula, S., 2002, 'University Education in Kenya: Current Developments and Future Outlook', *The International Journal of Education Management*, 16 (3), pp. 109-119

Mwebi, B. and Simatwa, E. M. W., 2013, 'Expansion of Private Universities in Kenya and Its Implication on Quality and Completion Rate: An Analytical Study', *Educational Research*, Vol. 4 (4), pp. 352-366.

Mwindi, B., 2009, 'Ethnic Political Bus Hits Varsity Polls', *Daily Nation*, May 22, 2009.

Mwiria, K., 1992, "*University Governance: Problems and Perspectives in Anglophone Africa*". *AFTED Technical Note, No. 3*, Washington, D.C.: The World Bank.

Mwiria, K., Ngethe, N., Ngome, C., Ouma-Odero, D, Wawire, V. and Wesonga, D., 2007, *Public and Private Universities in Kenya: New Challenges, Issues and Achievements*, Nairobi: East African Publishers.

Mwiria, K. and Nyukuri, M. S., 1994, *The Management of Double Intakes: A case of Kenyatta University*, Paris. UNESCO: International Institute for Educational Planning.

National College for School Leadership, 2008a, *ECM Premium Project: School Leadership, Every Child Matters and School Standards. Identifying Links between ECM and Improvements in School Standards*, Nottingham: National College for School Leadership. (http://www.ncsl.org.uk/ecm-premium-project summary.pdf). August 15, 2016.

National College for School Leadership, 2008b, *What We Are Learning About: Leadership of Every Child Matters (Report Summary)*, Nottingham: National College for School Leadership. (http://www.ncsl.org.uk/what-we-are-learning about.pdf). August 16, 2016.

Ndegwa, S., 2008, *Kenya: Private University Growth of Mixed Blessing*, (http://www.universityworldnews.com/article.php².story.). August 16, 2016.

Nganga, G., 2014, 'Student Numbers soar by 35%, University Funding Lags', *University World news: Global Window on Higher Education*, Issue No: 319, 09 May 2014. (http://www.universityworldnews.com/article.php?story=20140508075050866). August 1, 2016

Nganga, G., 2010, 'Kenya: Universities to Admit Extra Students', *University World News*. (http://www.universityworldnews.com/article.php?story=20100829095640755). August 2, 2016.

Ngolovoi, M., 2006, 'Means Testing of Student Loans in Kenya', paper presented at the Comparative and International Higher Education Policy: Issues and Analysis Workshop: University at Albany.

Ngome, C., 2003, 'Kenya', in D. Teferra, and P.G. Altbach (eds.) *African Higher Education: An International Reference Handbook*. Bloomington: Indiana University Press, pp. 359 - 371

Nyaigotti-Chacha, C., 2004, 'Reforming Higher Education in Kenya: Challenges, Lessons, and Opportunities', Paper presented at the State University of New York Workshop, Naivasha, Kenya in August 2004.

Nyangau, J. Z., 2014, 'Higher Education as an Instrument of Economic Growth in Kenya', *FIRE: Forum for International Research in Education, 1*(1). (http://preserve.lehigh.edu/fire/vol1/iss1/3). August 2, 2016.

Oanda, I, Chege, F and Wesonga, D., 2008, *Privatisation and Apprivate Higher Education in Kenya:Implications for Access, Equity and Knowledge Production*, Dakar: CODESRIA.

Obondo, A.T., 2000, 'Politics of Participatory Decision-Making: The Case of Kenyatta University and the University of Nairobi', *French Institute for Research in Africa "Les Cahiers,* Review no 19, November-December.

Obonyo, M., 2013, 'The Contributions of Affirmative Action Policies and Interventions on access of Students from Arid and Semi-arid Areas in Kenya', unpublished PhD Thesis, Kenyatta University, Nairobi, Kenya.

Odebero, O. S., 2010, 'Crisis in Financing and Management of Kenyan Higher Education: Implications for Planning Reform Agenda', paper presented at EMSK Workshop, held at Migori Teachers College on 12th to 14th April, 2010.

Odhiambo, G., O., 2011, 'Higher Education Quality in Kenya: A Critical Reflection of Key Challenges', *Quality in Higher Education*, vol. 17(3), pp. 299-315

OECD., 2003, *The Changing Patterns of Governance in Higher Education: Education Policy Analysis*, OECD.

Ogot, B. O., 2002, 'The Enterprise University: Real or Pseudo?', paper presented at the Seminar on the Occasion of the First Exhibition by Kenya Universities, May, 23-25, 2002, Nairobi, Kenya.

Oketch, M. O., 2003, 'The Growth of Private Education in Kenya: The Promise and Challenge' *Peabody Journal of Education*, 78 (2), pp. 18-40.

Okioga, C. K., Onsongo, E. N., and Nyaboga, Y.B., 2014, 'Quality Issues in the Expansion of University Education in Kenya, the Human Resource Challenges and Opportunities', *Chinese Business Review*, Vol. 11, No. 6, pp. 596-605.

Okwakol, M. J. N., 2008, 'Challenges and Prospects for Quality Assurance in Science and Technology Education in African Countries', *The Uganda Higher Education Review*. Journal of the National Council for Higher Education, Vol. 5, No. 2, pp. 17-26.

Olel, M. A., 2006, 'The Effect of Privately Sponsored Students Programme on Efficiency and Equity in Public Universities in Kenya and Uganda, an unpublished PhD Thesis, Maseno University, Kisumu, Kenya.

Onsongo, Jane, 2007, 'The Growth of Private Universities in Kenya: Implications for Gender Equity in Higher Education'. *JHEA/RESA* Vol. 5, No. 2&3, 2007, pp. 111–133.

Otieno, J. J., 2005, 'University Executives' Perception of Student Leaders: The Case of East African Universities', Unpublished Paper, Centre for Higher Education Transformation (African Student Leadership Network) and Moi University, Kenya.

Otieno, J. J., 2004, 'Student Participation in the Governance of Higher Education in Africa', Paper prepared of the Centre for Higher Education Transformation. (http://www.chet.org.za on). November 18, 2011.

Osseo-Asare, A. E., Longbottom, D. and Murphy, W. D., 2005, 'Leadership Best Practices for Sustaining Quality in UK Higher Education from the Perspective of the EFQM Excellence Model', *Quality Assurance in Education*, 12 (2), pp. 148-170.

Owuor, N. A., 2012, 'Higher Education in Kenya: The Rising Tension between Quantity and Quality in the Post-Massification Period', *Higher Education Studies*, vol. 2(4), pp. 126-136.

Parrish, D., n.d., 'Effective Leadership in Higher Education: The Circles of Influence', (http://www.aare.edu.au/10pap/2437Parrish.pdf). November 18, 2011.

Persson, A., 2003, *Student Participation in Governance of Higher Education in Europe*, Council of Europe Survey.

Petlane, T., 2009, 'Integrating Governance Education into University Education in Africa: Perspectives, Challenges and Lessons', Occasional Paper No 43, South African Institute of International Affairs.

Pounder, J. S., 2001, 'New Leadership' and University Organizational Effectiveness: Exploring the Relationship', *Leadership and Organizational Development Journal*, 22 (6), pp. 281-290.

Rabb, T. and Suleiman, E., 2003, *The Making and Unmaking of Democracy: Lessons from History and World Politics*, New York: Routledge.

Ramsden, P., 1998, *Learning to Lead in Higher Education*, London: Routledge.

Rantz, R., 2002, 'Leading Urban Institutions of Higher Education in the New Millennium', *Leadership and Organizational Development Journal*, 23 (8), pp. 456- 466.

Reisberg, L., 2010, *Challenges for African University Leadership*, (http://www.insidehighered.com/blogs/the_world_view/challenges_for_african_university leadership). November 18, 2011.

Republic of Kenya, 2012, *The Universities Act No. 42 of 2012*, Nairobi: Government Printers.

Republic of Kenya, 2006, *Transformation of Higher Education and Training in Kenya to Secure Kenya's Development in Knowledge Economy: Report of the Universities Inspection Board (Kinyanjui Report)*, Nairobi: Government Printers.

Republic of Kenya, 2005, *Sessional Paper No. 1 of 2005: Policy Framework for Education Training and Research Nairob*i, Ministry of Education, Science and Technology.

Republic of Kenya, 2003, *The Economic Recovery Strategy for Wealth and Employment Creation. 2003 - 2007*, Nairobi: Government Printers.

Republic of Kenya, 1999, *Charter for the United States International University*, Nairobi: Government Printers.

Republic of Kenya,1965, *African Socialism and Its Application to Planning in Kenya*, Nairobi: Government Printers.

Robinson, V. M. J., 2008, Forging the Links between Distributed Leadership and Educational Outcomes', *Journal of Educational Administration*, 46, pp. 241–256.

Rost, J. C., 1993, 'Leadership Development in the Millennium', *The Journal of Leadership and Organizational Studies*, 1 (1), pp. 91 – 110.

Rowley, J., 1997, 'Academic Leaders: Made or Born?', *Industrial and Commercial Training*, 29 (3), pp. 78 – 84.

Sabin, J.E. and Daniels, N., 2001, 'Managed Care: Strengthening the Consumer Voice in Managed Care', *Psychiatric Services,* 52, pp. 461–64.

Saha, L. J., 1993, 'Universities and National Development: Issues and Problems in Developing Countries', in Morsy, Z. and Altbach, P.G. eds, *Higher Education in International Perspective: Towards the 21st Century,* New York: Advent Books.

Saint, W., 2004, 'Comments on "Challenges Facing African Universities"', *African Studies Review*, 47 (1), pp. 61 – 65.

Santiago, P., Tremblay, K., Basri, E. and Arnal, E. 2008. *Tertiary Education for the Knowledge Society. Volume 1,* Paris: Organization for Economic Co-operation and Development.

Santiso, C., 2001, 'Good Governance and Aid Effectiveness: The World Bank and Conditionality'. *The Georgetown Public Policy Review,*Volume 7 Number 1 Fall 2001, pp. 1-22.

Saint, W., 2004, 'Comments on "Challenges Facing African Universities"', *African Studies Review*, 47 (1), pp. 61 – 65.

Sawyerr, A. 2004. "Challenges Facing African Universities: Selected Issues." *African Studies Review*, 47 (1), pp. 1 – 59

Schmidt, M., 2002, 'Political Performance and Types of Democracy: Findings from Comparative Studies', *European Journal of Political Research*, 41, pp. 147 – 162.

Schumpeter, J. A., 1950, *Capitalism, Socialism and Democracy*, New York: Harper and Row,

Serageldin, I., 2000, 'University Governance and the Stakeholder Society', Keynote Address, 11th General Conference: Universities as Gateway to the Future, Durban, 20–25 August 2000, International Association of Universities.

Sethi, M., 2000, 'Return and reintegration of African Nationals', in Tapsoba, S., Kassoum, S., Houenou, P. V., Oni, B., Sethi, M.and Ngu, J., eds, *Brain Drain and Capacity Building in Africa*, Dakar, Senegal: ECA/IRDC/IOM, pp. 38-48.

Sharma, Y., 2009, *Expansion of Private Higher Education*, (http://www.universityworldnews.com/article.php?story=20090707152 445674). August 11, 2016.

Sherman, M. A. B., 1989, 'The African University and the Challenge of Endogenous Development in Africa, a paper presented at the 32nd Annual Meeting of the African Studies Association, held in Atlanta, Georgia, November 4, 1989.

Sifuna, D. N., 2013, 'Leadership in Kenyan Public Universities and the Challenges of Autonomy', *JHEA/RESA* Vol. 10, No. 1, 2012.

Sifuna, D. N., 2010, 'Some Reflections on the Expansion and Quality of Higher Education in Public Universities in Kenya', *Research in Post-Compulsory Education*, 15(4), pp. 415-425.

Sifuna, D. N., 1998, 'The Governance of Kenyan Universities', *Research in post compulsory Education*, 3, 2, 175-212.

Softkenya, n.d., 'Universities in Kenya – Public, Private, Courses, Ranking, and Best Universities in Kenya', (http://softkenya.com/university/). August 1, 2016.

Smart, J. C., 2003, 'Organizational effectiveness of 2year colleges: the centrality of cultural and leadership complexity', *Research in Higher Education,* 44 (6), pp. 673-703.

SQW Limited, 2005, *Research to Inform the Management and Governance of Children's Centres, Final Report to Department for Education and Skills,* London: SQW Limited. (http://www.sqw.co.uk/file). August 15, 2016.

Standa, E., 2007, 'Institutional Autonomy and Academic Freedom. The Uganda Higher Education Review', *Journal of Higher Council for Education,* 4 (1), pp. 17-20.

Stark, J. S., Briggs, C. L., & Poplawski, J. R., 2002, 'Curriculum Leadership Roles of the Chairpersons in Continuously Planning Departments', *Research in Higher Education, 43* (3), pp. 329-356.

Task Force on Higher Education and Society, 2000, *Higher Education in Developing Countries:Peril and Promise,* Washington, D.C.: The International Bank for Reconstruction and Development.

Teferra, D. and Altbach, P. G., 2004, 'African Higher Education: Challenges for the 21st Century', *Higher Education,* 47(1), pp. 21-50.

Terenzini, P.T., Pascarella, E.T. and Blimling, G.S., 1996, 'Students' Out-of-class Experiences and their Influence on Learning and Cognitive Development: A literature Review', *Journal of College Student Development,* 37, pp. 149–62.

Trow, M., 2000, *From Mass Higher Education to Universal Access: The American Advantage,* Research and Occasional Paper Series, Center for Studies in Higher Education: UC Berkeley.

Teune, H., 2001, *Universities as Sites of Citizenship and Civic Responsibility: United States Study,* Philadelphia: International Consortium for Higher Education Civic Responsibility and Democracy.

The Independent Commission for Good Governance in Public Services, 2004, *The Good Governance Standard for Public Services,* London: OPM and CIPFA. (http://www.opm.co.uk/resources/papers/policy/Good_Gov_Standard). August 15, 2016.

Thierborn, G., 1977, 'The Rule of Capital and the Rise of Democracy', *New Left Review,* 103, pp. 3-41.

Thompson, L. and Uyeda, K., 2004, *Family Support: Fostering Leadership and Partnership to Improve Access and Quality,* Los Angeles, CA: National Centre for Infant and Early Childhood Health Policy.

Thurmond, V. A., 2001, 'The Point of Triangulation', *Journal of Nursing Scholarship,* 33 (3), pp. 253-258.

UNESCO, 2005a, *Private Higher Education in Kenya,* Paris: UNESCO/IIEP.

UNESCO, 2005b, *EFA Global Monitoring Report: The Quality Imperative,* Paris: UNESCO.

UNESCO, 1994, 'The Role of African Student Movements in the Political and Social Evolution of Africa from 1900 to 1975', *UNESCO General History of Africa,* Vol. 2. Paris: UNESCO.

United States International University, 2015a, 'USIU, Africa's Premier Institution of Education', Available online on: http://www.usiu.ac.ke/ Accessed: October 2, 2015.

United States International University, 2015b, *Constitution of the USIU-Africa Student Affairs Council (SAC),* Nairobi: USIU.

United States International University,n.d., *Institutional Profile,* Nairobi, United States International University.

University of East Anglia with the National Children's Bureau, 2005, *Realizing Children's Trust Arrangements: National Evaluation of Children's Trusts. Phase 1 Report (Department for Education and Skills Research Report 682)*, London: Department for Education and Skills. (http://publications.dcsf.gov.uk/eOrderingDownload/ RR682.pdf). August 15, 2016.

Utting, D., Painter, A., Renshaw, J. and Hutchinson, R., 2008, *Better Outcomes for Children and Young People: from Talk to Action*, London: DCSF, (http://www.rcslt.org/news/from_talk_to_action). August 15, 2016.

Van Ameijde, J. D., Nelson, P. C., Billsberrry, J., and Meurs, V. N., 2009, 'Improvng Leadership in Higher Educational Institutions'. *Journal of Higher Education, 58, pp.* 763-779.

Wainwright, H., 2005, *Why Participatory Democracy Matters - And Movements Matter to Participatory Democracy*, (https://www.tni.org/es/node/14262). August 24, 2016.

Wangenge-Ouma, G., 2012, 'Public by Day, Private by Night: Examining the Private Lives of Kenya's Public Universities', *European Journal of Education*, 47(2), pp. 213-227.

Waweru, S. N., 2013, 'The Role of Private Universities in Meeting Demand for Higher Education in Kenya', *International Journal of Education and Research*, Vol. 1, No. 12. (On line).

Wawire, V, Elarabi, N. and Mwanzi, H., 2010, *Access and Retention Opportunities for Students with Disabilities in Higher Education in Egypt and Kenya.*

Wondimu, H., 2003, 'Ethiopia', in Teferra, D. and Altbach, P.G., eds, *African Higher Education: An International Reference Handbook*, Bloomington: Indiana University Press, pp. 316 – 325.

Wood, D., 1993, 'Faculty, Student, and Support Staff Participation in College Governance: An Evaluation', paper presented at the Annual Conference of the Association of Canadian Community Colleges, Edmunton, Alberta, Canada.

World Bank, 2009, *Accelerating Catch-up: Tertiary education for growth in sub-Saharan Africa,* Washington DC: The World Bank.

World Bank, 2002, *Constructing Knowledge Societies: New challenges for Tertiary Education,* Washington DC: The World Bank.

World Bank, 2000a, *Higher Education in Developing Countries: Peril and Promise*, Washington D.C: World Bank.

World Bank 2000b, *The Quality of Growth,* New York: Oxford University Press.

World Bank, 1994, *Governance: The World Bank Experience*, Washington, DC: The World Bank.

World Bank, 1992, *Governance and Development*, Washington, D.C.: The World Bank

World Bank, 1989, *World Development Report 1989: Financial Systems and Development.* New York: Oxford University Press.

Yesufu, T. M., ed., 1973, *Creating the African University: Emerging issues of the 1970s,* Ibadan: Oxford University Press.

Zuo, B. and Ratsoy, E.W., 1999, 'Student Participation in University Governance', *Canadian Journal of Higher Education,* 29, pp. 1–26.

Websites

www.gdrc.org/u-gov/governance-understand.html
http://www.goodgovernance.org.au/about-good-governance/what-is-good-governance/
http://www.businessdictionary.com/definition/corporate-governance.html
http://www.helb.co.ke/about-helb/history/
http://australianpolitics.com/democracy/key-terms/liberal-democracy

Appendices

Appendix I: Research Instruments

Survey Instrument

Questionnaire Number..
Survey of Student Involvement in University Governance in Kenya

Dear Respondent,
This questionnaire is part of a CODESRIA funded research that is designed to gain a better understanding of student involvement in university governance in Kenya. Your contribution to this project is very important. You are in a unique position to provide information that will enable us to understand the nature, role and state of student involvement in university governance in Kenya and to draw appropriate conclusions and make fitting recommendations. By completing this survey you will help identify what may facilitate more democratic governance of our institutions of higher learning.

Though participation in this study is voluntary and one is at liberty to withdraw at any stage, you are strongly encouraged to participate because the study is for an educational purpose. The information you will provide will be kept confidential. Answers to all questions will be used only in combination with the responses from other participants and no names or any information that could be used to identify particular respondents will be employed in reporting the research findings. All surveys will be destroyed at the end of the study. The results will be disseminated through a publication available the public and other channels such as journals, seminars and workshops.

Request for further clarifications can be channeled through any of the following:

Prof. Munyae M. Mulinge
United States International University (USIU)
P.O. Box 14634-00800
Nairobi
Tel. 20-3606434

Dr. Josephine N. Arasa
United States International University (USIU)
P.O. Box 14634-00800
Nairobi
Tel. 20-3606181

Dr. Violet K. Wawire-Ochieng
Kenyatta University
P. O. Box 43844-00100
Nairobi
Tel. 20-810901-19 Ext. 57495

Instructions for Completing the Survey

I would appreciate if you could take some time to respond to the questions on the following pages of the questionnaire. Most questions require that you simply check the appropriate box for the response that most accurately represents your present work situation. Please use a pencil and ensure that your answer marks are heavy enough to distinguish them from any erased answer marks. The survey should take between 20 to 25 minutes to complete and you are encouraged to complete it all at once. Please answer the questions in order without skipping around. Be sure to read each question carefully.

A number of questions you are asked to respond to seem repetitious. Don't worry about this. It is not a trick. Rather, it is a deliberate methodological safety net. That is, it will facilitate the researcher to assess the validity and reliability of the measures. The assessment of these two attributes is a methodological necessity whenever variables are measured using scales like is the case in this study.

There are no "right" or "wrong" answers to any of the questions. However, you should be as candid as possible and also ensure that responses to closely related questions *are not contradictory.*

I want to thank you in advance for your time and cooperation.

© ....
© ....
© ....
© ....

I. Institutional Policy on Student Involvement in Governance

Q1. The following questions are designed to collect information on your awareness of institutional policies on student involvement in University governance. Respond by selecting from the following scale to indicate awareness or lack of awareness with respect to the following statements [Only one answer should be selected for each statement].

1 Agree	2 Disagree	
	1	2
1. The statutes governing my university makes reference to student involvement in the governance process		
2. My university has a published policy on student involvement in governance		
3. My university's strategic plan has 'student involvement in governance as one of its priority action areas.		
4. My university communicates the importance of student involvement in governance to all members of the university community		
5. My university has put in place mechanisms for the implementation and enforcement of policies on student involvement in governance		
6. My university provides opportunities for public debate /discussion of matters affecting student involvement in governance		
7. My university makes necessary amendments and revisions of policies on student involvement in governance		
8. In my university student involvement in the variou9s governance structures and in decision making is a matter of policy		
9. My university's policy on student involvement in governance has a constitutional and legal basis.		

II. Involvement in Governance Structures and Decision Making

Q2. The following questions are designed to collect information on the overall involvement by students in University governance. Respond by selecting from the following scale to indicate your agreement or disagreement with the following statements [Only one answer should be selected for each statement].

1	2	3	Strongly
Strongly Agree	Agree	Disagree	Disagree

	1	2	3	4
My university considers students participation in governance to be mandatory				
Students in my university have sufficient role in university governance				
Students in my university are involved in policy formulation				
Students in my university are involved in policy implementation				
My university has effective policies for student involvement in the decision making process				
In my university students constitute valuable sources of information on decision issues				
In my university students wield very strong influence on management decision making				
Students in my university exercise a sufficient voice in university policies, planning and budgeting				
In my university students have effective mechanisms for providing input into all decisions				

Q3. The following questions are designed to assess the level of student involvement in various governance structures and in the making specific decision in your university. Respond by selecting from the following scale to indicate your rating of that involvement [Only one answer should be selected for each statement].

1	2	3	4
Not involved at all	Low Involvement	High Involvement	Very High Involvement

	1	2	3	4
Involvement in Governance Structures				
1. University Council/ Board of trustees				
2. Management Council				
3. Senate				
4. All university wide committee				

5.	Deans' committee			
6.	All faculty-/ School-wide committees			
7.	All departmental-/ programs-wide committees			
	Involvement in Decision Making Activities			
1.	Formulation of university vision and missions			
2.	Strategic planning			
3.	Academic planning			
4.	Formulation of policies			
5.	Admission of new students			
6.	Orientation of new students			
7.	Curriculum design			
8.	Curriculum approvals			
9.	Program reviews			
10.	Curriculum development			
11.	Quality assurance			
12.	Student assessment			
13.	Student evaluation			
14.	Grading policy			
15.	Recruitment of faculty and staff			
16.	Faculty appraisal and promotions			
17.	Dispute resolution			
18.	Graduation planning			
19.	Disciplinary matters			
20.	Student support and advising committees			
21.	Procurements			
22.	Support services committees (e.g. library, ICT)			
23.	Closure and opening of the university			
24.	Increment of tuition and other fees			
25.	Other [Specify]			
	•			
	•			

Q4. The following questions are designed to gauge the importance (value) you attach to student involvement in governance structures and in the making of specific decision in your university. Select from the following scale to indicate the *importance* you attach to each of the provided items. [Only one answer should be selected for each statement].

1 Not important at all	2 Of little importance	3 Important	4 Very important			
			1	2	3	4
Involvement in Governance Structures						
1. University Council/ Board of Trustees						
2. Management Council						
3. Senate						
4. All university wide committee						
5. Deans' committee						
6. All faculty-/ School-wide committees						
7. All departmental-/ programs-wide committees						
Involvement in Decision Making Activities						
1. Formulation of university vision and missions						
2. Strategic planning						
3. Academic planning						
4. Formulation of policies						
5. Admission of new students						
6. Orientation of new students						
7. Curriculum design						
8. Curriculum approvals						
9. Program reviews						
10. Curriculum development						
11. Quality assurance						
12. Student assessment						
13. Student evaluation						
14. Grading policy						
15. Recruitment of faculty and staff						
16. Faculty appraisal and promotions						
17. Dispute resolution						
18. Graduation planning						
19. Disciplinary matters						
20. Student support and advising committees						
21. Procurements						
22. Support services committees (e.g. library, ICT)						
23. Closure and opening of the university						
24. Increment of tuition and other fees						

Appendices

Q5. The following items are designed to measure your level of satisfaction with student involvement in various governance structures and involvement in the specific decision making activities in your university. Respond by selecting from the following scale to indicate your level of satisfaction [Only one answer should be selected for each statement].

1 Very Dissatisfied	2. Dissatisfied	3. Satisfied	4 Very Satisfied			
			1	2	3	4
Involvement in Governance Structures						
1. University Council/ Board of Trustees						
2. Management Council						
3. Senate						
4. All university wide committee						
5. Deans' committee						
6. All faculty-/ School-wide committees						
7. All departmental-/ programs-wide committees						
Involvement in Decision Making Activities						
1. Formulation of university vision and missions						
2. Strategic planning						
3. Academic planning						
4. Formulation of academic and other university-wide policies						
5. Admission of new students						
6. Orientation of new students						
7. Curriculum design						
8. Curriculum approvals						
9. Program reviews						
10. Curriculum development						
11. Quality assurance						
12. Student assessment						
13. Student evaluation						
14. Grading policy						
15. Recruitment of faculty and staff						
16. Faculty appraisal and promotions						
17. Dispute resolution						
18. Graduation planning						
19. Disciplinary matters						
20. Student support and advising committees						
21. Procurements						
22. Support services committees (e.g. library, ICT)						
23. Closure and opening of the university						
24. Increment of tuition and other fees						
25. Other [Specify]						
•						
•						

Q6. The following questions are designed to capture the adequacy of involvement by student leadership (or representation) in different aspects of the university governance process. You are requested to select from the following scale to rate that adequacy [Only one answer should be selected for each statement].

1 Inadequate		2	Adequate	
			1	2
1.	Attendance in meetings			
1.	Input/ contributions during meetings			
1.	Representation of student issues			
1.	Voting power			
1.	Ability to influence decision making			
1.	Capacity to contribute solutions to problems faced by students			
1.	Feedback to students			

Q7. Please indicate your satisfaction with the involvement of student leadership (or representation) in the enumerated aspects of university governance processes [Only one answer should be selected for each statement].

1 Very Dissatisfied	2 Dissatisfied	3 Satisfied	4 Very Satisfied			
			1	2	3	4
1.	Attendance in meetings					
2.	Input/ contributions during meetings					
3.	Representation of student issues					
4.	Voting power					
5.	Ability to influence decision making					
6.	Capacity to contribute to the solution of problems faced by students					
7.	Feedback to students					

Q8. Indicate who you consider to be the major "players" in decision making in your university by rank ordering the following from the most import to the least important, (where 1 = most important and 11 = least important).

Player	Rank
1. Deans	
2. University Council	
3. Regular Students	
4. Vice-Chancellor	
5. Deputy Vice-chancellors	

Appendices

6. Registrars	
7. University senate	
8. Student Representative	
9. Faculty	
10. Government/ state	
11. Heads of Departments/ Programs	

Q9. To what extent are you satisfied with student involvement in the governance of your university?
1. Very dissatisfied
2. Dissatisfied
3. Satisfied
4. Very satisfied

III. Services for Support of Student Involvement in Governance

Q10. Select from among the following to rate the support services that your university has put in place to enhance student involvement in university governance? [Answer by circling all applicable support services]

	1 Not at all	2 Sometimes	3 Often	4 Always		
1.	Legal/ policy frameworks			1	2	3	4
2.	Provision of facilities (e.g. office space)						
3.	Special office to coordinate student involvement in governance						
4.	Periodic democratic elections						
5.	Institutionalized channels of communication at all levels						
6.	Formal appeal and complaints structures						
7.	Existence of student self-governance structures; i.e. clubs and associations				x		
8.	Allowances						
9.	Tuition waivers						
10.	Free meals						
11.	Free accommodation						
12.	Free transport						
13.	Leadership training						
14.	Mainstreaming of governance issues in the curriculum and other activities						x
15.	Short and long refresher courses						

16.	Retreats			
17.	Public addresses/symposiums			
18.	Invited guest speakers			
19.	Other [Specify]			
•				
•				

IV. Student Involvement in Self-Governance

The following questions are designed to collect information on the nature and process of student self-government governance in universities.

Q11. Select from among the following to indicate the different student self-governance organizations in your university:

1. Sports clubs
2. Professional/ subject related clubs
3. National association
4. Ethnic associations
5. Recreational associations
6. Student government/ councils
7. Other [Specify]:

....
....
....

Q12. What are specific mandates of the student self-governance organizations (bodies)? [Answer by circling all applicable mandates]

1. Student welfare
2. Academic issues
3. Recruitment of staff
4. Moderating management and other organs of decision making
5. Quality assurance of student programs, services and institutions
6. Other [Specify]

....
....
....

Q13. Which of the following are selection and appointment criteria for membership to student self-governance organizations? [Respond by circling all appropriate criteria]

1. Predetermined qualities (area of study, ethnicity, disability etc.)
2. Voluntary
3. Other [specify]

....
....

Q14. What are the minimum criteria for being an official in student self-governance bodies? [Respond by circling all applicable criteria]
1. Academic performance
2. Personality
3. Popularity/democratically elected
4. Leadership skills
5. Program of study
6. Seniority
7. Age
8. Gender
9. Disability
10. Other [specify]

....
....

Q15. Use the provided scale to indicate the extent to which the following aspects of the student governance processes are influenced by national politics and political parties [Only one answer should be selected for each aspect]:

1 Not influenced at all	2 Sometimes influenced	3 Often influence	4 Always influenced			
			1	2	3	4
a.	Formulation of constitutions and other legal frameworks					
b.	Clubs/societies/ associations meetings and activities					
c.	Nomination process for elections					
d.	Campaign for elections					
e.	Actual elections					
f.	Set up of governance structure					
g.	Student *barazas/ kamukunjis*					
h.	Representation of student grievances					
i.	Agenda for public discussion, debates and fora					
j.	Invited guests					
k.	Social activities					
l.	Personal matters					

V. Impediments to Student Involvement tn Governance

Questions in this section focus on the impediments to effective student involvement in university governance processes from the perspective of different stakeholders.

Q16. List up to five (5) positive consequences of student involvement in university governance?

....
....

Q17. List up to five (5) negative consequences of student involvement in university governance?

....
....

Q18. Give suggestions of how the negative outcomes can be addressed

....
....

Q19. Indicate the major challenges that undermine effective student involvement at different levels of university governance [Respond by circling all applicable challenges]:

1. Lack of adequate recognition of the role of students in governance
2. Lack of constitutional basis for participation
3. Lack of leadership capacity among students
4. Mistrust of student leaders among the student body
5. Being compromised by management
6. Fear of victimization by management
7. Student apathy
8. Lack of financial, physical and other supportive resources
9. Lack of opportunities for complaints and appeals
10. Limited power and authority among students
11. Intimidation of student leadership by top management
12. Lack of awareness of student needs
13. Affiliation with political parties
14. Tendency for management to impose decisions while ignoring student contributions
15. Low moral
16. Non-conducive university environment

17. External interference
18. Internal manipulation
19. Poor communication
20. Poor implementation of involvement policies and strategies
21. Inadequate feedback mechanisms
22. Excessive bureaucracy
23. Lack of adequate information
24. Poor enforcement of involvement policies and strategies
25. No voting power
26. Students leaders not being in a position to effectively represent the interest of their groups
27. Lack of transparency and consultative democratic processes in governance process
28. Lack of amendments /revision of policy to make them current
29. Any others (specify)

....
....

Q20. Suggest ways that can be used to overcome the above challenges?
....
....

VI. Inclusivity of Involvement in Governance Structures

Q21. Select from the following scale to indicate your agreement or disagreement with the following areas [Only one answer should be selected for each statement].

1 Strongly disagree	2 Disagree	3 Agree	4 Strongly Agree			
			1	2	3	4
1.	It is university policy to observe diversity in the representative of students in various structures of governance					
2.	The election of student representatives to university governance structures caters for the diversity of the study body					
3.	The following aspects of diversity must be observed in the representation of students in overall university governance and student self-governance structures:					
i. Age						
ii. Gender						
iii. Ethnicity						

iv. Nationality				
v. Study Program				
vi. Year of Study				
vii. Mode of study				
viii. Disability				
ix. Sexual orientation				

VII. Respondents' Demographic Characteristics

Q22. Which of the following best describes you?
1. Full-time student
2. Part-time student
3. School based student
4. Open learning student
5. Evening/ Saturday student
6. Other [Specify]

....
....

Q23. In which faculty/school is your program of study housed?

....
....
....

Q24. What is your year of study?
1. First year
2. Second year
3. Third year
4. Fourth year
5. Postgraduate

Q25. What is your gender?
1. Male
2. Female

Q26. What is your age?
1. Below 21
2. 21 to 25 years
3. 26- 30 years
4. 31- 35 years
5. 36-40 years
6. 41-50 yeas
7. 51+years

Q27. What is your marital status?
- 1. Single (never married)
- 2. Married
- 3. Divorced
- 4. Separated
- 5. Cohabitation
- 6. Widowed

Q28. Indicate your nationality: ..
....
....

Q29. Please indicate your ethnic background:
....
....

Q30. Do have any of the following challenges [tick as appropriate]:
- 1. Physical
- 2. Visual
- 3. Hearing
- 4. Other [Specify] ....
....

Thank you very much for your cooperation

Interview Guide: In-Depth Interviews

University Administrators:

a) Policy

1. How do the key governance statements of the university (Mission, vision policy) make reference to student governance?

   Probe for:
   - Details in terms of dissemination/communication
   - Enforcement and feedback mechanisms
   - Implementation strategies

2. Does the university have a published policy on student involvement in governance?

   Probe for:
   - The document it is contained in (statues, strategic plan, hand book etc.)
   - If it involves all levels of university governance
   - Whether internally or externally driven
   - Awareness of policy
   - How they interpret it and use it
   - Amendments and revisions of policy and why
   - Constitutional and legal basis of policies

3. What mechanisms are in place to ensure to ensure full implementation and enforcement of these policies?

   Probe for:
   - Offices
   - Resources
   - Facilities
   - Opportunities for appeals
   - Expression of unpopular and descending view

4. Does the university provide opportunities for public debate /discussion of matters affecting students?

   Probes:
   - Nature of opportunities
   - How they impact on student impressions of processes of university governance, Regulation mechanisms.

5. Comment on the involvement of the public and other stakeholders in the governance of the university?

    Probe for involvement of:
    - Alumni
    - Government
    - Bodies regulating higher education

b) University Organizational Structures:

6. How is university governance structured?

    Probe for
    - Role/functions of each level
    - Student involvement in various levels
    - Student roles in various levels
    - The specific issues at each level that require the approval of student leadership (e.g. program development/review, disciplinary matters/expulsion, closure and opening of universities, increments of tuition and other fees etc.).

7. In what ways are students involved in curriculum design?

    Probe for:
    - Student involvement in school and university committees;
    - Issues of course content
    - Grading policy
    - Recruitment of faculty
    - Program development reviews
    - Appraisal of faculty (courses and instruments)
    - Formulation of university missions and visions

c) Nature and Role of Student Involvement in Self-governance:

8. What organizations exist within the university to facilitate student self-governance?

    Probe for:
    - Clubs
    - Societies
    - Associations

9. What are the specific mandates of the student governance bodies?
   Probe for:
   - Student welfare
   - Academic issues
   - Recruitment of staff
   - Moderating management and other organs of decision making
   - Quality assurance of student programs, services and institutions

10. What are the criteria for general members and selection of officials?
    Probe for:
    - Pre-determined qualities
    - Voluntary

11. What are the minimum criteria for being an official in student governance bodies?
    Probe for:
    - Academic performance
    - Personality
    - Popularity
    - Program of study
    - Seniority
    - Age
    - Gender etc.

12. How would you rate the adequacy of student involvement in the governance process in your university?
    Probe for:
    - Attendance of meetings
    - Input in decision making
    - Representation of student issues
    - Voting power
    - Feedback to students

13. How does national politics including diversity in political parties influence student involvement in governance processes?
    Probe for:
    - Campaign rallies for student elections
    - Nomination process

- Actual election
- Set up (structure)
- Student government

14. Comment on the quality of student involvement in governance:
    Probe for:
    - Trust and satisfaction by students, administration

d) Impediments

15. What challenges (e.g., capacity, financial, motivation etc) undermine the effective involvement of students in governance through the student governance body?
    Probe for:
    - Challenges at different levels(financial, capacity, motivation)

16. What limitations (set boundaries) have been placed on student involvement in the governance of universities in general?
    Probe for:
    - Specific limitations
    - Rationale for placing limitations
    - Acceptance by students
    - Overall impact
    - Limitations on student involvement in governance of university

e) Support Systems

17. What support services are put in place to address the challenges of involving students in university governance?
    Probe for:
    - Infrastructure
    - Allowances
    - Leadership training
    - Mainstreaming of governance issues in the curriculum and other activities
    - Short and long courses
    - Retreats

- Public addresses/symposiums,
- Guest speakers

18. What mechanisms exist to allow students staff and faculty to raise governance issues with management?
    Probe for:
    - Actual channels of communication
    - Responsible persons
    - Feedback mechanisms
    - Appeal channels, procedures for due process

f) Inclusivity

19. How does the representation in the student governance body cater for the diverse needs of the students?
    Probe for:
    - Age
    - Gender
    - Ethnicity
    - Nationality
    - Study program
    - Year of study
    - Mode of study
    - Disability

Student Government Officials

a) Policy

1. How do the key governance statements of the university (mission, vision policy) make reference to student governance?
   Probe for:
   - Awareness of the details of this statements
   - Details in terms of dissemination/communication
   - Enforcement and feedback mechanisms
   - Implementation strategies.

2. Does the university have a published policy on student involvement in governance?
   Probe for:
   - Awareness of the details of this statements
   - The document it is contained in (statues, strategic plan, hand book etc.)
   - If it involves all levels of university governance
   - Whether internally or externally driven
   - Awareness of policy
   - How they interpret it and use it
   - Amendments and revisions of policy and why
   - Constitutional and legal basis of policies

3. What mechanisms are in place to ensure to ensure full implementation and enforcement of these policies?
   Probe for:
   - Offices
   - Resources
   - Facilities
   - Opportunities for appeals
   - Expression of unpopular and descending view

4. Does the university provide opportunities for public debate /discussion of matters affecting students?
   Probes for:
   - Nature of opportunities
   - How they impact on student impressions of processes of university governance, Regulation mechanisms

5. Comment on the involvement of the public and other stakeholders in the governance of the university?
   Probe for involvement of:
   - Alumni
   - Government
   - Bodies regulating higher education

b) **University Organizational Structures:**

6. How is university governance structured?
   Probe for
   - Role/functions of each level
   - Student involvement in various levels
   - Student roles in various levels
   - The specific issues at each level that require the approval of student leadership (e.g. program development/review, disciplinary matters/expulsion, closure and opening of universities, increments of tuition and other fees etc.).

7. In what ways are students involved in curriculum design?
   Probe for:
   - Student involvement in school and university committees,
   - Issues of course content,
   - Grading policy
   - Recruitment of faculty
   - Program development reviews
   - Appraisal of faculty (courses and instruments)
   - Formulation of university missions and visions.

c) **Nature and Role of Student Involvement in Self-governance**

8. What organizations exist within the university to facilitate student self-governance?
   Probe for:
   - Clubs
   - Societies
   - Associations

9. What are the specific mandates of the student governance bodies?
   Probe for:
   - Student welfare
   - Academic issues
   - Recruitment of staff

- Moderating management and other organs of decision making
- Quality assurance of student programs, services and institutions

10. What are the criteria for general members and selection of officials?
    Probe for:
    - Pre-determined qualities
    - Voluntary

11. What are the minimum criteria for being an official in student governance bodies?
    Probe for:
    - Academic performance,
    - Personality
    - Popularity
    - Program of study
    - Seniority
    - Age
    - Gender etc.

12. How would you rate the adequacy of student involvement in the governance process in your university?
    Probe for:
    - Attendance of meetings
    - Input in decision making
    - Representation of student issues
    - Voting power
    - Feedback to students

13. How does national politics including diversity in political parties influence student involvement in governance processes?
    Probe for:
    - Campaign rallies for student elections,
    - Nomination process
    - Actual election
    - Set up (structure)
    - Student government

14. Comment on the quality of student involvement in governance:
    Probe for:
    - Trust and satisfaction by students, administration

d) Impediments

15. What challenges (e.g., capacity, financial, motivation etc.) undermine the effective involvement of students in governance through the student governance body?
    Probe for:
    - Challenges at different levels (financial, capacity, motivation)

16. What limitations (set boundaries) have been placed on student involvement in the governance of universities in general?
    Probe for:
    - Specific limitations,
    - Rationale for placing limitations
    - Acceptance by students
    - Overall impact
    - Limitations on student involvement in governance of university

e) Support Systems

17. What support services are put in place to address the challenges of involving students in university governance?
    Probe for:
    - Infrastructure
    - Allowances
    - Leadership training
    - Mainstreaming of governance issues in the curriculum and other activities
    - Short and long courses
    - Retreats
    - Public addresses/symposiums
    - Guest speakers

18. What mechanisms exist to allow students staff and faculty to raise governance issues with management?
    Probe for:
    - Actual channels of communication
    - Responsible persons
    - Feedback mechanisms
    - Appeal channels, procedures for due process

f) Inclusivity

19. How does the representation in the student governance body cater for the diverse needs of the students?
    Probe for:
    - Age
    - Gender
    - Ethnicity
    - Nationality
    - Study program
    - Year of study
    - Mode of study
    - Disability

Guide for Focused Group Discussions

a) Policy

1. How do the key governance statements of the university (Mission, vision policy) make reference to student governance?
   Probe for awareness of the details of this statement
   - Details in terms of dissemination/communication
   - Enforcement and feedback mechanisms
   - Implementation strategies.

2. Does the university have a published policy on student involvement in governance?
   Probe for awareness of the details of this statement
   - The document it is contained in (statutes, strategic plan, hand book etc.)

- If it involves all levels of university governance
- Whether internally or externally driven
- Awareness of policy
- How they interpret it and use it
- Amendments and revisions of policy and why
- Constitutional and legal basis of policies

3. What mechanisms are in place to ensure to ensure full implementation and enforcement of these policies?
   Probe for:
   - Offices
   - Resources
   - Facilities
   - Opportunities for appeals
   - Expression of unpopular and descending view

4. Does the university provide opportunities for public debate /discussion of matters affecting students?
   Probe for:
   - Nature of opportunities
   - How they impact on student impressions of processes of university governance, Regulation mechanisms

5. Comment on the involvement of the public and other stakeholders in the governance of the university?
   Probe for involvement of:
   - Alumni
   - Government
   - Bodies regulating higher education

b) University Organizational Structures

6. How is university governance structured?
   Probe for:
   - Role/functions of each level
   - Student involvement in various levels
   - Student roles in various levels

- The specific issues at each level that require the approval of student leadership (e.g., program development/review, disciplinary matters/expulsion, closure and opening of universities, increments of tuition and other fees etc.)

7. In what ways are students involved in curriculum design?
   Probe for:
   - Student involvement in school and university committees
   - Issues of course content
   - Grading policy
   - Recruitment of faculty
   - Program development reviews
   - Appraisal of faculty (courses and instruments)
   - Formulation of university missions and visions

c) **Nature and Role of Student Involvement in Self-governance**

8. What organizations exist within the university to facilitate student self-governance?
   Probe for:
   - Clubs
   - Societies
   - Associations

9. What are the specific mandates of the student governance bodies?
   Probe for:
   - Student welfare
   - Academic issues
   - Recruitment of staff
   - Moderating management and other organs of decision making
   - Quality assurance of student programs, services and institutions

10. What are the criteria for general members and selection of officials?
    Probe for:
    - Pre-determined qualities
    - Voluntary

11. What are the minimum criteria for being an official in student governance bodies?

    Probe for:
    - Academic performance
    - Personality
    - Popularity
    - Program of study
    - Seniority
    - Age
    - Gender etc

12. How would you rate the adequacy of student involvement in the governance process in your university?

    Probe for:
    - Attendance of meetings
    - Input in decision making
    - Representation of student issues
    - Voting power
    - Feedback to students

13. How does national politics including diversity in political parties influence student involvement in governance processes?

    Probe for:
    - Campaign rallies for student elections,
    - Nomination process
    - Actual election
    - Set up (structure)
    - Student government

14. Comment on the quality of student involvement in governance:

    Probe for:
    - Trust and satisfaction by students, administration

d) **Impediments**

15. What challenges (e.g., capacity, financial, motivation etc.) undermine the effective involvement of students in governance through the student governance body?

Probe for:
- Challenges at different levels(financial, capacity, motivation)

16. What limitations (set boundaries) have been placed on student involvement in the governance of universities in general?
Probe for:
- Specific limitations
- Rationale for placing limitations
- Acceptance by students
- Overall impact
- Limitations on student involvement in governance of university

e) Support Systems

17. What support services are put in place to address the challenges of involving students in university governance?
Probe for:
- Infrastructure
- Allowances
- Leadership training
- Mainstreaming of governance issues in the curriculum and other activities
- Short and long courses
- Retreats
- Public addresses/symposiums
- Guest speakers

18. What mechanisms exist to allow students staff and faculty to raise governance issues with management?
Probe for:
- Actual channels of communication
- Responsible persons
- Feedback mechanisms
- Appeal channels, procedures for due process

f) Inclusivity

19. How does the representation in the student governance body cater for the diverse needs of the students?
    Probe for:
    - Age
    - Gender
    - Ethnicity
    - Nationality
    - Study program
    - Year of study
    - Mode of study
    - Disability

8.2 Appendix II: Cross-Tabulation Tables

Table A21: Cross University Differences in Policies and Practices on Student Involvement in Governance

	Policy/ Practice	χ^2 Value	d.f.	p-value
1	My university's policy on student involvement in governance has a constitutional and legal basis.	27.197	2	.000
2	The statutes governing my university make reference to student involvement in the governance process	5.429	2	.066
3	My university's strategic plan has 'student involvement in governance as one of its priority action areas.	8.637	2	.013
4	In my university student involvement in the various governance structures and in decision making is a matter of policy	25.936	2	.000
5	My university has a published policy on student involvement in governance	8.083	2	.018
6	My university communicates the importance of student involvement in governance to all members of the university community	7.092	2	.029
7	My university makes necessary amendments and revisions of policies on student involvement in governance	5.971	2	050
8	My university has put in place mechanisms for the implementation and enforcement of policies on student involvement in governance	22.913	2	.000
9	My university provides opportunities for public debate of matters affecting student involvement in governance	12.408	2	.002

Table A 22: Cross University Differences in Opportunities for Involvement in Governance Structures and Decision Making

	Governance Structure/Decision Making	χ^2 Value	d.f.	p-value
1	My university offers sufficient avenues for university-wide communications for students	12.978	3	.005
2	In my university students constitute valuable sources of information on decision issues	3.002	3	.391
3	Students in my university are involved in policy implementation	6.597	3	.086
4	My university considers students participation in governance is mandatory	3.993	3	.262

5	Students in my university are involved in policy formulation	21.941	3	.000
6	Students in my university have sufficient role in university governance	5.675	3	.129
7	In my university students wield very strong influence on management decision making	2.366	3	.500
8	In my university, policies for student involvement in the decision making process are effective	4.200	3	.241
9	In my university students have effective mechanisms for providing input into all decisions	5.365	3	.147
10	Students in my university exercise a sufficient voice in university policies, planning and budget	1.882	3	.597

Table A 23: Cross University Differences in Level of Involvement in Governance Structures and Decision Making Activities

Governance Structures		χ^2 Value	d.f.	p-value
1	University Council/ Board of trustees	3.082	3	.379
2	Board of Management/ Management Council	2.835	3	.418
3	Senate	7.034	3	.071
4	All university wide committee	1.367	3	.713
5	Deans' committee	6.361	3	.095
6	All School-wide committees	6.404	3	.094
7	All departmental-/ program-wide committees	6.041	3	.110
Decision Making Activities				
8	Formulation of university vision and missions	3.020	3	.389
9	Strategic planning	3.964	3	.265
10	Academic planning	0.397	3	.941
11	Formulation of policies	6.830	3	.078
12	Admission of new students	5.623	3	.131
13	Orientation of new students	33.638	3	.000
14	Curriculum design	3.825	3	.281
15	Curriculum approvals	4.357	3	.225
16	Program reviews	4.699	3	.195
17	Curriculum development	0.732	3	.866
18	Quality assurance	5.425	3	.143
19	Student assessment	10.364	3	.016
20	Student evaluation	5.659	3	.129
21	Grading policy	2.724	3	.436

22	Recruitment of faculty and staff	6.455	3	.091
23	Faculty appraisal and promotions	15.430	3	.001
24	Dispute resolution	4.678	3	.197
25	Graduation planning	29.636	3	.000
26	Disciplinary matters	3.116	3	.374
27	Student support and advising committees	9.491	3	.023
28	Procurements	3.116	3	.374
29	Support services committees (e.g. library, ICT)	19.262	3	.000
30	Closure and opening of the university	3.538	3	.316
31	Increment of tuition and other fees	0.996	3	.802

Table A 24: Cross University Differences in Importance Attached to Participation in Decision Making

Governance Structures		χ^2 Value	d.f.	p-value
1	University Council/ Board of trustees	3.491	3	.322
2	Board of Management/ Management Council	6.777	3	.079
3	Senate	7.823	3	.050
4	All university wide committee	6.983	3	.072
5	Deans' committee	4.984	3	.173
6	All School-wide committees	3.841	3	.279
7	All departmental-/ program-wide committees	7.872	3	.049
Decision Making Activities				
8	Formulation of university vision and missions	11.503	3	.009
9	Strategic planning	12.690	3	.005
10	Academic planning	15.033	3	.002
11	Formulation of policies	1.485	3	.686
12	Admission of new students	2.756	3	.431
13	Orientation of new students	8.462	3	.037
14	Curriculum design	4.367	3	.225
15	Curriculum approvals	6.776	3	.079
16	Program reviews	3.488	3	.322
17	Curriculum development	11.171	3	.011
18	Quality assurance	0.643	3	.887
19	Student assessment	0.280	3	.964
20	Student evaluation	3.403	3	.334
21	Grading policy	2.246	3	.523
22	Recruitment of faculty and staff	11.785	3	.008
23	Faculty appraisal and promotions	9.430	3	.024

24	Dispute resolution	13.228	3	.004
25	Graduation planning	5.404	3	.145
26	Disciplinary matters	10.947	3	.012
27	Student support and advising committees	10.042	3	.018
28	Procurements	5.832	3	.120
29	Support services committees (e.g. library, ICT)	6.566	3	.087
30	Closure and opening of the university	14.530	3	.002
31	Increment of tuition and other fees	2.616	3	.455

Table A25: Cross University Differences in Adequacy of Involvement in Decision Making Activities

	Decision Making Activity	χ^2 Value	d.f.	p-value
1	Attendance in meetings	2.125	2	.346
2	Input /contributions during meetings	13.094	2	001
3	Representation of student issues	9.788	2	.007
4	Voting power	5.611	2	.060
5	Ability to influence decision making	0.308	2	.857
6	Capacity to contribute to the solution of problems faced by students	4.294	2	.117
7	Feedback to students	3.119	2	.210

Table A 26: Cross University Differences in Satisfaction with Participation in Decision Making

	Governance Structures	χ^2 Value	d.f.	p-value
1	University Council/ Board of trustees	12.413	3	.006
2	Board of Management/ Management Council	3.252	3	.354
3	Senate	8.667	3	.034
4	All university wide committee	4.632	3	.201
5	Deans' committee	3.048	3	.384
6	All School-wide committees	3.218	3	.359
7	All departmental-/ program-wide committees	8.196	3	.042
Decision Making Activities				
8	Formulation of university vision and missions	5.251	3	.154
9	Strategic planning	1.970	3	.579
10	Academic planning	5.167	3	.160
11	Formulation of policies	0.539	3	.910
12	Admission of new students	7.896	3	.048

13	Orientation of new students	9.018	3	.029
14	Curriculum design	3.802	3	.284
15	Curriculum approvals	0.409	3	.938
16	Program reviews	1.204	3	.752
17	Curriculum development	0.673	3	.879
18	Quality assurance	1.646	3	.649
19	Student assessment	3.395	3	.335
20	Student evaluation	3.139	3	.371
21	Grading policy	1.894	3	.595
22	Recruitment of faculty and staff	1.918	3	.590
23	Faculty appraisal and promotions	4.941	3	.176
24	Dispute resolution	5.041	3	.169
25	Graduation planning	20.882	3	.000
26	Disciplinary matters	9.555	3	.023
27	Student support and advising committees	11.766	3	.008
28	Procurements	9.966	3	.019
29	Support services committees (e.g. library, ICT)	23.431	3	.000
30	Closure and opening of the university	13.932	3	.003
31	Increment of tuition and other fees	1.095	3	.778

Table A27: Cross University Differences in Satisfaction with Student LeadershipInvolvement in Decision Making Activities

	Decision Making Activity	χ^2 Value	d.f.	p-value
1	Attendance in meetings	3.806	3	.283
2	Input /contributions during meetings	4.254	3	.235
3	Representation of student issues	2.851	3	.415
4	Voting power	6.328	3	.097
5	Ability to influence decision making	0.034	3	.998
6	Capacity to contribute to the solution of problems faced by students	1.040	3	.792
7	Feedback to students	1.266	3	.737

Table A 28: Differences in Support Services for Enhancing StudentInvolvement in Governance

	Support Services	χ^2 Value	d.f.	p-value
1	Legal/ policy frameworks	2.179	3	.536
2	Provision of facilities (e.g. office space)	3.023	3	.388
3	Special office to coordinate student involvement in governance	13.404	3	.004

4	Periodic democratic elections	11.331	3	.010
5	Institutionalized channels of communication at all levels	12.555	3	.006
6	Formal appeal and complaints structures	6.167	3	.104
7	Existence of student self-governance structures; i.e. clubs and associations	74.548	3	.000
8	Allowances	2.997	3	.392
9	Tuition waivers	40.026	3	.000
10	Free meals	18.390	3	.000
11	Free accommodation	6.320	3	.097
12	Free transport	14.123	3	.003
13	Leadership training	19.362	3	.000
14	Mainstreaming of governance issues in the curriculum and other activities	2.501	3	.475
15	Short and long refresher courses	1.563	3	.668
16	Retreats	3.158	3	.368
17	Public addresses/symposiums	8.669	3	.034
18	Invited guest speakers	12.205	3	007

Table A 29: Cross University Differences in External Political Influence

Support Services		χ^2 Value	d.f.	p-value
1	Formulation of constitutions and other legal frameworks	2.828	3	.419
2	Clubs/societies/associations meetings and activities	8.087	3	.044
3	Nomination process for elections	25.937	3	.000
4	Campaign for elections	41.771	3	.000
5	Actual elections	27.525	3	.000
6	Set up of governance structure	25.195	3	.000
7	Student *barazas/kamukunjis*	19.746	3	.000
8	Representation of student grievances	4.059	3	.255
9	Agenda for public discussion, debates and fora	14.399	3	.002
10	Invited guests	0.385	3	.943
11	Social activities	8.423	3	.038
12	Personal matters	9.859	3	.020

Index

A
AAU (Africa Association of Universities), 81
about-good-governance, 42–43
academic freedom, 5, 33–34, 45–46, 53, 69, 149, 165
Academic Freedom. The Uganda Higher Education Review, 176
academic planning, 101–2, 109–10, 119, 132, 135, 146, 183–85, 210–12
academic staff, 26, 29–30, 35–36, 54, 68, 81
accountability, 3, 5, 9, 33–34, 41–43, 45, 50–52, 62, 68, 73, 83, 149, 153, 162
accreditation, 5, 17, 35, 51–52, 66, 83, 87
adherence, 28, 33–34, 43–44, 50
administration, 55, 66–67, 70–73, 82, 84, 90, 168, 197, 202, 206
administrators, 7, 31, 33, 42, 47, 49, 59, 63, 70, 74–75, 149–50
admission, 19–20, 26–27, 49, 67
admission of new students, 101, 110, 118–19, 132, 136, 146, 183–85, 210–12
Adventist University, 16–18, 88
Adventist University of Africa (AUA), 16–18, 88
advising committees, 102, 109–10, 119, 132, 135–36, 146, 183–85, 211–13
Africa, 1–3, 5, 14, 16–18, 25–26, 45, 53–58, 63–64, 80, 82–83, 153, 155, 165–67, 169–71, 173–76
Africa Association of Universities (AAU), 81
Africa Nazarene University (ANU), 16–17, 88
African Charter, 46, 165
african continent, 2, 4, 21, 23, 27, 45, 68
african countries, 4, 6, 24, 29, 33–34, 44, 46, 48–50, 54–55, 153, 173
African Higher Education, 167, 171–73, 176–77

African International University (AIU), 16–18, 88
African Studies Review, 165, 175
african universities, 2, 5, 44–45, 48, 59, 64, 71, 159, 167, 172, 174–75, 177
emergent, 2
family Ties Bind, 31
african universities lack, 45
Aga Khan University (AKU), 16, 18
age, 115–17, 139, 189, 191–92, 196, 198, 201, 203, 206, 208
agenda, 41, 58, 72, 124–25, 127, 133, 137, 144, 157, 189, 214
country's development, 6, 24
Ahmad, 31, 34, 36, 50, 166
AIU (African International University), 16–18, 88
AKU (Aga Khan University), 16, 18
Altbach, 3–5, 11, 20, 29, 63, 165, 167, 172–73, 175–77
ambits, decision-making, 135
Amendments, necessary, 98, 100, 131, 141, 181, 209
ANU (Africa Nazarene University), 16–17, 88
Anyang, 54, 165
apathy, 60, 125–26, 133, 144–45, 155–56, 162–63
high levels of, 111, 143, 154, 156
appeal management decisions, 129
Appendices, 179, 181, 183, 185, 187, 189, 191, 193, 195, 197, 199, 201, 203, 205, 207
APPENDICES.indd, 179–214
Apprivate Higher Education, 173
areas
decision-making, 134, 146

lower-level, 135–36
associations, 65, 70, 81–82, 97, 110–13, 117, 121, 124, 128, 133, 136, 143–44, 147, 161, 164–65
associations meetings, 124–25, 133, 144, 189, 214
Astin, 57, 60–62, 155, 165, 167
attendance, 112, 114, 118, 120, 135, 143, 186, 212–13
AUA. See Adventist University of Africa
authority, 21, 38, 52, 56, 58, 60, 68, 70, 125, 127, 144, 149, 190
autonomous Kenyan institution, 83
avenues, sufficient, 108, 131, 134, 145, 209
award, 66–67, 82–83
awareness, 62, 181, 190, 198–99, 203
   management's lack of, 126, 128

B

background, 1
Badat, 57–58, 165
Bailey, 1–2, 11–13, 20, 165, 167
Basham, 39–40, 150, 159, 166
Bloom, 1, 3, 31, 34, 36, 50, 166
Board of Management, 65, 84–85, 101, 109, 112, 140–41, 148, 154, 210–12
Board of trustees, 84, 101, 106, 109, 112, 118–19, 128, 132, 136, 140–42, 146–47, 151, 182, 184–85, 210–12
bodies, 35, 62, 76, 81, 105, 136, 188, 195, 199, 201, 204
   university-level governance, 57
Bollen, 76, 166
Bretton Woods Institutions (BWI), 56
Brookes, 5, 40–41, 50, 166
BSc, 12, 83–84
BWI (Bretton Woods Institutions), 56

C

capacity, 4, 36, 38, 42, 44, 112, 114, 117–18, 120, 135, 186, 197, 202, 206–7, 212–13
   co-decision, 59, 148
Cape Town, 170–71
careers, 4, 21
Castells, 1, 3, 166

Catholic University of East Africa, 17
Catholic University of Eastern Africa. See CUEA
cent, 108–9, 119, 129, 141
Centre for Higher education Transformation, 165, 167, 171, 174
Centre for Higher Education Transformation. See CHET
century, 167, 175–76
challenges, 4, 8–9, 12, 25, 34, 47, 61, 126, 145, 166–68, 172–76, 191, 197, 202, 206–7
Challenges Facing African Universities, 175
Chancellor, 55, 66, 68, 71, 81, 84, 97, 106, 147
Chandaria School, 83–84
channels, institutionalized, 122–23, 133, 136, 143, 146, 187, 214
chartered universities, 86, 93
   fully-fledged, 17–18
   private, 15, 92
charters, 17–18, 46, 49, 51, 68, 83–84, 87, 96–97, 99, 106, 113, 140, 147, 158, 174
   institutional, 5, 49, 51
Chege, 54–56, 166, 173
CHET (Centre for Higher Education Transformation), 165, 167, 171, 174
civil society, 1, 42
classrooms, 26–29, 170
Cloete, 1–2, 11–12, 20, 165, 167
closure, 64, 69
closure and opening, 102, 109–10, 113, 118, 120, 132, 135–36, 146, 183–85, 211–13
closure and opening of universities, 195, 200, 205
clubs, 77, 85, 110–12, 117, 121, 124–25, 133, 136, 144, 161, 163, 188–89, 195, 200, 205
clubs and associations, 111, 121, 133, 143, 187, 214
Coalition for Reform and Democracy (CORD), 124
CODESRIA, 165, 173, 179
commercial ventures, 26–27
Commission, 35, 65–66
Commission for Higher Education, 65, 170
Commission for University Education. See CUE

Commission of Higher Education, 83
commitment, 31, 41, 62, 126, 128, 145, 147–48, 153, 157
committees, 5, 51–52, 56–57, 62, 101, 109, 111, 113, 119, 141, 143, 147, 182, 184–85, 210–12
  student support and advising, 102, 109–10, 119, 132, 135–36, 146, 183–85, 211–13
communication, 72, 105, 122–23, 133, 136, 143, 146, 187, 194, 198, 203, 207, 214
communication technology, 28–29, 170
concept, 9, 12, 37–39, 41
conditions, 14, 44, 50, 54, 67, 75
conflict, 44, 52–53, 60, 62–63, 97
congress, 54, 82, 116
consequences, 42, 103–5
  positive, 103, 141, 190
constituent colleges, 12–13, 19, 67, 80–81, 87
  public university, 14–15, 18–19
constitutions, 99, 110–11, 113, 124–25, 127, 140, 147, 176, 189, 214
consultative democratic processes, 125, 127, 191
Contemporary Higher Education, 169
contributions, 4, 19, 42, 112–14, 117–18, 132, 135, 143, 146, 149, 151, 173, 179, 186, 212–13
CORD (Coalition for Reform and Democracy), 124
corruption, 42, 45, 48, 64, 104, 152, 155, 158–59
Council, 58, 66–67, 81, 85, 111, 113, 140, 188
Council on Higher Education, 35
country, 1, 3–6, 9, 11–14, 17–18, 20–25, 32–34, 38, 45–46, 64–67, 69, 80, 84, 145, 158–59
courses, 12, 14, 25–26, 32, 83, 162, 175, 195, 200, 205
  general education, 162–63
Cress, 60–61, 167
cross-university differences, 130, 133–36, 145–46
CUE (Commission for University Education), 16–19, 26, 28, 30, 32, 34–35, 49–50, 66, 68, 81, 83, 88, 167
CUEA (Catholic University of Eastern Africa), 15–17, 88
curriculum, 26, 54–55, 122–23, 163, 187, 197, 202, 207, 214
curriculum approvals, 101, 110, 119, 183–85, 210–11, 213
Curriculum design, 101, 110, 119, 183–85, 195, 200, 205, 210–11, 213
Curriculum development, 102, 110, 119, 132, 135, 146, 183–85, 210–11, 213

D

Damtew and Altbach, 3–5, 11, 20, 29
data management, 79, 91–92
deans, 55, 67, 71–72, 81, 101, 107, 109, 113, 141–42, 147, 151, 158, 161, 163, 186
Deans' committee, 101, 109, 118–19, 183–85, 210–12
decision-makers, five, 106–7, 142
Decision Making, 182, 209, 211–12
decision-making activities, 100, 107, 109, 117, 119, 133–34, 141–43, 145
Decision Making Activities, 101, 110, 132, 183–85, 210–13
decision-making organs, 112, 150, 152
decision-making structures, 70, 126, 158
  institutional, 147
decisions, 5–8, 41–42, 47–48, 52–53, 74–75, 77, 103–4, 108, 111–12, 120–21, 126–27, 148–55, 161–63, 181–83, 209–10
  democratic, 105
  key, 73, 159–60
  major, 6, 53, 105, 142, 163
democracy, 3, 34, 41, 60, 73–77, 126, 145, 159, 165, 167–68, 174–76, 178
  direct, 75–76, 159
  liberal, 76, 159–60, 166
democratic culture, 46, 149, 156–57, 159–60, 162
democratic governance, 7–8, 57, 139, 148–49, 179
democratic governance processes, 154
democratic institutional governance form, 59
democratic theory, 73–74, 159, 167–68
democratization, 6, 8, 53–54, 61, 68, 70, 77, 103, 148, 150–51, 157, 159–60
Department, 7, 27, 40–41, 50, 66–67, 71, 74, 81, 85, 107, 163, 167–68, 176–77, 187

departmental, 57, 101, 109, 113, 118–20, 132, 134, 136, 141, 146, 160, 163, 183–85, 210–12
Departmental Leadership, 168
Deputy Vice Chancellors, 66–68, 71, 81, 106–7, 112–13, 142, 147, 161
Developing Countries, 52, 166, 175–77
development, 1–3, 5–6, 9, 12, 14, 20, 23–24, 27, 38, 44–45, 56, 162, 164, 166, 175–77
economic, 2, 55, 165–67
Development Series, 166, 168
differences, 70, 92, 126, 130, 134–36, 145, 166
significant, 92, 130, 133, 135–36, 145–46
direction, 26, 40, 66, 68–69, 76
direct representation, 111–12, 120, 128, 133–36, 148–49, 154, 160
Disabilities in Higher Education in Egypt, 177
disability, 73, 115–17, 121, 143, 189, 192, 198, 203, 208
Disciplinary, 102, 110, 119, 132, 183–85, 211–13
dispute resolution, 102, 109–10, 118–19, 132, 135, 146, 183–85, 211–13
dissemination, 2, 6, 20, 24, 85, 194, 198, 203
diversity, 43, 57, 115–16, 191, 196, 201, 206
Dynamics of Student Unrests in Kenya's Public Higher Education, 170

E

East Africa, 12–13, 17, 54, 84
East African, 12, 83, 95, 140
The East Africa University (TEAU), 16
Eastern Africa, 15, 17, 88
education, 1, 3–4, 8–9, 11, 13, 19–29, 31–32, 34–35, 40–41, 52, 66–67, 70, 80, 165–70, 173–77
relevant, 6, 11–12, 25, 50
Educational Research, 166, 170, 172
education institutions, 39
recognized, 66
Education Management, 170, 172

education market, 152
education sector, 18, 22
higher, 44, 48, 55–56
effectiveness of students' participation in governance processes, 155, 161
Effective Students' Participation, 125, 127
Efficiency and Equity in Public Universities, 174
elections, 52, 63, 69–70, 73, 115, 122, 124–25, 136, 144, 154, 156, 158
periodic democratic, 122–23, 133, 136, 143, 146, 187, 214
Embeywa, 4, 8, 11, 24, 27, 153, 169
enforcement, 98, 100, 131, 141, 181, 194, 199, 204, 209
Engaging Higher Education in Social Change, 165
Enhancing Students' Involvement, 95, 121–23, 133, 136
enrolments, 4, 19–20, 25, 27–29, 153
entrenchment, 155, 157
equality, 74–75
Equity in Public Universities, 174
European Higher Education, 170
Evaluation of Quality of University Education, 169
evidence, 1, 6–7, 33–34, 44, 49–50, 64, 68, 71, 85, 147, 160
example, 1–2, 4–5, 19–20, 25, 27, 29, 47, 49, 54, 69–71, 126, 148
existence, 33–34, 48–49, 59, 62–63, 75–76, 86, 115, 122, 124, 133–34, 136, 141, 143–45, 149–52, 155–56
Existence of student self-governance structures, 123, 133, 187, 214
expansion, 5, 17, 19–22, 153, 172, 175
Extended Schools, 167, 170
extent, 6–8, 51, 53, 70, 76, 92–93, 106, 115–16, 130, 139, 142, 145–46, 151–52, 187, 189

F

facilities, 4–5, 12, 27–29, 123, 187, 194, 199, 204, 213
faculty, 30, 33, 36, 47–49, 51–53, 59, 65–67,

71–72, 84–85, 101–2, 106–7, 160, 163, 183–85, 211
faculty appraisal and promotions, 102, 110, 118–19, 132, 134–35, 141, 145–46, 183–85, 211, 213
faculty appraisals, 102, 118, 134–35, 141, 145–46
Faculty Boards, 57, 66–68, 106, 147
faculty councils, 5, 51
Faculty Involvement in Institutional Governance, 169
fair degree of state, 34, 50
fair degree of state and higher education system enmeshment, 34, 50
Family Ties Bind African Universities, 169
feedback, 103, 112, 114, 117–18, 120, 126, 135, 143, 186, 196, 201, 206, 212–13
feedback mechanisms, 194, 198, 203, 207
feedback to students, 103, 114, 118, 135, 143, 186, 196, 201, 206, 212–13
fees, 67, 102, 105, 110, 113, 118, 120, 151–52, 183–85, 195, 200, 205, 211–13
females, 20, 84, 95, 117, 139–40
FGDs (focus group discussions), 79, 89–90, 92, 96, 99–100, 102–3, 110–16, 120–22, 124, 126–27, 140–45, 151, 154
finance, 5–6, 17, 47, 81, 121
Financing and Management of Kenyan Higher Education, 173
findings, 95, 97, 99, 101, 103, 105, 107, 109, 111, 113, 117–21, 133–37, 139–40, 146–47, 160–62
  earlier, 121, 133–34
Findings.indd, 95–138
focus group, 79, 89, 96, 102–3, 113, 124, 126, 140, 151
focus group discussants, 89–90, 111, 114–15, 140, 147, 151
focus group discussions. See FGDs
followers, 39–40, 48, 64
Formulation, 101–2, 110, 119, 124–25, 132, 134, 146, 183–85, 189, 195, 200, 205, 210–12, 214
forums, 72, 85–86, 115, 124, 137, 144
frameworks, 41, 43, 58
Frequency Per cent, 103–5, 127, 129

functions, 5, 24, 34, 41, 48–51, 67, 85–86, 121, 124–25, 144, 151, 157, 195, 200, 204
funding, 25, 27, 33, 50, 58, 158, 167
  declining, 25, 29

G
gender, 115–17, 143, 174, 189, 191–92, 196, 198, 201, 203, 206, 208
Globally Competitive Quality Education for Sustainable Development, 172
GLUK (Great Lakes University of Kisumu), 16–17, 88
good governance, 5, 9, 33–34, 37, 40–45, 47–48, 51–53, 71, 103, 153, 176
  core principles of, 6
  key principles of, 5, 45
  practice of, 3, 46, 153
  principles of, 33–34, 44–45, 48–50, 149
  shared governance principle of, 6, 70
Good governance and leadership, 44
governance, 5–9, 37–78, 95–100, 102–8, 110–15, 120–23, 125–31, 133–36, 139–54, 156–63, 168–71, 173–77, 181–82, 202–4, 209
  collaborative, 6–7, 53
  cooperative, 33, 46, 149
  impediments to effective student participation in, 95
  impediments to effective students' participation in, 90, 125, 127
  internal, 45, 51, 59, 147
  poor, 6, 9, 22, 25, 33, 42, 44, 50, 68–69
  student, 8, 171–72, 194, 198, 201, 203
  student participation in, 7, 90, 95, 99, 122, 128
  student self-, 200, 205
  student self-government, 188
  students' participation in, 57, 71, 95, 100, 105–6, 122, 130, 133, 139, 143–45, 147, 161
  term, 38
governance activities, monitor student, 105
Governance and Leadership Development in Democratisation of Universities, 169
governance arrangements, 40–41, 71
governance body, 75, 202
governance crisis, 5, 44, 48, 65

Governance Education, 174
Governance in Policy Documents, 96
governance issues, 45, 198, 203, 207
  mainstreaming of, 122–23, 187, 197, 202, 207, 214
Governance Matters, 105, 170
governance organs, 82, 99, 107, 140, 142
governance practices, good, 86, 103
governance processes, 8–9, 33, 96–98, 100, 111, 113, 123–24, 140–41, 148, 152, 154–62, 164, 196, 201, 206
governance purposes, 155–56
governance structures, 7–8, 40, 96–98, 100–101, 106–7, 109, 116–19, 124–25, 130–36, 139–44, 146–47, 182–85, 189, 191, 209–12
  high-level, 147
  lower-level, 112
governance structures and decision-making activities, 100, 109, 117, 119, 142–43
Governance Structures and Decision Making Activities, 210
governance systems, 44, 153
Governing Council, 5, 51
Governing Higher Education, 169
government, 2–4, 11, 13–14, 20–23, 25, 32–33, 37–38, 45–46, 54–56, 58, 61, 68–69, 75–76, 107, 168–69
government funding, 25–27
Government Printers, 168, 170, 172, 174–75
Grading policy, 59, 102, 110, 119, 183–85, 195, 200, 205, 210–11, 213
graduates, 2, 6, 9, 23–24, 28–30, 32, 69, 116
graduation planning, 102, 109–10, 118–19, 132, 134, 136, 145–46, 183–85, 211–13
Great Lakes University of Kisumu (GLUK), 16–17, 88
groups, 3, 7, 39–40, 42–43, 47, 60, 73, 76, 89, 92, 117, 140, 153, 191, 203
growth, 4, 12–14, 17, 19, 22–23, 26, 29, 35, 48, 50, 55–56, 81, 84, 87, 177
  phenomenal, 18, 22–23, 25
Gudo, 4, 8, 19–21, 28–31, 153, 168

H

hallmark, 151–53
handbooks, 5, 51
Health Sciences, 80, 83–84, 96
HELB (Higher Education Loans Board), 66
higher education, 1–4, 11, 13–14, 17–18, 20–25, 33, 37–39, 43–51, 53–57, 59, 61–63, 65–67, 69–71, 165–74, 176–77
  associated, 3
  external, 49
  facing, 33
  principles of good governance in, 49–50
  private, 14, 175–76
  regulating, 195, 199, 204
Higher Educational Institutions, 12, 177
Higher Education Civic Responsibility and Democracy, 176
higher education community, 62, 148
higher education enrolments, 14
higher education governance, 39, 167
Higher Education.indd, 37–78
Higher Education in International Perspective, 175
Higher Education in Public Universities, 175
higher education institutions, 1, 9, 26, 29, 38, 40, 44, 46–47, 52, 57, 63–64, 91
Higher Education Loans Board (HELB), 66
higher education participation rates, 1
higher education policy, 58
higher education policy formulation, 57
higher education programmes, 63
higher education provision, 22
Higher Education Quality, 173
Higher Education Quarterly, 169
higher education reforms, 63
higher education research, 167
Higher Education Studies, 174
Higher Education Support Fund, 171
higher education system enmeshment, 34, 50
higher education systems, 4, 33, 170
  largest, 18
Higher Education Teaching Personnel, 46
Higher Education Transformation, 165, 167, 171, 174
higher education vol, 168, 170
high importance, 100–102, 141

Humanities, 80, 83–84, 88, 96, 139
human resources, 1–2, 13, 20, 35, 168

I

IAU (International Association of Universities), 81, 175
ICEF Monitor, 19, 26, 169
ICT, 102, 109–10, 120, 132, 134, 170, 183–85, 211–13
impediments, 8, 90, 95, 125–29, 139, 144–45, 190, 197, 202, 206
implications, 12, 32, 55, 92, 106, 121, 152, 158, 165–66, 172–74
Inadequacies in teaching and learning facilities in public universities, 28
incentives, 8, 22, 30, 115, 121–23, 128, 139, 144, 156, 163
   material, 122–23, 143–44
   structural, 121–23, 143–44
individuals, 2, 4, 11, 21, 40, 45, 47, 73, 76, 90, 150, 162
influence, strong, 108, 182, 210
influence decisions, 62, 112, 114, 118, 120, 186, 212–13
informants, 110, 114, 120, 142, 144
information, 28, 42–43, 62, 71, 73, 89–93, 170, 179, 181–82, 188
input, 24, 108, 114, 117–18, 120, 126–27, 132, 135, 143, 146, 182, 186, 206, 210, 212–13
   constructive, 59, 149
institutional goals, 71, 159
institutional governance, 34, 38, 47, 58, 63, 150, 169
institutional governance procedures, 148
institutional governance structure, 148
Institutional Policy on Student Involvement in Governance, 181
institutional practices, 54, 98–100, 130, 141, 145
Institutional Strategic, 98
Institutional structures, 44, 59
institutions, 4–8, 17–18, 26–28, 30–31, 35–40, 43–54, 58–60, 80–81, 83–84, 86–89, 91–93, 99–100, 140, 148–53, 155–59
   educational, 60
   governed, 33, 44
   public, 18, 66, 86, 97
   registered, 17, 19
institution's governance process, 131
interests, 39, 42–44, 58, 60, 70, 73, 76–77, 103–4, 126, 128–29, 142, 151–52, 156–57, 161, 163
   lack of, 115, 145, 154, 156–58, 162
internal governance structures, 67, 140
International Association of Universities (IAU), 81, 175
International Consortium for Higher Education Civic Responsibility, 176
International Handbook of Higher Education, 165
International Higher Education, 165, 172
International Higher Education Policy, 173
International Journal of higher education research, 167
Inter-University Council for East Africa (IUCEA), 81
interviewees, 91, 95–97, 100–102, 104–5, 108, 114–18, 124, 126, 141
interviews, 79, 89–90, 92, 140
Involvement in Decision Making Activities, 183–85, 212
Involvement in Governance in Policy Documents, 96
involvement in governance structures and decision-making activities, 100, 109, 119, 142
Involvement in Governance Structures and Decision Making Activities, 210
involvement policies, 128, 191
items, 90, 98, 101, 107–9, 118–19, 135, 142, 152, 183
IUCEA (Inter-University Council for East Africa), 81

J

JKUAT (Jomo Kenyatta University of Agriculture and Technology), 15, 35, 80, 87
Johnson, 48, 59–60, 68, 79, 149, 165, 169
Jomo Kenyatta University of Agriculture and Technology. See JKUAT
Journal of Assessment and Evaluation in Higher Education, 168
Journal of Higher Education, 177
justification, 8–9

K

Kabarak University (KABU), 16–18, 88, 168
KABU. See Kabarak University
Kaburu, 4, 8, 11, 24, 27, 153, 169
KACE (Kenya Advanced Certificate of Education), 21
Kamuzora, 61–62, 73, 169
Kauffeldt, 1–2, 4–5, 11, 20, 25, 27–30, 33–34, 44–47, 49–50, 149–50, 170
KCAU (KCA University), 16–17, 88
KCA University (KCAU), 16–17, 88
KCSE (Kenya Certificate of Secondary Education), 21
KeMU (Kenya Methodist University), 16–18, 88
Kenya Advanced Certificate of Education (KACE), 21
Kenya Certificate of Secondary Education (KCSE), 21
Kenya Education Sector Support Programme, 22
Kenya government, 13, 17, 35, 46, 91–92
Kenya government's goal, 24
Kenya government's grip, 17
Kenya Highlands Evangelical University (KHEU), 16–18, 88
Kenya.indd, 11–36
Kenya Methodist University (KeMU), 16–18, 88
Kenya National Bureau, 25, 170
Kenya National Examination Council (KNEC), 32
Kenyan Commission for Higher Education, 87
Kenyan context, 21, 72
Kenyan Higher Education, 173
Kenyan Ministry of Education, 83
Kenyan Public Universities, 175
Kenyans, 3, 6, 13, 20–21, 23–24, 29, 73, 84, 158
Kenyan situation, 11, 28, 68
Kenyan society, 4, 158
Kenyan universities, 6–8, 24, 30, 65, 68, 100, 106, 123, 142, 150, 156, 158, 162, 166, 175
Kenyan universities lecturers, 30
Kenya's Commission of University Education, 35
Kenya's Higher Education, 169
Kenya's Public Higher Education, 170
Kenya's Public Universities, 177
Kenya's universities, 17, 172
Kenya's university education sector, 6
Kenyatta, 63, 172–73
Kenyatta College, 13, 80
Kenyatta University. See KU
Kenyatta University College (KUC), 13, 80
Kenyatta University Students Association. See KUSA
Keriri Women's University of Science and Technology (KWUST), 16, 18
key informants. See KIs
KHEU (Kenya Highlands Evangelical University), 16–18, 88
KI interviews and FGDs, 110–11, 113, 116, 120
KIs (key informants), 89–90, 93, 96, 99, 120, 124, 126–27, 140, 143–44, 147, 149
KIs and FGDS, 99, 111–12, 115, 120–22, 126–27, 141–42, 144–45
Klemenčič, 6–7, 53, 57–60, 63, 68, 149–50, 156, 170
KNEC (Kenya National Examination Council), 32
knowledge, 1, 4, 6, 8–9, 11, 24, 31, 43, 62, 73, 75, 86, 99, 167, 175
relevant, 1–2, 20
Kouzes, 39, 170
KU (Kenyatta University), 14–15, 80–82, 86–89, 91–92, 95, 102–3, 110–11, 113, 116, 120–22, 126–27, 136–37, 139–40, 142–46, 154
KU and USIU students, 135, 145–46
KUC (Kenyatta University College), 13, 80
KU counterparts, 128, 135–36, 145
KUSA (Kenyatta University Students Association), 82, 99, 110–11, 113, 116, 121, 127–28, 140, 142, 154–55, 157, 170
KU students, 112, 114, 122, 130–31, 134–36, 144–46
KWUST (Keriri Women's University of Science and Technology), 16, 18

Index

L

lack of student interest, 115, 156
laws, 39, 43, 49, 61, 74, 76, 80, 83
leaders, 39–41, 48, 52, 57, 61, 64–65, 74, 80, 103–4, 115, 126, 155, 159, 161–62, 172
   institutional, 45, 60
leadership, 37, 39–41, 44–45, 48, 61–62, 64–65, 103, 105, 126, 150–51, 155–56, 158–59, 161–64, 170–72, 174–75
   distributed, 39–40, 172, 175
   effective, 41, 166, 174
   participative, 40, 150, 159
   self-seeking, 104, 142
   transformational, 39, 48
Leadership and Institutional Change in South African Higher Education, 170
Leadership Best Practices for Sustaining Quality in UK Higher Education, 174
leadership capacity, lack of, 126–27, 190
Leadership Development in Democratisation of Universities, 169
Leadership Foundation for Higher Education, 166
Leadership in Kenyan Public Universities, 175
Leading Urban Institutions of Higher Education, 174
learning, 22, 27–28, 32, 34, 61, 81, 104, 150, 167–69, 172, 174, 176
   higher, 2, 5, 7, 14, 44–46, 84, 87, 155, 157, 161, 171, 179
learning facilities, 9, 25–29, 64
lecturers, 29–32, 45, 81, 113
lecture sessions, 89, 91
legal basis, 51, 97–98, 126, 128, 130–31, 140, 145, 147, 181, 194, 199, 204, 209
Lessons, 166–67, 173–74
Letter of Interim Authority. See LIA
Leuscher-Mamashela, 6, 59, 68, 149
level governance structures, 111, 143
level of satisfaction, 8, 106, 117–18, 135, 139, 143, 185
level of students' participation in governance processes, 60, 156
levels, 7–8, 23, 45–47, 71–72, 99–102, 111–13, 122–23, 133–36, 142–44, 146–48, 160–61, 163–64, 194–95, 199–200, 204–5

lower, 112, 120, 134, 143, 148–49, 151, 160
LIA (Letter of Interim Authority), 16–17, 19
libraries, 5, 26–27, 35, 64, 102, 109–10, 120, 132, 134, 183–85, 211–13
limitations, 10, 79, 92, 197, 202, 207
Limitations on student involvement in governance of university, 197, 202, 207
list, 106, 122, 129, 142, 190
London, 12, 166–68, 171, 174, 176–77
London Leadership Foundation for Higher Education, 168
lower levels of education, 32
lower levels of management, 114, 143, 163
Luescher-Mamashela, 7, 9, 54, 56–58, 62–64, 153, 155, 171
Lukenya University, 16–17

M

mainstreaming, 7, 90, 95, 97–99, 122, 126, 140–41, 147
Mainstreaming of Involvement in Governance in Policy Documents, 96
males, 20, 84, 95, 139–40
management, 43–45, 63, 68–69, 99–101, 103–6, 108–9, 112, 114, 125–28, 140–44, 151–56, 159–64, 169–72, 190, 210–12
   financial, 5, 51–52
management communication, 129
Management Council, 85, 101, 109, 112–13, 118–19, 128, 140–42, 148, 151, 154, 182, 184–85, 210–12
Management Councils and Senate, 109, 147
management decision, 108, 182, 210
management honesty, 129
management interference, 157
Management of Kenyan Higher Education, 173
Management University of Africa (MUA), 16
manipulation, 22, 129, 154, 157–58, 160
Martin, 5, 41, 44, 171
Masinde Muliro University of Science and Technology (MMUST), 13, 15, 87
Mass Higher Education, 176

massification, 4, 8, 11, 21, 23–24, 53
Master of Business Administration (MBA), 84
matter, 37, 88, 97–98, 106, 130–31, 133, 141, 145, 151–52, 181, 209
MBA (Master of Business Administration), 84
mechanisms, 50, 57, 68, 73, 194, 198–99, 203–4, 207
meetings, 34, 112, 114–15, 117–18, 120, 126, 132, 135–36, 143, 146, 186, 196, 201, 206, 212–13
   attendance in, 114, 118, 135, 143, 186, 212–13
   decision-making, 120
members, 39–40, 55, 57–58, 62, 67, 76, 81–82, 85, 89–90, 97–100, 131, 141, 149–50, 159, 162
   general, 196, 201, 205
   pertinent, 97, 99, 107, 140, 142, 147, 152
Methodology, 79, 81, 83, 85, 87, 89, 91, 93
Methodology.indd, 79–94
Ministry of Education (MoE), 3, 6, 18–20, 22–26, 32, 34, 49, 65–67, 172, 174
Ministry of Higher Education, 66
Mistrust of student leaders, 125, 127, 144, 190
Mixed Methods Research, 169
MKU. See Mount Kenya University
MMUST. See Masinde Muliro University of Science and Technology
Moderating management, 188, 196, 201, 205
Module II, 26–27
MoE. See Ministry of Education
Mohamedbhai, 64, 69, 153, 172
Moi University (MU), 13–15, 35, 87, 170, 174
money, 32, 34, 36, 115, 152
monitor, 35, 38, 40, 43, 74–75
motivation, 73, 197, 202, 206–7
Mount Kenya University (MKU), 16–18, 88
MU. See Moi University
MUA (Management University of Africa), 16
Mulinge, 179
Munene, 8, 11, 19, 24–29, 32, 34–35, 50, 54, 153, 172
Mutula, 6, 8, 12–14, 19–20, 22, 26–29, 31–32, 34, 44, 50, 68–70, 150–51, 153, 172
Mwebi and Simatwa, 11, 22, 27–28
Mwiria, 7, 12, 22, 44, 56, 68–71, 153, 172

N

NACOSTI (National Council for Science Technology and Innovations), 91–92
Nairobi, 12–14, 18, 54–55, 63, 80, 82–83, 87–88, 154, 168, 170, 172–76, 179–80
National association, 121, 188
National College for School Leadership, 41, 172
National Council for Science Technology and Innovations (NACOSTI), 91–92
nationality, 115–17, 121, 192–93, 198, 203, 208
national politics, 123–25, 127, 144, 161, 189, 196, 201, 206
nations, 1, 20, 82, 166
Nature and Role of Student Involvement in Self-governance, 195, 200, 205
negative consequences, 46, 104–5, 141–42, 161, 190
Negative Consequences of Students' Participation in Governance, 104–5
New York, 165, 167, 174–75, 177
Nganga, 8, 11, 19–20, 24–26, 34, 50, 153, 173
Ngome, 4–5, 11–12, 19–20, 22, 29, 69, 172–73
Nottingham, 167, 170, 172
number, 4–5, 13–14, 17–22, 25, 34–35, 45, 55–56, 66, 68, 121, 151, 153, 160, 162, 169
   total, 17–19
nurture, 8, 51, 103, 105, 121, 129, 139, 142–43, 159–60
Nyaboga, 2, 4, 8, 11, 153, 173
Nyangau, 3, 8, 11–13, 20, 23–29, 32–34, 50, 153, 173

O

objectives, 6–7, 9–10, 24, 28, 40, 51, 82, 85–86, 92, 160
Obondo, 5, 7, 40, 44, 47, 60, 63, 65, 68, 72, 150, 159, 164, 173
Odebero, 28, 30, 173
OECD, 5, 39, 47, 173
offices, 7, 28, 30, 55, 71, 73, 85, 113, 134, 136, 146, 156–58, 194, 199, 204
officials, 7, 74, 85, 113, 115, 156
   general members and selection of, 196, 201, 205
Ogot, 28, 30, 173

Okioga, 2, 4, 8, 11, 14, 20–22, 24–25, 27–28, 30, 34, 36, 153, 173
Okwakol, 27–28, 173
Onsongo, 2, 4, 8, 11, 13–14, 17, 21, 153, 173–74
Organizational Development Journal, 174
organizational structures, 39, 71, 90, 95
Organizational Structures and Nature of Students' Involvement in Governance, 71
organizations, 36, 38–41, 58, 62, 66, 73–74, 81–82, 85, 110–11, 113, 142, 153, 157, 170, 175
orientation of new students, 101–2, 109–10, 118–19, 131–32, 134–36, 145–46, 183–85, 210–11, 213
Origins and Growth of University Education, 12
Origins of Students' Participation in University Governance, 53
Owuor, 19, 30, 174

P

Pan Africa Christian University, 16–18, 88
Paris, 166, 169, 172, 175–76
Parrish, 39–40, 47–48, 153, 159, 174
participation, 8–9, 33, 40–42, 57, 60–61, 63–64, 70–75, 99–100, 105–9, 118–19, 121–22, 130–36, 143–48, 152–57, 159–62
  management-controlled, 148, 161
  stakeholder, 40, 153
participation principle, 47
participatory, higher education institutions practice, 39
participatory democracy, 74–75, 159, 161, 166, 177
participatory governance, 54, 60
participatory institutions, 75
participatory processes, 74–75
people, 2, 29, 37–42, 47, 61, 64, 73–76
Persson, 62, 72–73, 148, 174
pharmacy, 18, 83–84
Pillay, 1–2, 11–12, 20, 165, 167
place mechanisms, 98, 100, 131, 141, 181, 209
players, 106–7, 186
policies, 38, 40, 42, 45, 71, 97–102, 105, 115, 128–31, 141–42, 145, 194, 198–99, 203–4, 209–12
  implementation and enforcement of, 98, 100, 131, 141, 181, 209
  institutional, 90, 95, 160, 181
  public, 42, 74
  published, 97–98, 130–31, 145, 181, 194, 199, 203, 209
  university's, 97–98, 130–31, 140, 147, 181, 209
  vision, 194, 198, 203
policy documents, 13, 96–98, 130, 140, 145
policy documents and practices, 97–98, 140
policy formulation, 6, 47, 66, 74, 85, 99, 103, 108, 131, 134, 145, 150, 182, 210
policy-formulation, 42, 77
political meddling, 8, 22, 34, 49, 69, 127, 145
  external, 104, 136–37, 146
political parties, 54, 58, 76, 124, 126, 128, 144, 158, 161, 189–90
politicians, 49, 126–28
Politics of Higher Education Transformation, 165
poor quality, 28, 31–32, 35
Positive Consequences of Students' Participation in Governance, 103
Posner, 39, 44, 170
power, 21, 38–41, 47–48, 51, 67, 73, 104, 150, 155
Pre-determined qualities, 196, 201, 205
Presbyterian University of East Africa (PUEA), 16
President, 68, 81–82, 112, 154
principles, 7, 9, 33–34, 37, 45–46, 48, 59–60, 68, 70–71, 73, 76–77, 96, 140, 148, 160
principles of good governance in universities, 48, 149
Principles of Good Governance in University Education, 45
Private Initiatives in Higher Education, 167
private institutions, 14, 16–19, 152
private sectors, 17–19, 22, 26, 46, 66, 86, 92, 113, 130, 150, 156, 163
private universities, 14, 17–20, 22–23, 26, 28–29, 32–33, 35, 65–68, 70–71, 87–88, 96, 147–48, 150–58, 160–63, 172
  accredited, 17
  established, 87
  fully-fledged chartered, 17

growth of, 23, 174
new, 66
single, 18
Privatisation and Apprivate Higher Education, 173
Probe, 90, 194–208
problems, 22, 72, 100, 103, 112–14, 120, 143, 168, 171–72, 175, 186
  solution of, 117–18, 135, 186, 212–13
processes, 7–8, 37–38, 41–43, 46–48, 74–75, 77, 89, 91, 93, 124, 126, 144–45, 147–48, 198–99, 203–4
  decision-making, 38, 42–43, 45, 47, 54, 104, 106, 113–14, 139–40, 143, 145, 147, 149–51, 157, 159
  making, 7–8, 33, 104, 108, 111, 162, 182, 210
Procurements, 102, 110, 120, 132, 136, 146, 183–85, 211–13
programmes, 2, 13, 18, 22, 26, 35, 51–52, 66, 80, 121, 160
program reviews, 101, 110, 119, 183–85, 210–11, 213
promotions, 33–34, 49, 53, 66–67, 86, 102, 110, 118–19, 132, 134–35, 141, 145–46, 183–85, 211, 213
proxy, 112–13, 120, 133, 140, 151–52
public-private universities comparison, systematic, 8
public universities, 13–14, 18–23, 25–29, 34–35, 50, 55–56, 65–72, 80, 84, 87, 124, 127, 151–53, 157, 174–75
  enrolments in, 19–20
  fastest-growing, 87
  forced, 25
  fully-fledged, 18
  fully-fledged chartered, 14, 18
  respective, 71
  single, 18
public universities manifests, 27
PUEA (Presbyterian University of East Africa), 16
p-value, 131, 135, 209–14

Q
qualitative approaches, 79
qualitative data, 79, 114, 122, 124, 126, 145
Qualitative Study, 172
quality, 4–6, 8–9, 11, 21–29, 31–32, 34–35, 41, 44–46, 52–53, 61–63, 65, 73, 92–93, 168–69, 172–76
  declining, 25, 31, 64
quality assurance, 47, 65, 102, 109–10, 119, 121, 166, 174, 183–85, 188, 196, 201, 205, 210–11, 213
quality education, 23, 25, 27–29, 33, 35, 44, 51, 165, 168
  competitive, 6, 24
  delivery of, 31
Quality Education Development, 168
Quality Teaching, 168
quality university education, 4, 23, 29
questionnaire, 79, 89–91, 179–80
questions, following, 181–83, 186, 188

R
recognition, 2–4, 47, 49, 65, 128–29
recommendations, 12–13, 97, 106, 139, 141, 143, 145, 147, 149, 151, 153, 155, 157, 159, 161–63
Recommendations.indd, 139–64
recruitment of faculty and staff, 102, 109–10, 119, 121, 132, 135, 141, 146, 183–85, 211, 213
References.indd, 165–78
Registered Private Institutions, 16–17
Reisberg, 4–5, 45, 174
relation, 37, 39, 42, 52, 58, 60, 72–73, 140
relationship, 1, 7, 9, 37, 39, 62, 64, 72, 75, 154–55, 158, 171, 174
remainder, 18, 95, 97
representation, 57, 76–77, 100–101, 103, 112, 114–18, 124–26, 128, 135, 143, 151, 163–64, 186, 189, 212–14
  adequate, 56–57
  formal, 57
  proxy, 134, 151–52, 154, 164
representatives, 67, 72, 76–77, 85, 103, 107, 112, 120, 128, 142, 147, 151, 156–57, 159, 162–63

proxy, 151–52, 164
Republic, 3, 13, 21, 66–67, 106, 147, 174–75
research, 2–4, 6, 24, 26, 31, 34, 36, 44, 46, 66–67, 72, 166, 168, 173, 175–77
Research Design, 10, 79
Research Design and Methodology, 79–94
researchers, 79, 88–91, 180
Research in Higher Education, 176
Research Leadership in Higher Education, 172
research universities, 35, 46
Resources for Quality Education Development, 168
respondents, 86, 89–92, 95–96, 99–109, 114–16, 118, 123–24, 128–30, 137, 140–42, 151, 153, 156, 179
  actual, 88–89
  primary, 88–91, 140–44
  survey, 121–22, 125, 129, 141
responsibilities, 23, 31, 33–34, 38, 40–43, 45, 48–51, 60, 66–67, 71, 81, 84–85, 112, 120, 149
revisions, 4, 71, 98, 100, 128, 131, 141, 181, 191, 194, 199, 204, 209
rights, clear, 5, 33, 45, 48–49, 149
Rost, 39, 48, 64, 175
rules, 38, 42–43, 51–52, 58, 63, 73–74, 176
  democratic, 74, 76
  institutional, 60, 63, 156

S

SAC (Student Affairs Council), 84–85, 97, 99, 111–13, 115, 121, 126, 128, 140, 142, 155, 157, 176
samples
  combined public-private universities, 97
  primary, 86, 88, 139–40
Santiso, 38, 41–42, 175
SAPs (Structural Adjustment Programmes), 22, 56
scales, following, 181–83, 185–86, 191
scholarships, 65–66, 166
School Leadership, 41, 172
School of Humanities and Social sciences, 80, 83–84, 88
School of Pharmacy and Health Sciences, 83–84

School of Science and Technology, 83–84
schools, 67, 71, 80, 83, 88–91, 112–13, 116, 120, 134, 139, 160, 192, 195, 200, 205
Schools of Education and Business in Kenyatta University, 88
school-wide committees, 101, 109, 118–19, 141, 183–85, 210–12
Science and Technology, 13, 15–16, 66, 83–84, 87, 96, 139, 166, 174
Scott Christian University (SCU), 15, 17–18, 88
SCU (Scott Christian University), 15, 17–18, 88
secretary, 3, 67, 82, 116, 154
sector, 1–6, 8–9, 11–12, 14, 17, 20, 22–25, 36, 45, 50, 53, 61, 69, 92, 155
  public, 19–20, 22, 26, 28, 38, 42, 46, 65, 69–70, 86, 92, 151, 158, 161
Secure Kenya's Development in Knowledge Economy, 174
SEKU (South Eastern Kenya University), 15, 87
selection, 33, 49, 68, 86, 88–89, 188, 196, 201, 205
self-governance, 55–56, 70, 85, 115, 135, 150, 161, 188, 195, 200, 205
  academic, 44, 48
  managerial, 44, 48
self-governance bodies, 160, 162
self-governance organizations, 110, 121, 142, 157
self-governance processes, 151, 157–58
self-governance structures, 57, 90, 95, 121, 124, 136, 144, 146, 155, 159, 163–64
  university governance and student, 116–17, 191
Senate, 51, 66–68, 71, 81, 101, 109, 118–20, 132, 134, 136, 140–41, 146–47, 182, 184–85, 210–12
sentiments, 23–24, 26–27, 29, 31–32, 39, 41, 60, 74, 100, 112, 141, 155
services, 18, 26, 43–44, 52, 58, 67, 115–16, 121, 187–88, 196, 201, 205
shared governance, 5–6, 33, 45–48, 51–52, 59, 68, 70, 149–50, 153
  principle of, 33, 47
shortage, 28–30, 50
  public universities experience, 27
Sifuna, 12, 26, 29, 45, 55, 72, 175

Simatwa, 11, 22, 27–28, 172
skills, 1, 4, 6, 20, 23–24, 31, 39–41, 50, 61–62, 86, 99, 167, 169, 176–77
social institution, 1
Social Sciences, 18, 20, 80, 83–84, 88, 96, 139, 168–69
society, 5–6, 23–24, 33, 37–39, 43–54, 59–61, 63–64, 113, 121, 124–25, 144–45, 149–50, 155, 161–62, 175–76
socio-economic development, 1, 3–4, 6, 11, 20, 23–24, 61
Softkenya, 19, 175
South Africa, 64, 170–71
South African Higher Education, 170
South African Universities Closed, 165
South Eastern Kenya University (SEKU), 15, 87
SPU (St Paul University), 16–17, 88
stability, financial, 5, 33, 45, 49, 52, 149
staff, 29, 54, 56–57, 63, 65, 67–70, 72, 102, 109–10, 119, 121, 146, 164, 183–85, 211
   recruitment of, 113, 188, 196, 200, 205
stakeholders, 42–45, 47–52, 59, 62, 68, 73–76, 99, 103, 149–50, 153, 159–61, 164, 190, 195, 199
   important, 99, 147–48
   internal, 48–49
Stakeholder Society, 169, 175
statements, 97, 99, 140–41, 181–83, 185–86, 191, 198–99, 203
   key governance, 194, 198, 203
Status of Higher Education Teaching Personnel, 46
statutes, institutional, 71
story, 165, 171, 173, 175
St Paul University (SPU), 16–17, 88
strategic plan, 71, 97–98, 130–31, 147, 181, 194, 199, 203, 209
Strategic planning, 56, 101, 110, 119, 132, 135, 146, 183–85, 210–12
strategies, 25–26, 35, 126, 128, 162, 191
Strathmore University, 16–18, 88
Structural Adjustment Programmes (SAPs), 22, 56
structures, 37–38, 57–58, 68, 72, 74–75, 77, 101, 117, 121, 134–35, 147, 152, 160–61, 164, 167

Student Affairs Council. See SAC
student assessment, 102, 109–10, 119, 132, 134, 145, 183–85, 210–11, 213
student body, 7, 9, 55, 58, 64, 84, 112, 114–16, 128, 148, 154, 162, 190
student community, 82, 155–56, 161
student elections, 60, 154, 156–60, 196, 201, 206
Student evaluation, 102, 109–10, 118–19, 183–85, 210–11, 213
student governance bodies, 72, 196–97, 200, 205–6
student governance body cater, 198, 203, 208
Student Government Association, 110, 172
student government councils, 121
student governments, 7, 55, 57–63, 73, 124, 144, 156, 170, 188, 197, 201, 206
student KIs, 100, 112, 122, 141, 144
student leaders, 47, 55, 61–64, 72–73, 77, 89, 93, 105–6, 122, 125–29, 140, 144–45, 152, 154–56, 159–62
   reward, 129
student leadership, 6–8, 63–64, 72, 79, 90, 93, 104–6, 122, 126, 128–30, 150, 156–57, 162–63, 186, 190
   intimidation of, 129
   proactive, 105, 142
   quality of, 7
student leadership and university activities, 105, 142
student leadership bodies, 129–30
student leadership organizations, 129
student movements, 54, 60, 165
student organizations, 57–58, 85
student participation, 7, 33, 62–63, 90, 95, 104, 108, 122, 126, 128, 162, 170–71, 174, 182, 209
Student Participation in Governance of Higher Education, 174
student power, 105, 142, 170–71
student protests, 58, 63–64
student representation, 33, 57, 114–15, 121, 141, 143, 148
student representatives, 59–60, 67, 75, 107, 114, 117, 120, 140, 171, 187
   election of, 115–16, 191
student self-governance bodies, 70, 155, 189

student self-governance organizations, 121, 188
student self-governance processes, 139
student self-governance structures, 115–17, 121, 123, 133, 187, 191, 214
Students' Involvement, 53, 57, 60, 71, 73, 98, 101, 106, 114, 116, 118, 130–31, 133–35
students leaders, 104, 126, 128, 191
Students' Participation, 53, 103–5
Students' Self-Governance Processes, 123, 125, 144
student support, 102, 109, 118, 134–36, 145–46, 155
student unions, 58–59, 64, 71–72, 77, 155
student unrests, 63–64, 69, 165, 170, 172
study, 6–10, 79–80, 86, 88–93, 95–97, 113–17, 121–25, 136–37, 139–41, 143–48, 150–53, 155–62, 170–71, 179–80, 192
study findings, 93
study objectives, 89, 140
study program, 117, 192, 198, 203, 208
study programme, 115–16
study representation, 115
study respondents, 10, 95, 126
study subjects, 9, 104, 107, 109, 124, 129, 142
support services, 123, 130, 133–34, 136, 145, 187, 197, 202, 207, 213–14
Support services committees, 102, 109–10, 120, 132, 136, 146, 183–85, 211–13
Support Staff Participation in College Governance, 177
support systems, 72–73, 90, 95, 122, 160, 197, 202, 207
Survey of Student Involvement in University Governance, 179
systems, 13, 24–25, 38–39, 43, 58–59, 152, 164
representative management, 64, 155

T

Table, 14, 18, 86–87, 95–109, 114–19, 121–27, 129–31, 134, 136, 147, 209–14
Tanganyika African Welfare Society (TAWS), 54
Task Force, 45, 47, 50–53
Task Force for University Education and Society, 153
Task Force on Education and Society, 52

Task force on Higher Education and Society, 33, 38–39, 44, 46–51, 59, 63, 70, 149–50, 176
Task Force on University Education and Society, 43, 45, 50–53
Task Force on University Education in Society, 51–52
Task on University Education and Society, 5, 52
TAWS (Tanganyika African Welfare Society), 54
teaching, 2, 17, 27–28, 30–32, 34, 36, 51–52, 64, 165, 171
TEAU (The East Africa University), 16
Technology, 13, 15–16, 18, 66, 80, 83–84, 87–88, 96, 139, 166, 174
Teferra, 29, 167, 172–73, 176–77
Tertiary Education, 34, 170, 172, 175, 177
tools, 9, 28, 37, 45, 50–53
top, 48, 106–7, 112–13, 125, 129, 137, 140–42, 144, 151
top governance structures, 128, 151
top management, 47, 70, 99, 111–12, 115, 121, 147, 149–52, 154–55, 157–58, 190
top management officials, 89, 140
top managements of universities, 70, 147
top organs, 112, 120–21, 160, 164
top university management, 161
transparency, 42–43, 51–52, 62, 74, 129, 162–63, 191
trustees, 83–84, 101, 106, 109, 112, 118–19, 128, 132, 136, 140–42, 146–47, 151, 182, 184–85, 210–12
tuition, increment of, 102, 110, 118, 120, 183–85, 195, 200, 205, 211–13

U

UEAB (University of Eastern Africa, Baraton), 15, 17, 88
Uganda Higher Education Review, 173
UK Higher Education, 174
UNESCO (United Nations Educational, Scientific and Cultural Organization), 3, 14, 22, 29, 46, 63, 172, 176
unions, 110, 121, 124, 128, 142–44, 155, 160
United Nations Educational, Scientific and Cultural Organization. See UNESCO
United States, 14, 76, 83, 87

United States International University. See USIU
universities
  establishing, 49, 147
  fully-fledged, 13–14, 18–19, 80, 87
  joining, 21, 29
  new, 4, 66
  parent, 14, 34
  private sector, 4, 106
  second, 13, 168
Universities, Kenya, 173
Universities Act, 65, 67, 69, 83–85, 106, 147, 158, 174
Universities Education Act, 66
universities student leaders, 99
University College of Nairobi, 12
University Council, 55, 57, 66–68, 71, 81, 84, 101, 106–7, 109, 118–19, 136, 146–47, 182, 184–86, 210–12
university education, 3–5, 11–14, 17–26, 30, 34–35, 43, 45, 50–53, 64–68, 80–81, 84, 103, 153, 167–68, 171–72
  access to, 3, 73
  development of, 12, 168
  expansion of, 20, 169, 173
  facing, 8, 34
  governance in, 43
  governance of, 37, 65
  growth of, 11–36
  massification of, 4–5
  private, 14, 17, 22
  private sectors of, 26, 130
  quality of, 12, 23, 25, 30, 169
  relevant, 6, 24
University Education and Society, 46, 153
University Education in Africa, 174
university education sector, 9, 23
university education system, 3–4, 20, 23
university governance
  democratic, 57
  good, 9
  impediments to effective students' involvement in, 125, 139, 144
  student participation in, 99, 104, 128, 171, 177

university governance policy documents, 71
university governance practices, 54, 147
university governance processes, 6, 53, 110, 118, 121, 142, 186, 190
  permeated, 152
university governance structures, 104, 112, 115–16, 150, 161, 163, 191
  principle top, 112
university governance zeroing, 159
university institutions, 21, 59, 149
university management, 7, 9, 47, 64, 85–86, 103, 129, 157
  intimidation of student leadership by, 129
university missions, 86, 96, 140, 195, 200, 205
University of East Africa, 12
University of Eastern Africa, 15, 17, 88
University of Eastern Africa, Baraton (UEAB), 15, 17, 88
University of Nairobi (UoN), 12–15, 18, 35, 69, 80, 87, 124, 165, 171
university policies, 59–60, 105, 108, 116, 149, 182, 191, 210
university's governance structures, 133, 135
university students, 19, 31–32, 60, 72, 108, 158, 182, 209–10
university vision, 101, 110, 119, 132, 135, 146, 183–85, 210–12
university-wide communications, 108, 131, 134, 145, 209
University World News, 171, 173
UoN. See University of Nairobi
USIU (United States International University), 16–18, 80, 82–89, 95–96, 99–100, 110–13, 120–22, 126–28, 136–37, 139–40, 144–46, 151–52, 154–56, 176, 179–80
USIU Charter, 99, 140
USIU counterparts, 130–31, 134–35, 145
USIU students, 112, 130, 133–36, 145–46, 151

V

Vice Chancellor, 45, 55, 66–68, 71, 81–82, 84–85, 106, 142, 147, 161
visions, 6–7, 24, 39, 41, 53, 71, 86, 99, 195, 200, 205
vision statements, 56, 96, 99, 140

voices, 2, 42, 47–48, 54, 57, 76, 79, 120, 126, 150–51, 156, 160, 163
vol, 165–74, 176–77
voting power, 112, 114, 118, 120, 135, 143, 186, 191, 196, 201, 206, 212–13

W

Wainwright, 74–76, 177
WASC (Western Association of Schools and Colleges), 83
Washington, 170, 172, 176–77
Washington DC, 166, 177
Wawire, 22, 69, 73, 172, 177
Western Association of Schools and Colleges (WASC), 83
Western higher education systems, 2
what-is-good-governance, 42–43
work, 26–27, 30, 35–36, 46, 61, 68, 71, 74–75, 85, 88, 152
World Bank, 1–3, 11, 20, 25, 28, 33, 38, 42–43, 50, 56, 166, 168–70, 172, 175, 177
www, 37, 43, 165–68, 170, 173, 176
www.goodgovernance.org, 42–43
www.goodgovernance.org.au, 42–43, 178
Wynberg, 165, 167, 171

www.ingramcontent.com/pod-product-compliance
Lightning Source LLC
Chambersburg PA
CBHW050532300426
44113CB00012B/2058